SACRAMENTO PUBLIC LIBRARY
828 "I" Street
Sacramento, CA 95814
02/19

D0432172

SHRUBS

SHRUBS

Discover the Perfect
Plant for Every Place
in Your Garden

ANDY McINDOE

Timber Press
Portland, Oregon

Contents

7   About This Book

11   A Few Good Reasons
to Plant Your Garden with Shrubs

23   ## Choosing the Right Shrub, Planting, and Care

25   Assessing your situation

40   Planting: Give new shrubs the best possible start

43   Care during establishment

45   ## Shrubs for Challenging Growing Conditions

47   Shade, including dry shade

61   Exposed and coastal situations

75   Wet and compacted soil, including clay and new construction

89   Alkaline and chalk soils

103   Acid soils: Moist and peaty, dry and sandy

117   Hot and dry conditions, including prolonged drought

131   Harsh winters

145 Shrubs for Restricted Planting Spaces

147 Pots and containers

161 Small gardens

175 Narrow beds and borders

189 Steep slopes and banks

203 Wall shrubs, alternatives to climbers

217 Shrubs with Desirable Characteristics

219 Architectural and dramatic foliage effects

233 Fast movers for impact, screening, and shelter

249 Shrubs grown as trees

263 Long-blooming shrubs

277 Shrubs with fragrant flowers

291 Shrubs to attract wildlife

305 Deer- and rabbit-resistant shrubs

318 Further Reading

319 Photography Credits

320 Index

About This Book

Compiling this book has been interesting, rewarding, and often challenging. The obvious garden situations are the easiest to make recommendations for. Shade, sun, and acid soil are just some that are constantly asked about. Those of us who advise on gardens have our favourites for such conditions, and these are the first plants that spring to mind. However, I have tried to include as extensive a palette of shrubs as possible and avoid duplications, but it is surprising how the obvious contenders for one situation are the forerunners for the next. Thinking of alternatives is where the challenge begins.

Our garden at Sandhill Farm, Hampshire, UK, contains a variety of shrubs and trees planted for year-round interest.

I have tried to be definite in my recommendations. It would be easy to say "any potentilla will do," but that leads to the question of which one. I've included my first choices in the shrub entries, and the reader can then choose alternatives. For example, I may recommend *Potentilla fruticosa* 'Abbotswood' in one situation and *Potentilla fruticosa* 'Primrose Beauty' in another. Unless I say otherwise, the two are really interchangeable. I have included them because they are both good plants.

I advise you to use my selections as a guide, but see what is available locally or from your usual source of plant material. Selections vary with nursery and country. If you can choose the plants personally, so much the better. It is preferable to have a good plant of a close substitute than a poor plant of your first choice. Many planting schemes are ruined by the inflexibility of the designer.

In most cases choosing the shrubs for each situation was easy and the selection could have been far more extensive; in other instances it was challenging. Some will undoubtedly question why I have not included shrubs that seem obvious choices to them. We all use a group of plants that are familiar to us, and I always recommend plants that I have some experience of. Also it is important to remember that all plants behave differently in different gardens. For example, I never recommend sarcococcas for pots and containers because I never have success with them. However I have met several gardeners who claim to have wonderful specimens that have thrived in pots for years. Similarly I usually find that *Daphne odora* has a lifespan of ten to fifteen years. Yet I have met gardeners who claim that theirs has been with

them for more than thirty. Two things are certain: we all lose track of time and plants have not read the rule book.

The shrub descriptions include an indication of potential size. It will certainly depend on the growing conditions, and it can depend on the original specimen you plant, its condition, and possibly the clonal selection. Some cultivars vary considerably according to the clone being propagated and even where the cutting material is taken from on the parent plant. Some shrubs are multiplied by micropropagation and the offspring can appear slightly different from the parent even if they are genetically identical. Take a look at a batch of *Pittosporum* 'Garnettii' on a nursery bed and you will probably see variation in leaf size, shape, and growth habit, even though they are all true to type.

The subject of hardiness is perhaps the most difficult to be specific about. For gardeners in the UK, the Royal Horticultural Society's hardiness ratings are a relatively recent introduction. They are perhaps more useful in the colder areas; those of us gardening in the warmer south pay little heed to them. Also we are an island and the warming effect of the sea is profound, even in the Far North. However, we get caught out by an unusually cold winter every few years.

In North America zonal information is far more relevant. I have consulted as many sources as possible before stating these and they are an average, in some cases of widely varied opinions. This is not surprising as the microclimates in gardens vary so much. Urban areas are usually warmer. The presence of walls and buildings may mean more tender subjects survive. Exposure to cold winds or drainage of cold air down a slope can mean failure of a plant which should survive in that zone.

At the end of the day it is up to the gardener to determine the risk he or she wishes to take. We all like to push the boundaries; that is part of the fun of gardening.

I hope you find this book a useful companion when selecting shrubs. I also hope you find it inspirational and that it helps you to extend the palette of plants you use. If I may I would like to suggest keeping the following in mind:

- Never reject those hardy familiar shrubs that are widely used: they are a great foundation and support for the desirable treasures which may or may not succeed.

- Always consider foliage first and flowers second. Leaves last for longer and are the fabric of a planting scheme; flowers are fragile embroidery.

- Always buy good-quality shrubs, plant them well, and look after them; they will reward year after year.

- If a shrub fails to perform, does not please, or declines, remove it and plant something else. A space in a bed or border is a wonderful planting opportunity.

Happy gardening.

HARDINESS RATINGS

Knowing a plant's hardiness rating will help you to determine whether it will survive in your climate.

For the UK the RHS has devised a system of hardiness (H) ratings for garden plants based on temperature ranges. Download the table here: rhs.org.uk/plants/pdfs/2012_rhs-hardiness-rating.pdf.

USDA hardiness zones are based on average annual minimum temperatures. The lower the zone number, the colder the winter temperatures. To see temperature equivalents and to learn in which zone you garden, see the U.S. Department of Agriculture Hardiness Zone Map at planthardiness.ars.usda.gov/PHZMWeb/.

For Canada, go to planthardiness.gc.ca/.

For Europe, go to uk.gardenweb.com/forums/zones/hze.html.

A Few Good Reasons to Plant Your Garden with Shrubs

The fabulous Venus dogwood, a flowering specimen with exceptionally large bracts, rarely shows its potential in the garden centre or nursery, is slow to produce, and therefore is also more expensive to buy. However, when established in the garden it proves its worth.

Shrub is a familiar word in the world of plants and gardening, but one that means different things to different people.

To the botanist it means a plant with several woody stems growing from ground level. These stems are permanent structures that do not die back to ground level in winter. They usually branch, they can be evergreen or deciduous, and they have the ability to grow longer with each growing season. A shrub has the ability to last from year to year; it does not just grow from a seed, then flower, produce its own seeds, and die in just a year like an annual. It does not produce an underground food- and water-storage structure like a flower bulb or rhizome, which enables it to survive a dormant season when flowers and leaves wither and die. A shrub has a magical ingredient in its stems, a reinforcement called lignin, a substance that makes those stems permanent and built to last.

To the nursery professional shrubs are a group of long-term garden and landscape plants, usually sold in medium-sized pots and containers. Gardeners tend to buy them in small quantities, and some varieties are used in larger numbers in landscape projects. Some are flowering, some have colourful foliage, some are very appealing, but many are slow sellers that never look good in a nursery or garden centre pot. Most shrubs are slow to grow in the early stages of their life and more difficult to propagate than fast-growing perennials and annuals. Propagation probably involves taking cuttings, grafting, budding, or layering, skilled operations that require years of experience and patience. Numbers produced are fewer, the process more costly than growing bedding plants and perennials.

To the garden designer the shrub can be a plant that is either making a comeback or distinctly out of fashion. It is often seen as rather a utilitarian subject that has been superseded by perennials, grasses, or garden structures. When he or she uses shrubs in a design, they are clearly in vogue and their use nothing short of ground-breaking. Some designers are very selective in their use of shrubs. There are some that he or she would never be caught using, however suited to the situation. Even if they are good, basic, hard-working garden plants, their widespread use makes them less desirable, *Euonymus fortunei* 'Silver Queen', for example.

Topiary and trimmed hedges provide structure in a contemporary show garden. Although they are not necessarily regarded as shrubs in the recognized use of the word, they are simply extreme cases of controlled pruning.

There are elements of truth in all opinions and meanings. However, the botanist excludes all those plants that are not true shrubs even though they are used as shrubs in gardens: evergreen perennials including phormiums and cordylines, woody salvias, and euphorbias. What about multi-stemmed trees and those subjects that fall into both categories: amelanchier, magnolia, cercis, and the flowering dogwoods. They can get taller and broader than most shrubs, so when does a shrub become a tree?

The professional horticulturist is probably the most discriminatory. He excludes roses, conifers, hedging plants, and some shrubs we grow as climbers from his definition. These are even segregated at the point of sale, banished onto different beds in garden centres, confined with their own kind. This can cause even more confusion for both the experienced and the new gardener. Heathers and woody herbs, because of their size, are usually excluded from the main shrub selection; therefore we also tend to overlook them when choosing shrubs for a garden.

The garden designer often uses woody plants without considering them as shrubs. He disregards those plants regularly used in traditional and contemporary designs as vegetable masonry and living structure: yew and box as hedging and topiary, Japanese maples, step-over fruit trees, and other trendy woody plants. If they are not shrubs, what are they?

In many ways the gardener comes closest to defining what he or she thinks a shrub is: a long-term

Phormiums fulfil the role of evergreen shrubs with perennials at the Beth Chatto Gardens, Essex, UK.

garden plant that will grow easily and perform year after year, at least for the foreseeable future. A shrub means reliability, permanence, and colour, a rewarding plant that requires little care and maintenance.

Defining a plant as a shrub conveys an expectation that the plant will last, if not forever, at least for several years. The gardener expects it to survive through the winter, providing that it is deemed to be hardy enough to grow in that area. For some reason this changes the perceived value of a plant. Even if that young shrub costs the same as a seasonal bedding plant or short-lived perennial, it is expected to give far longer service for the same investment.

The definition of a shrub is confused with that of a tree, and so it should be; there is little difference. There are small trees and large shrubs, standard shrubs, and multi-stemmed trees. The definition is up to the individual. Today the traditional plant categories are becoming less defined in other ways. Plants sold as bedding plants are often seed-raised perennials. Varieties that grow quickly, look good in a pot, and flower as quickly may be sold as annuals or biennials.

As far as I am concerned shrubs include roses, bushy conifers, heathers, woody herbs, phormiums, cordylines, and yuccas. All can be used in similar ways in gardens; all are long-term, permanent garden plants. For some reason I do not normally regard bamboos as shrubs; I do not know why. They are usually grouped with grasses even though their woody

'Spring-break Princess', a new variety of *Lavandula stoechas*, joins a great many lavenders introduced every year. Differences among cultivars may be small; however, new plants like this always have great appeal.

stems mean they are closer to shrubs in character. Bamboos are plants I recommend with caution. Even the clump-forming ones can be problematic when their strong shoots erupt from the ground and shoot skywards. The spreading ones are invasive and have to be contained. These are often plants for the brave; once established most are difficult to control and impossible to remove. That is how they differ from most shrubs: the latter are better behaved and respond to pruning.

Are shrubs on trend?

With some the word *shrub* may conjure a feeling of nostalgia: memories from a childhood garden, plants or cuttings you were given in the past, that bony plant you took with you when you moved house. Undoubtedly this is why shrubs sometimes are regarded as old-fashioned garden plants.

Those of us who write about gardens and gardening are often asked for comment on trends. Certainly fashions change in the world of gardening as they do with most things. Over the years the resurgence of interest in shrubs has been proclaimed on many occasions. I have to admit to having exclaimed that "shrubs are back" more than once. Actually I cannot recall a time when they ever went away. Tastes may have changed, but that is also influenced by the palette of plants now available to gardeners, a palette so much more extensive than it was a quarter of a century ago.

Gardens are smaller, so big shrubs such as flowering currant, forsythia, and lilac may not be so widely planted. But smaller shrubs, especially those that perform quickly, are planted in vast numbers. Take lavenders for example. New varieties of lavender appear on the scene every year. A newly planted lavender makes an impact in the first season, it flowers the first summer, it never gets too large, and so it never presents a challenge for long-term cultivation. At the time of purchase it may be seen as a long-term garden plant; in reality it will probably only survive for a couple of seasons, but it is easily replaced.

Many of us will still attempt to grow lavender even if we do not have ideal growing conditions. This is a plant with an emotional attraction that overcomes horticultural reason—the smell of the foliage, the colour of the flowers, its attraction to bees and

Hydrangea macrophylla Magical Amethyst is just one of a new generation of hydrangeas that have great appeal both as a plant and a cut flower. The whole Magical Series of hydrangeas helps to show what is sometimes regarded as an old-fashioned shrub in a new light.

Photinia serratifolia Pink Crispy was introduced in 2015. A very different variegated variety of a popular evergreen shrub, it undoubtedly has sales appeal, but its long-term value as a garden plant has yet to be proved.

butterflies. The scent is both nostalgic and fashionable, featuring in fragrances of all types: calming, warm, floral, and sweet with hints of pine. Familiarity is probably its most enduring and magnetic attraction.

The appeal of lavender may be consistent, fuelled by the introduction of many new varieties, but there are other shrubs that have enjoyed a major boost in popularity. The hydrangea, for example, has enjoyed a meteoric rise from being a relic from yesterday's garden to one of our most desirable choice shrubs. This boost has been assisted by the introduction of new varieties that perform more reliably and the extensive use of hydrangea blooms for floral decoration.

Both lavender and hydrangeas have one quality in common that has a profound impact on their use in gardens. Breeders have developed varieties that look good in a pot at the point of sale. As increasing numbers of plants are bought in pots on garden centres and in other retail outlets, sales appeal is paramount. Compact plants that bloom reliably, travel well, have a long shelf life, and create instant impact in the garden are bound to be winners.

In today's sophisticated retail world, marketing is an important influence on the popularity of a shrub, especially when it is first introduced. Garden plants are often given a selling name, which can vary in different countries. This is different from its original cultivar name, which could have less sales appeal. Plant breeders and growers are under constant pressure to come up with new varieties. These capture media attention and provide nurseries and suppliers with stories at shows and events. A new plant launch is always the most certain way of capturing media attention. Some new plants become enduring favourites, many fall by the wayside. Time alone can tell if a new shrub is a good performer in a wide range of situations.

Why choose a shrub?

In most cases a shrub is a long-term garden plant which lasts for a number of years. It may cost a little more than a perennial or seasonal bedding plant, but

Choisya ternata, Mexican orange, is worth planting as a larger specimen which will make a more instant impact and buy a year or two of growing time.

it is usually longer lived and will earn its keep after a year or two. Its initial impact in the garden varies, not only according to variety but also size of plant chosen.

Some shrubs have instant effect. Buy a clipped boxwood ball, for example, and it looks the same in the garden as when you buy it. It will have taken a long time to produce on the nursery; therefore it costs more than a young plant of *Buxus sempervirens* which would take a few years of clipping and training to achieve the same effect.

Larger specimen shrubs create a greater impact in the garden when first planted. Basically you are buying time by investing in a larger specimen. Evergreens such as euonymus, choisya, osmanthus, and pittosporum are often purchased as larger shrubs. They respond well to an extra year or two in a pot if grown well on the nursery and look good in the garden as soon as they are planted out.

Deciduous shrubs are less popular as large specimens and some do not respond well to the confines of a pot for longer than necessary. These are the shrubs the gardener has to be a little more patient for; philadelphus or mock orange, deutzia, and lilac are good examples. You are never really going to get an idea of the potential from a pot-grown specimen on a garden centre. You are planting the promise of flowers, fragrance, and foliage in years to come.

Most garden owners perceive shrubs as low-maintenance plants that have the potential to reduce their work load. It is interesting that although

above Most shrubs have the ability to take care of themselves, regardless of the gardener's attention. Even when not in flower or leaf they maintain a presence. Evergreen shrubs such as rhododendrons are particularly valuable for their year-round contribution to a planting scheme.

top left *Philadelphus coronarius* never shows its potential in a pot. Although young plants bloom, they need time to grow and develop their elegant arching branches which produce garlands of flowers.

top right Evergreen *Hebe rakaiensis* makes excellent ground-cover and requires far less regular maintenance than an area of grass.

gardening is a hobby and a pleasurable pastime, it is also seen as hard work. Anything that makes gardening easier (was it really that difficult in the first place?) has to be good news. Of course if the focus of the garden was previously on plants that require more input, such as perennials, bedding, and vegetables, then easy-care shrubs could well make the garden easier to maintain.

Reluctant gardeners, with little thought for the aesthetic value of a garden, think that they are making life easier by grassing over the planting areas. Doing away with beds and borders means no more weeding? In reality, a well-planted bed where shrubs achieve excellent groundcover requires far less regular maintenance than an area of grass. The planting suppresses any weed growth, once established, and it does not require mowing once a week during the growing season.

What makes shrubs low maintenance?

Shrubs are perceived as low maintenance because they are survivors. Once a shrub is planted it will probably still grow and do what is expected of it even if conditions are less than ideal. It does not need to be lifted, divided, and replanted every few years to maintain its vigour, like a perennial. It does not need replacing every year, like a seasonal bedding plant. It is unlikely to be as prone to pests and diseases or crop failure as vegetables which seem to demand daily attention through the growing season.

A shrub does not require the gardener to provide support of its weak stems, like a climber or tall perennial. It takes care of itself and maintains its appearance without tedious staking and tying. It does not die back to the ground in winter, like an herbaceous

above The thick, woolly leaves and stems of *Phlomis italica* make it resistant to sun and drought, perfect for hot, dry situations.

top *Nandina domestica* Obsessed is a dwarf form of sacred bamboo with attractive evergreen foliage that colours brilliantly in winter.

Potentilla fruticosa 'Abbotswood' and *Syringa* 'Red Pixie', blooming freely in midsummer despite competition from a vigorous *Parrotia persica* growing alongside on dry, sandy soil. No irrigation and no regular feeding.

perennial, leaving a heap of faded stems and foliage for the gardener to clear up. Even if it loses its leaves it maintains a presence in winter, bringing structure and texture to beds and borders throughout the year.

Shrubs are adaptable plants and many seem able to modify their growth rate and proportions according to the growing conditions. Often leaves are smaller on poor dry soils, reducing transpiration and photosynthesis. Their woody stems also make them drought resistant and survivors where watering would be difficult or expensive. Thick leathery leaves, silvery reflective foliage, and sometimes a woolly coating all help to reduce water loss from the most drought-resistant subjects. Deciduous shrubs also have the ability to shed their foliage if conditions are tough; they leaf up again when water becomes plentiful. Therefore shrubs are the ideal plants for sustainable planting schemes.

In gardens, the ability of shrubs to survive without fuss and special care costs them the attention they deserve and is probably why they are seen as the ultimate low-maintenance plants. Roses are fed regularly and often sprayed with various chemicals to keep them disease free throughout the growing season. Seasonal bedding plants are treated to regular watering with liquid fertilizers throughout their brief lives. Their faded flowers are picked off meticulously to encourage further blooms. Tomatoes are fed, watered, trimmed of side shoots, and monitored for disease almost daily.

But flowering and foliage shrubs, which just carry on regardless, are lucky if they get a handful of general fertilizer occasionally. Pruning is often indiscriminate tidying, snipping off the ends of straying branches or a hatchet operation with hedge shears. Perhaps pruning does not happen at all until things get out of hand and the loppers are brought into action. Despite this, those reliable shrubs still manage to put on a performance.

What do shrubs contribute in a garden?

If you choose the right shrubs you have hard-working garden plants with more than one season of interest. Some flower in spring and produce fruits in fall. Some have attractive foliage and colourful winter stems. Many are evergreen and look good throughout the year. Shrubs are the most effective garden plants when it comes to adding long-lasting colour to the planting picture. Varieties with coloured and variegated foliage are essential for holding a planting scheme together through the seasons. When it comes to specific flower colours, you may have more choice with the perennial and annual planting palette, but the individual contributions are short lived and often unreliable.

Shrubs provide perfect planting solutions in all areas of the garden. Many make excellent subjects for permanent planting in pots and containers. This avoids not only the tedious and expensive task of replanting once or twice a year, but also the down time between seasons that comes with bedding plants and flower bulbs.

Shrubs offer a wide selection of excellent subjects for planting in shade, especially evergreens with colourful and variegated foliage. These add colour to shady corners where flowers fail. Shade tolerance is particularly relevant for today's small urban gardens surrounded by housing.

With a little thought and planning you will find a shrub for every situation. Whatever the growing conditions, you could plant your entire garden exclusively with shrubs. However, most like to use them with perennials, grasses, climbers, and trees, even if the shrubs predominate. Seasonal bedding and flower bulbs also play an important role, providing injections of colour that change the picture at certain times of the year.

Choosing the Right Shrub, Planting, and Care

In the mild climate of Abbotsbury Gardens in Dorset, UK, *Cornus controversa* 'Variegata' (right) grows luxuriantly alongside phormium, cordyline, and cotinus. I look enviously as it grows to tree proportions in ideal conditions, unlike those in my garden.

opposite With a little planning and careful selection, the shrubs in your garden can create a colourful and interesting picture during every season. Fall foliage can be particularly pleasing if you choose those shrubs that colour well on your soil type.

Few gardeners are lucky enough to have perfect growing conditions: deep, well-drained, fertile soil that never dries out, a sheltered, sunny situation,

and a mild climate with plenty of regular rainfall. We look enviously at gardens that come close, jealously admiring how well our favourite shrubs grow there. In our garden, a favourite shrub, *Cornus controversa* 'Variegata', grows slowly. Every year it gains a branch and in the process loses at least one of its lower ones. At the foot of a slope it catches the cold, then the early morning sun. Late frosts can therefore cause foliage damage as frozen leaves are warmed by the early light. Our poor sandy soil is dry, so growth is never lush and vigorous. I know it is not the right plant for our garden, but that does not stop me from growing it. If it eventually turns up its roots and dies, I will undoubtedly plant another.

On a more positive note we have plenty of space, a large garden where the main restriction to the size of beds and borders is the time needed to create and maintain them. In a smaller garden we might need to be more selective, choosing shrubs of more modest proportions.

Most gardens, even small ones, have a variety of growing conditions. Variable amounts of shade, according to the time of day and the time of year. Areas where soil is moist or dry. The pH of the soil and the soil type may vary in different parts of the garden. Some areas of the garden may be more sheltered, others cold or exposed. Although most shrubs are adaptable plants that cope with a wide range of growing conditions, choosing the right plant for a particular situation needs some consideration. Choosing the wrong subject is rarely disastrous, but it can be disappointing.

ASSESSING YOUR SITUATION

Impulse is a dominant factor in the selection of plants for today's gardens. We see a plant at its best in a pot in a garden centre, beautifully photographed in a book or magazine, or on a website. The information on the label or the description may be limited, but would we heed the advice anyway? The appeal of flowers and foliage is always greater than the reason of written or symbolic instruction.

For the shrubs in your garden to work together to create a continually pleasing picture, it is worth giving the situation some thought. It is human nature to take a chance on some, just because we like them. However, the shrubs that hold the planting in the garden together should be ones that are certain to succeed.

Soil type and fertility

Nearly all sources of advice put a lot of emphasis on the pH of the soil, in other words the degree of acidity or alkalinity. Neutral soils have a pH of 7. The nearer

above Common heather, *Calluna vulgaris*, grows on poor, dry, slightly acidic soil with golden oregano, *Origanum vulgare* 'Aureum'. Plants like these still thrive on soils without improvement.

Rhododendron 'Scintillation' is a hardy rhododendron that thrives on acidic soil. It will not succeed on soils with a pH greater than 7.

Cornus sanguinea 'Midwinter Fire', a dogwood grown for its amazing winter stems, also has good fall foliage colour. A very tolerant shrub, it grows on heavy, wet soil and provides six months of colour in the garden at a time of year when many shrubs look their worst.

your soil is to this, the wider the range of plants you will be able to grow. Soils with a higher pH are unsuitable for ericaceous and other acid-loving plants. Soils with a pH much below 7 are not ideal for some of the popular flowering and foliage shrubs. You can measure soil pH using a simple soil testing kit.

Some experts will advise testing for all the main plant nutrients or having a detailed soil analysis. In a garden situation this is rarely necessary. Most soils contain enough nutrients for plant growth; however, you will be demanding a lot of the plants you are growing, so best results will be achieved if you supplement with a balanced, slow-release fertilizer. You need to choose a specific one for ericaceous plants, and it is always best to use a specific rose fertilizer for roses because they are so demanding.

The drainage and moisture content of the soil at different times of the year is more important than the nutrient content. Heavy clay soils are often wet and soggy in winter, then bake hard in summer. If the ground is heavy and compacted, water may lie on the soil surface in the wettest months. This can prove challenging to plants that hate these conditions, which should definitely influence your plant choice.

It will limit it: you may really want lavender, but its chances of survival are slim if it is grown in the open ground. Grow the lavender in pots and plant something that thrives in wet ground.

In contrast, your soil may be light and free draining. This usually means low fertility and very dry conditions in the summer months. Plants need to be able to survive with minimal moisture; in other words, they need to be drought tolerant. This is where sustainable planting comes in. By choosing shrubs that grow in these conditions, you should not have to irrigate when the plants are established.

Most soils can be improved by the addition of organic matter, which both improves their structure and boosts the humus content. This increases the ability of the soils to retain moisture and plant nutrients, making them accessible to plants growing on them. You may also be able to improve drainage, in more extreme circumstances by installing simple land drains or by digging in grit or gravel on heavy soils. If this all sounds rather extreme, then choosing the right shrubs that will cope with the existing conditions is the best solution.

Sun and shade

Equally important as soil type, the amount of direct sunlight has a profound effect on the success of a shrub. Too often failure in gardens is down to choosing sun-loving shrubs for heavily shaded conditions. This can be particularly difficult to assess in a new garden because sunlight varies so much with the time of year.

Although we have a big garden it receives very little direct sunlight after midmorning during the winter months. As a northeast-facing slope it gets the morning sun, but that soon disappears behind the ridge of trees, casting long shadows from around midday. If I was assessing the site in early summer I would consider it open and sunny, not realizing that some of the beds are totally shaded from late summer through to midspring.

Also the conditions have changed gradually over the years since the trees have grown. Beds that were once sunny are now quite shaded. Therefore the selection of plants changes with the growing conditions.

As a shrub needs replacing, one more suited to the more shaded conditions takes its place, at least theoretically.

Under deciduous trees, conditions can often be improved by selective crown thinning. If some lower branches are removed and small branches through the centre of the tree are selectively thinned, the canopy becomes lighter, allowing more air, light, and rainfall through to the planting below. We do this with our birches, cutting only when the trees are in leaf or immediately after leaf fall to avoid bleeding. This vastly increases the transparency of the trees, casting only dappled shade on the planting below.

In nearly all gardens planting situations change with time as plants grow and cast shade and building development changes the surroundings. In a new garden, whether you are starting from scratch or taking on an established plot, it is worth waiting to see how the light changes through the seasons before making major planting decisions.

The light conditions in a garden can change significantly during the day. In our garden, by midsummer the shadows are already lengthening by midafternoon as the sun moves behind the trees at the top of the slope.

Ceanothus 'Italian Skies' grows quickly and flowers from year one. Sadly it is short lived, especially on our light, sandy, slightly acidic soil.

Viburnum plicatum f. *tomentosum* 'Mariesii' is broad and spreading in habit, with wonderful layered branches. In this naturalistic setting it has room to grow. In a restricted space, pruning would rob it of its natural beauty.

Size and timescale

The ultimate size of any shrub varies according to growing conditions and often with the individual specimen. Many sources state the ultimate size of a shrub in ideal growing conditions, often after many years. This can limit your choice of shrubs dramatically if you take it too literally. Obviously it is important not to plant to create problems in the future. However, we all want to see results and increasingly gardeners are looking for instant impact.

I tend to consider the size of a shrub in five to ten years, and that is the timeframe for the sizes in the shrub descriptions; for many shrubs that is their useful lifespan. It is a misconception to think that a shrub is a permanent feature in the garden. Some are, but many are past their best after a few years and may well need replacing. Mediterranean subjects such as cistus, ceanothus, and lavender rarely last more than seven to ten years, and they are unlikely to outgrow their situation in that time, if you choose the right ones.

A cherry laurel, however, is a long-lived shrub of great vigour and potentially vast proportions. It may well be a widely planted, fast-growing screening solution, but it may also be a potential problem in a relatively short time frame. Certainly it can be pruned or trimmed regularly to restrict its size and spread, but that requires regular input from the gardener, which is another consideration.

The most unfortunate decisions follow the choice of a flowering shrub that is too large for the situation. This frequent mistake often leads to indiscriminate pruning to control the unhappy plant. The result is usually an unattractive shrub that fails to bloom and perform, the very reason for its selection in the first place.

Pittosporum tenuifolium 'Variegatum' is evergreen, providing colour and structure throughout the year. *Berberis thunbergii* f. *atropurpurea* 'Admiration' adds changing foliage colour from spring to fall. They work with seasonal bedding plants to create an attractive planting combination.

Restricted planting spaces

Gardens are getting smaller, especially in towns and suburban areas. These may limit the choice of shrubs to more compact varieties and ones suitable for growing in narrow borders and small beds. Some situations may be even more restricted—without any open ground to plant in, everything has to be grown in pots and containers. However, courtyards, patio gardens, and balconies can all be planted for year-round interest if the right shrubs and pots are chosen.

This does not necessarily mean choosing only small shrubs. Scale is just as important in small gardens as it is in large ones. It is often better to have a few large containers with significant shrubs, with long seasons of interest, rather than a larger number of smaller containers. The right plants teamed up with good containers can transform what appeared to be a hopeless garden situation into a green oasis.

Ongoing maintenance is worth considering at the outset. An outside tap in close proximity is highly desirable, if not essential. This also enables the installation of a simple micro-irrigation system which will water pots efficiently and economically through the growing season and when the garden owner is away. Even for the non-technically minded like myself, these are easy to install and programme. They are controlled by simple computers that fit onto garden taps and can be set to operate by timer or by light level, watering at daybreak and nightfall.

Pittosporum tenuifolium is a versatile evergreen shrub that grows quickly to a substantial size, but it can be kept within bounds by pruning. It also makes an excellent hedge if planted no closer than 90cm (3 ft.) apart and clipped regularly well before it reaches the required height.

Boundaries and privacy

We plant a large proportion of the shrubs in our gardens to define boundaries and create privacy. Hedging plants are rarely thought of as shrubs, but of course they are, and selection of the right variety is even more important than that of individual ornamental specimens. It is also essential to plant at the right spacing to achieve an attractive, well-branched hedge that responds well to clipping. Hedges can take up a lot of space in gardens, and they can also give the gardener a lot of extra, regular work. Planting a hedge needs more consideration than most give it.

Many shrubs are also planted to provide privacy and to screen eyesores. In these circumstances quick results are desirable. Sadly few shrubs grow quickly to two or three metres and then stop; instead they keep on growing, demanding regular pruning to control their size. Often control measures are not implemented until the subjects have grown well beyond easy reach, pruning then requiring a ladder or pruning platform and considerably greater efforts.

Rosa 'Jubilee Celebration' is a wonderful English rose that blooms in midsummer and again in late summer, providing dead-heading, often called summer pruning, is carried out after the first flush of flowers. Feeding and watering are also essential.

Spiraea japonica 'Firelight' in late summer, proving its worth with lovely fall foliage colour. The summer flowers have been removed by clipping lightly with shears.

Ease of maintenance

These points bring us to the need for easy maintenance. Even keen gardeners are often short of time, and the choice of plants for a garden has a major impact on the time required to maintain it. Planting with shrubs is often seen as a way to achieve a garden that is easier to manage. Shrubs do not require the regular lifting and dividing, cutting back, and support that perennials need. They do not require seasonal replacement and replanting, like bedding plants do.

Many shrubs require some pruning and their performance depends upon it. Roses, for example, need pruning twice a year. They need regular feeding, even on fertile soils. They also need watering in dry weather during the growing season. One or two roses in a planting scheme, to provide seasonal colour and fragrance, will not be an undue burden. However, a scheme based primarily on roses will be time consuming.

Other flowering shrubs, such as potentillas and spiraeas, are easy care. A clip over with a pair of shears after flowering or in late winter is really all that is required. If you forget for a year or two, it does not really matter. If you never feed them they will still grow and bloom, even on the poorest soil.

Season of interest

Selecting shrubs for certain qualities is extremely rewarding. Foliage shrubs are always the foundation of a successful planting scheme for good reason: they have the longest season of interest and are not just dependent on a few weeks of flowers. More than one season of interest or a prolonged period of interest is really important when selecting shrubs for small gardens. In this situation every plant has to work hard to earn its keep; two weeks of flowers but dull green leaves for the rest of the year is simply not enough.

Even in large gardens shrubs with limited periods of interest may be easier to accommodate, but if possible look for ones with other attributes. For example, the lovely witch hazel *Hamamelis ×intermedia* 'Jelena' has glorious deep orange flowers on the bare stems in winter. It is a reliable variety and a wonderful large shrub of spreading habit. The blooms are lightly fragrant, rather disappointing for a witch hazel. However, it does develop fantastic fall foliage colour in shades of orange and scarlet, more than doubling the value of the plant.

The appeal of any garden is enhanced by having something of interest at every time of year. This may be easier to plan for if starting from scratch, but most of us have to concentrate on filling the gaps. So if your garden, like most, peaks in early summer, then plant additions and replacements to avoid that season. If you keep working with this discipline you will eventually have a garden with year-round appeal.

Whether you are starting a whole garden from scratch or just planting a new bed or border, it is a mistake to go out and buy all the plants at the same time based on what is looking good. You could end up with a garden that all happens on the anniversary of your shopping trip, with little else for the rest of the year.

above *Hamamelis ×intermedia* 'Jelena' produces its ribbon-petalled blooms on bare branches in midwinter. The flowers are lightly fragrant but amazingly weather resistant.

top It also has the bonus of superb fall foliage colour as well as the winter flowers.

Desirable characteristics

Selecting for certain attributes is a way of focussing your planting choice. Of course the most familiar way of doing this is to choose plants for a specific colour scheme. However, the palette has to be appropriate to the setting and may be influenced by the growing conditions. For example, a pastel scheme of pinks, mauves, blues, and silver will be easy to put together for a sunny situation on dry soil but will be unlikely to succeed in shade. In contrast, green and white presents plenty of possibilities in a shady border, such as using green and white variegated evergreens with varying shades of plain green foliage.

Aromatic foliage and fragrant flowers are other important attributes that may influence some plant selections. Woody culinary herbs are attractive shrubs which are appealing not only for their ornamental value but also their use in the kitchen; the productive aspect of gardens has gained a lot of interest in recent years. Fragrant flowers always delight, whether stars of the summer or winter garden. Shrubs excel in the fragrance department at all times of the year from the daphnes which scent the winter garden to philadelphus, stars of summer fragrance.

Planting for wildlife has become a major priority for many gardeners. Shrubs that provide a valuable source of nectar and pollen or seed or fruits for wild birds can form the foundation of an entire planting scheme. Gardens are vital to the preservation of wildlife in urban and rural areas and ornamental shrubs are valuable food sources, helping to maintain continuity of supply. Although in some parts the emphasis is on native plants, most recognize the value of ornamentals in the provision of food throughout the year, particularly important with changing climate.

above Berry-bearing shrubs such as *Cotoneaster naoujanensis* 'Berried Treasure' (similar to *Cotoneaster franchetii*) provide nectar for pollinators in spring and food for wild birds in fall.

top Winter-flowering shrubs such as the fragrant *Mahonia japonica* provide valuable pollen and nectar for early-flying bees and other pollinators.

Planting for survival

Gardeners living in more rural locations may face an even more limiting factor in the selection of shrubs for their gardens: the threat of deer and rabbits. These can wreak havoc, especially on new plants. It is sometimes amazing how they will ignore an established shrub, but plant a new specimen of exactly the same thing and they will demolish it overnight.

Some shrubs are more resistant to attack than others; these are bound to influence the planting of those living in deer country, although recommendations are never definitive. The preferences of deer populations seem to vary and their tastes sometimes change, making life even more difficult. A few shrubs are certain targets: roses, evergreen euonymus, *Viburnum tinus*, and dogwoods, especially *Cornus sanguinea*, to name but a few. *Clerodendrum trichotomum* var. *fargesii* 'Carnival' is an attractive autumn-flowering shrub with variegated foliage. Deer and rabbits avoid this plant because the foliage smells of rubber when lightly crushed. But even if you choose more resistant subjects, protection of newly planted specimens is advised.

Alliums and nepeta add pastel colour to this sunny border in early summer with the light and uplifting foliage colour of *Phlomis fruticosa* and *Euphorbia characias*. The soft textures contrast with the strong lines of the phormium behind.

Personal preference

To some the analysis of growing conditions will seem restrictive and limiting, choosing for season of interest and desirable attributes more appealing. Personal preference will always play a very important part in plant selection, and so it should. Gardens are personal spaces, and there is no point choosing a shrub that you really do not like just because it will succeed in a specific situation. This is often an obstacle to those of us who specify and recommend plants for gardens. I get frustrated when a client tells me that he or she only likes plants with small leaves, hates exotics, and dislikes yellow, or variegated foliage. But my frustration is unreasonable. Why should he or she like my recommendation just because I know it will grow there? After all, it is not my garden and I grow lots of unsuitable plants on my patch just because I like them.

Cornus controversa 'Variegata', one of my favourite shrubs, is not ideal on our poor sandy soil. But I still attempt to grow it.

PLANTING: GIVE NEW SHRUBS THE BEST POSSIBLE START

A shrub is a long-term garden plant. Its success in your garden depends on you. It is not only about where you plant it but also how you plant to ensure good root development and establishment, encouraging it to grow, develop, and thrive. In a nursery situation it will have been given care and attention to produce the appealing plant that you bought. You need to ensure that the growing conditions in your garden are as good as, or better than, those it enjoyed in the nursery.

Ground preparation

Preparation of the planting site is vital to encourage those roots to spread out from the growing medium or soil that the shrub started life in. Few gardens have deep, well-drained, fertile soil that needs little preparation. So fork over the area thoroughly to a depth greater than the roots of the shrubs you are planting and incorporate plenty of good garden compost, well-rotted manure, or any organic soil conditioner. This is especially important on poor, sandy, or chalky (shallow alkaline) soils, or on heavy clay. The organic matter helps to improve the soil structure. If existing shrubs, hedging, or conifers have been removed, be even more generous with the soil conditioner and add a concentrated organic fertilizer such as chicken manure pellets.

Poorly drained and very heavy clay soils can be improved by adding coarse grit or sharp sand. If the planting site is dry, water thoroughly and gently a day or two before planting.

opposite The hardy lilac, *Syringa vulgaris*, grows on most soils, including clay. However, good ground preparation prior to planting helps establishment and encourages a live display of flowers.

right Pot-grown rhododendrons have dense, fibrous root systems. They should be soaked thoroughly prior to planting, then planted undisturbed.

Planting container-grown shrubs

Most shrubs are grown in pots for sale through garden centres and other gardening outlets. Always look for healthy stock that does not appear pot bound or as if it has been struggling in the same pot for a few years. Before you plant, water the shrub in its pot thoroughly; submerging the pot in a bucket of water until it stops bubbling is ideal. If you plant when the growing medium is dry, water often fails to penetrate the rootball once it is in the ground.

Dig a hole at least twice the size of the pot and thoroughly fork over the base of the hole. Sprinkle a handful of balanced, slow-release fertilizer around the hole and into the soil you will use to backfill around the plant.

Now carefully remove the shrub from its pot. If the roots look nice and healthy and are fairly loose around the edge of the rootball, leave them undisturbed and position the plant carefully in the planting hole.

If the rootball is densely packed, the roots appearing knotted together, you can gently tease out some of the roots from the base of the rootball and spread them out in the planting hole. Some recommend cross-cutting the base of the rootball with a knife to encourage branching. This is a matter

of personal preference and is best only attempted on vigorous deciduous shrubs that are likely to grow easily.

Ericaceous subjects, such as rhododendrons, have dense, fibrous root systems and should be planted undisturbed. Roses have bony tap-root systems that never form a rootball. The growing medium is likely to fall away when they are planted, so adding mycorrhizal fungi to the planting hole is advisable to encourage establishment.

Settle the plant in the planting hole so that the surface of the growing medium is just slightly below ground level. Backfill with soil and fertilizer and firm around the rootball with your fist or foot. Ideally there should be a saucer-like depression around the shrub that will make watering easier. Now water thoroughly, even if the soil

is moist or rain is expected. This is important to settle the soil particles around the roots.

Planting root-balled shrubs

Some shrubs, especially conifers, are grown in the field, lifted during autumn and winter, and sold with the rootball and soil wrapped in hessian or burlap, sometimes with wire mesh around the outside. Lifting a root-balled plant is a skilled operation and great care is taken to keep the rootball intact with the soil to avoid breaking the roots. Take care when handling them and avoid dropping the rootballs when you move them. This easily breaks brittle young roots.

Ground preparation and planting are the same as for container-grown plants, but it is important not to

Roses, such as 'Felicia', are frequently planted as bare-root shrubs from late autumn through to early spring. Using mycorrhizal fungi in the planting hole aids establishment.

attempt to remove the hessian or the wire cage. The hessian rots in the ground and the roots grow through the wire, so leave both alone. However, when the plant is positioned in the hole and you are ready to backfill, you can cut away some of the hessian from the base of the plant if it is likely to be left above ground after planting. This looks tidier and prevents its acting as a wick, drawing moisture from the roots.

Watering after planting and regular checking to make sure that plants are firm in the ground and have not been rocked by the wind are particularly important.

Planting bare-root shrubs

Some hardy, easy-to-grow shrubs are grown in the field and lifted when dormant during late autumn and winter. Deciduous hedging plants and roses are often sold in this way. The soil is not retained around the roots, but the roots are protected from frost and drying out, either by temporary planting, known as heeling in, or by wrapping them.

Here again good soil preparation is important. The roots must be moist when planted. If they appear dry, soak them in a bucket of water for a couple of hours immediately before planting. Ideally dig planting holes that are large enough for the roots to be spread out. If you are planting a large quantity of deciduous hedging plants, or whips

as they are known, a mechanical soil auger to drill the planting holes is a massive benefit.

Using mycorrhizal fungi when planting aids establishment. This can be added as powder or granules, sprinkled onto and around the roots, or as a gel dip before placing the plant in the planting hole. The mycorrhizal fungi form a mycelium that grows in association with the shrub's roots, aiding water and nutrient absorption and stimulating growth.

Plants should be really firm in the ground after planting, and thorough watering is essential.

CARE DURING ESTABLISHMENT

Most hardy shrubs are easy to establish if planted with care in the first place. In temperate areas, where winters are not too severe, autumn planting is favourable because the soil is warm and moist and roots have time to establish before leaf growth is active. In colder areas it can be advisable to delay planting evergreens and borderline hardy subjects until spring.

When frost is expected beware of planting out shrubs that have been grown under the protection of a polytunnel or glass. Harden plants off by protecting at night or in severe weather until milder weather conditions prevail. However, it is a mistake to keep hardy deciduous subjects, such as Japanese maples, indoors before planting if they have previously been outside on a nursery. Keeping them indoors will stimulate soft, weak growth which is particularly vulnerable.

Protection

Deer and rabbits are always curious about newly planted stock and can do extensive damage even without eating. Where they are a problem make sure to protect new plants by surrounding them with wire or stiff plastic mesh. Various deterrent sprays and devices are also available; they may help but are rarely reliable.

Newly planted evergreens can be susceptible to desiccation in winter. Freezing wind draws water from the foliage which cannot be replenished by the roots if the ground is frozen. In more exposed situations during winter, use windbreak mesh around recently planted subjects.

Similarly in hot, dry situations if you plant tender subjects in late spring or summer it may be advisable to provide temporary shade. This will reduce transpiration from leaves, reducing the work the roots have to do to keep them supplied with water.

Watering

Attention to watering during the first season after planting is essential, especially during the first spring and early summer when growth is most active. Gentle watering that penetrates the soil is perfect, a sudden deluge from a watering can or hosepipe usually results in more runoff than water in the soil. Try to water during evening or morning when conditions are cooler, and get the water into the roots rather than all over the plants. Just wetting the soil surface is not sufficient, so take time to water properly.

Feeding

Applying additional fertilizer will not result in happier plants and increased growth. If you added a good, slow-release fertilizer at the time of planting, that will be sufficient for the first growing season. Applying too much fertilizer can be detrimental.

However, a growth stimulant, such as seaweed extract, applied as a liquid with a watering can, can help in the early stages as well as on shrubs that are struggling. Seaweed extract with added iron is especially beneficial when establishing ericaceous subjects.

Some mycorrhizal preparations can be applied after planting to aid root development. These are usually watered on in solution. They are useful to stimulate the root systems of shrubs that appear to be slow to establish.

Shrubs for Challenging Growing Conditions

With attractively coloured foliage in the early part of the year, *Sorbaria sorbifolia* 'Sem' is an easy-care, very hardy shrub that has proved its worth on soils of most types, including heavy, wet clay. 'Sem' is an excellent choice for the garden of a newly constructed house where the soil is compacted.

Shrubs and perennials paint a luxuriant picture with leaves beneath the light shade of a maple.

SHADE, INCLUDING DRY SHADE

Most gardens have shaded areas, often from the position of neighbouring buildings, surrounding walls and fences, or overhanging trees and large shrubs. An area of the garden may be shady throughout the day or only for part of it, or it may depend on the time of year. Shade may affect only a corner or one side of the garden, or the whole area may be in shade. As gardens get smaller and new houses are built closer together, shade becomes a more dominant factor, especially in urban areas.

Foliage may be the most important element in any garden, but in a shady garden leaves reign supreme. Most of our favourite flowering shrubs and perennials need around four hours of direct sun a day during the growing season if they are to perform well. With insufficient light they become drawn and weak with few flowers. However, foliage really shines in shade and has more depth and definition than it does in bright sunshine. Evergreens with glossy, reflective leaves are wonderfully cooling in summer and full of life in winter when most deciduous shrubs have little appeal. In reality the planting palette for shade is diverse and interesting and can provide colour and interest throughout the year in even the gloomiest situations.

Many different terms are used to describe degrees of shade, including semi-shade, partial shade, and dappled shade. If an area of the garden gets some direct sunlight it is worth experimenting with different plants that tolerate some shade, but sun-loving subjects should be avoided. If the area is shaded throughout the day, choose plants that thrive in shade, such as those in this selection.

Those with shaded gardens on acid soil have more choice when it comes to flowering subjects. Rhododendrons, pieris, camellias, and other lime-hating subjects thrive in semi-shade, especially under light deciduous trees such as birches and Japanese maples. The perennials that grow well with them, including ferns and hostas, also enjoy these conditions.

Dry shade is the most challenging growing condition. The soil beneath a conifer hedge or a large pine tree, for example, can be dust-dry with little organic content. A border along a shaded wall of the house, overhung by the eaves, can also be an inhospitable growing environment. Although some of the plants recommended here will grow in these situations, they will need help until they are established. Soil improvement and regular watering is essential to help the roots develop and find their way to survival.

Astelia 'Silver Shadow'

75 × 75cm (30 × 30 in.)
UK H4 USDA 8–11

Astelia is a surprising subject for shade with silver, softly shining, sword-shaped leaves in vase-like rosettes, reminiscent of those of a bromeliad. A native of Australian woodland, it is not the hardiest of plants, but 'Silver Shadow' is tougher than most and survives freezing conditions in a sheltered situation. Astelia thrives on most well-drained soils and is an excellent subject for a pot where its dramatic, architectural form can be displayed. Once established it is reasonably drought tolerant, but it prefers enough moisture in the soil for much of the year. Really an evergreen herbaceous perennial, astelia is used in a similar way to phormiums in a planting scheme: as a spiky contrast to the softer shapes of other plants. No pruning is required, but old, withered leaves should be removed as necessary.

Aucuba japonica 'Rozannie'

90 × 90cm (3 × 3 ft.)
UK H5 USDA 6–10

A compact form of the evergreen Japanese laurel with shining, dark green foliage and large scarlet berries from midsummer onwards. Although some may regard this plain evergreen as boring, the large, shining leaves with toothed margins are highly reflective and showy in a shady spot. When the bright red fruits develop, they contrast beautifully, giving a long-lasting display. This versatile shrub grows on any well-drained soil in the deepest shade and is compact enough for small gardens and use in pots and containers. In a planting scheme 'Rozannie' is a good contrast to variegated evergreens. Tolerant of atmospheric pollution, it is perfect for town gardens. Prune as required in spring to control shape and size.

Berberis darwinii

3 × 1.8m (10 × 6 ft.)
UK H5 USDA 7–9

Darwin's barberry is a dense, bushy evergreen shrub with small, shining, holly-like dark green leaves. In early spring the tiny blood-orange buds appear in drooping clusters. These open to bright orange blooms that hang like tiny lanterns; they last for several weeks, eventually covering the ground beneath the shrub in a carpet of tiny orange petals. It grows on most soils but is at its best in acid conditions. It thrives in sun or partial shade and is tolerant of deeper shade. Growing slowly at first, it eventually makes a large shrub that is an excellent structure plant. It also grows well as a hedge and responds well to clipping. Prune after flowering to control shape and size if necessary. There is a dwarf form, *Berberis darwinii* 'Compacta', which is similar but more compact, with red-tinted new growth. It is a better choice for small gardens.

Elaeagnus pungens 'Frederici'

1.2 × 1.2m (4 × 4 ft.)
UK H5 USDA 7–9

A more subtly coloured variegated oleaster than many of the other gold and green forms. The leaves are soft sulphur-yellow, edged with dark green and gently waved at the margins. The overall effect is light and pretty for an evergreen, creating a useful contrast to heavier plain-leaved subjects. This compact shrub with its stiff branched stems and leathery leaves is drought tolerant and will grow in sun or shade on any well-drained soil. Slow growth, reasonably compact habit, and year-round interest make it perfect for small gardens. It is also useful for coastal and windy sites. Prune as necessary in spring to control shape and size.

Euonymus fortunei 'Silver Queen'

60 × 90cm (2 × 3 ft.)
UK H6 USDA 4–9

The variegated forms of *Euonymus fortunei* are among the most widely planted and versatile evergreen shrubs. 'Silver Queen' is regarded by many as the finest with its dark green leaves, edged and variegated with rich cream, occasionally entirely cream on some of the shoots. Often overlooked among the leaves, tiny white summer flowers may develop to creamy seed capsules on mature plants. Frequently used as groundcover because of its horizontal, spreading habit, it can eventually make a striking shrub up to 90cm (3 ft.) or more in height although it is slow growing when first planted. It also makes an excellent short climber if grown against a shaded wall. Drought tolerant once established, it grows on any soil that is not excessively wet. Prune as necessary to control shape and size.

Fatsia japonica

1.8 × 1.5m (6 × 5 ft.)
UK H4 USDA 8–11

With its large, glossy, dark green, hand-shaped leaves, the evergreen Japanese aralia brings a touch of the exotic to temperate gardens. Creamy white flower heads, which resemble giant ivy flowers, appear at the tips of the upright stems in winter, sometimes followed by heavy clusters of green-black fruits. It can be grown as a large, dramatic subject in a shaded corner or used in a large pot or container to grace a courtyard or shaded balcony. It thrives on any well-drained soil and is tolerant of atmospheric pollution. The variegated form, *Fatsia japonica* 'Variegata', has creamy white edges to the tips of the leaves; it is a little less vigorous. Old, leggy plants can be cut back hard in spring to rejuvenate them.

Hedera helix 'Erecta'

75 × 90cm (30 in. × 3 ft.)
UK H6 USDA 5–9

An interesting form of common ivy with upright stems densely clothed in small, waved, arrow-head, deep green leaves. When the stems reach 60cm (2 ft.) or so in height they tend to lean over to the ground before growing vertically again. Eventually it can make a substantial low evergreen shrub of architectural appearance. Rarely offered by garden centres and nurseries, 'Erecta' deserves wider planting and is a good partner for the variegated forms of *Euonymus fortunei*. Like the species, it is drought tolerant and will thrive in the deepest shade on virtually any soil. It is also an interesting subject for a pot. Prune at any time, only to control spread. The species is invasive in parts of North America.

Mahonia aquifolium 'Apollo'

60 × 90cm (2 × 3 ft.)
UK H5, USDA 5–9

A low-growing evergreen shrub forming a clump of upright stems carrying shiny, softly spiny, holly-like leaves of darkest green. The foliage often flushes purple in winter and in situations with some direct sun. Crowded clusters of tiny bright yellow flowers open from yellow-green buds in early spring; these may be followed by blue-black berries later in the year, hence the common name, Oregon grape. Probably the showiest variety of this tough shrub, 'Apollo' will grow in dry shade under pines and other conifers, as well as under deciduous trees. It thrives on any soil that is nor waterlogged. Old plants can be hard pruned to rejuvenate them if they become straggly. Although a native of the Pacific Northwest, Oregon grape is considered invasive in parts of North America as well as in Europe.

Osmanthus heterophyllus 'Variegatus'

1.2m × 75cm (4 ft. × 30 in.)
UK H5, USDA 7–9

Often mistaken for a small variegated holly because of its spiny, soft green leaves edged with creamy white, this is an excellent slow-growing evergreen shrub. Compact in habit and bushy, it is useful in small gardens and a good choice for a pot when young. Tiny, fragrant flowers appear on the stems in autumn and can be inconspicuous apart from their perfume. It grows well on any well-drained soil in sun or shade. Prune only to control size and shape or to promote new growth on older plants. Left to grow naturally, it can make a substantial shrub after ten years or more.

Pachysandra terminalis

15 × 45cm (6 × 18 in.)
UK H6 USDA 4–8

Japanese spurge is a deceptive evergreen shrub that resembles a suckering herbaceous perennial with its short, upright stems and rosettes of shining green leaves. The leaves are diamond shaped and attractively toothed. Tiny greenish flowers appear in the centres of the rosettes in early spring. Surprisingly pachysandra is a close relative of buxus and is equally shade loving. In a sunny position it usually assumes an unhealthy chlorotic appearance. Pachysandra likes a fertile, reasonably moist soil to thrive where it will form dense mats of foliage making excellent groundcover. For best results plant a number of small plants 20cm (8 in.) apart rather than one or two larger specimens. No pruning is required.

Prunus laurocerasus 'Otto Luyken'

90cm × 1.2m (3 × 4 ft.)
UK H5, USDA 6–9

Another commercial landscape favourite, this is an excellent form of cherry laurel with a far more compact, manageable habit than the species. The upright stems grow at an angle. The narrow dark green leaves are exceptionally shiny and are held close to the straight stems. The dense foliage forms the perfect setting for the upright spikes of small, pure white spring flowers. Although it grows well on most reasonably fertile soils, it can be slow and chlorotic on shallow chalk. It tolerates shade and pollution so is an excellent choice for town gardens and landscape schemes. Prune after flowering to control size and spread. It can be trimmed with shears, but this destroys its attractive growth habit.

Ruscus aculeatus 'John Redmond'

30 × 30cm (12 × 12 in.)
UK H6 USDA 6-9

A dense, compact variety of butcher's broom, forming a tight clump of stiff, upright green stems with dark green flattened, spine-tipped stems resembling leaves. These produce tiny flowers that develop into sealing-wax berries. As this is a hermaphrodite form, it reliably produces fruit without the need for a male pollinator. The species has both male and female plants. A tough shrub that survives in deep shade and dry conditions where little else will grow—that is its appeal. It does not grow well in a pot and is slow to develop, therefore is rarely offered for sale. Where it succeeds it has a long season of winter interest. No pruning is required, fortunately, because it is an aggressive plant to handle; very deer and rabbit resistant.

Sarcococca hookeriana var. digyna

75 × 90cm (30 in. × 3 ft.)
UK H5 USDA 6-9

A tall variety of evergreen sweet or Christmas box, forming a clump of slender, upright, red-brown stems with very narrow, leathery, dark green leaves that create a bamboo-like effect. The tiny pinkish white flowers appear in mid- to late winter in the leaf axils. Because the leaves are quite upright on the stems, the flowers are more conspicuous than on some other varieties; the fragrance is sweet and powerful. Growing on any reasonable soil, especially chalk, this compact shrub will fit into any garden. However, it does not usually grow well in a pot; for containers Sarcococca hookeriana Winter Gem is a better choice. Sarcococca is excellent for cutting at any time of the year, especially when the flowers first open. No pruning is required.

Skimmia ×confusa 'Kew Green'

75 × 75cm (30 × 30 in.)
UK H5 USDA 7–9

Probably the most reliable skimmia, this excellent evergreen shrub forms a loose mound of apple-green leaves on green stems. Clusters of pale green buds, attractive through winter, open to fragrant creamy yellow flowers in spring. The scent is deliciously similar to that of lily of the valley. Growing on any reasonably fertile soil, this skimmia tolerates more sun than most without turning yellow, although it is at its best in shade. It makes a good subject for a pot and is useful to cut for floral decoration, both as sprigs of foliage and flower buds. No regular pruning is required, but pruning to control shape and size is best done immediately after flowering.

Viburnum davidii

75 × 90cm (30 in. × 3 ft.)
UK H5 USDA 7–9

A bold evergreen, making a mound of deep green, heavily veined leaves carried on red leaf stalks. Dense and dark, it is among the finest of evergreen structure shrubs and a useful contrast to lighter more feathery subjects. Clusters of whitish flowers develop into attractive blue-black berries on female plants. Plants of both sexes are needed for pollination; the only way to select female plants is to buy when they are fruiting. *Viburnum davidii* grows on any well-drained soil and tolerates deep shade. It thrives under trees and in pots and can even be used as a low hedge. It is ideal in small shaded gardens and tolerates atmospheric pollution. Prune in spring, if required, to control shape and size.

OTHER GOOD SHRUBS FOR SHADE

×*Fatshedera lizei*

Ilex ×*altaclerensis*
  'Golden King'

Ilex aquifolium 'Ferox
  Argentea'

Leucothoe fontanesiana
  'Rainbow'

Ligustrum ovalifolium
  'Argenteum'

Mahonia japonica

Prunus lusitanica 'Variegata'

Rhododendron
  'Cunningham's White'

Rubus tricolor

Symphoricarpos ×*chenaultii*
  'Hancock'

PLANTING PARTNERS FOR SHADE

Evergreen foliage forms the foundation of planting in shade, but there are plenty of plants, often of woodland origin, that can be added as enhancements and seasonal highlights. Flower bulbs are an obvious choice: shade-tolerant subjects such as chionodoxa, galanthus, narcissus, and scilla are well adapted to growing and flowering when trees and shrubs are bare and more light and rainfall reaches the soil. They retreat below the surface when competition from woody plants becomes greater. The secret of success is to choose them as part of the planting scheme as you would another shrub or perennial. For example, a few clumps of the common snowdrop, *Galanthus nivalis*, against the dark green foliage of *Viburnum davidii* alongside green and white *Euonymus fortunei* 'Silver Queen' is a winning combination. The white flowers emphasize the green and white scheme for a few weeks, but the foliage of the shrubs carries it through the rest of the year.

Bulbous plants are not only for spring. The autumn-flowering *Cyclamen hederifolium* is a great success in dry shade when planted with a carpet of small-leaved ivy or *Vinca minor*. It spreads easily by self-seeding but may be easier to establish initially from seed-raised plants rather than dry corms. This combination seems to work even in the dry, resinous areas under pine trees.

Epimediums, commonly known as barrenwort, are excellent plants for shade, although they can be somewhat slow to establish. *Epimedium* ×*versicolor* 'Sulphureum' is the best evergreen variety for dry shade. The new leaves are flushed red, becoming green in summer and often developing autumn tints. Once established it forms clumps up to 30cm (12 in.) in height, the delicate stems of sulphur-yellow, elfin flowers rising just above the leaves in spring. Some suggest removing some of the old leaves to show the flowers to advantage, but this seems to defeat the object of an evergreen groundcover.

Liriope muscari, lilyturf, is a grass-like perennial forming dense clumps of narrow, strap-shaped, dark green, shiny leaves up to 20cm (8 in.) in height. In autumn spikes of bright purple-blue flowers rise above the foliage, adding welcome colour to a shady situation. The flowers are often followed by black berries. Liriope succeeds under trees and in narrow borders at the base of walls and fences. It makes a lovely planting partner for the soft yellow and green foliage of *Elaeagnus pungens* 'Frederici'.

Plants that hug the ground under shade-loving evergreens are particularly valuable. Some varieties of lamium, deadnettle, are particularly successful. *Lamium maculatum* 'Beacon Silver' and 'White Nancy', with their soft leaves boldly marked with shining silver, can be particularly showy under subjects like *Aucuba japonica* 'Rozannie'. These are even more effective when established with the shining purple, green, or variegated leaves of ajugas, the bugles, with their spikes of sapphire flowers in summer.

top The autumn-flowering *Cyclamen hederifolium* with small-leaved variegated ivies on a dry bank under a pine tree.

above left *Viburnum davidii* with *Euonymus fortunei* 'Silver Queen', a good evergreen foundation in a green and white planting scheme for a shady situation.

left *Brunnera macrophylla* 'Looking Glass' shines in shade under deciduous shrubs and trees.

Hellebores and scillas light up the ground beneath deciduous trees and shrubs in early spring before their foliage reduces the light and rainfall reaching the soil.

Pulmonarias, lungworts, thrive if the shade is not too dry; arid conditions result in foliage wilting and developing mildew. *Brunnera macrophylla*, Siberian bugloss, is also normally recommended for moist shade; however, the varieties 'Jack Frost' and 'Looking Glass' have proved to be tolerant of dry conditions. The heart-shaped, silver leaves are delicately edged and veined with dark green; the whole plant gives a shining silvery effect. It forms a neat clump of foliage by midspring when the tiny brilliant blue flowers are carried on fine stems in a cloud above the leaves. This little plant, growing to 30cm (12 in.) in height and spread, will fit into any shady corner.

Most geraniums thrive in sunny borders, but *Geranium macrorrhizum* is shade tolerant and survives even dry shade. The foliage and stems are highly aromatic, making the plant resistant to the ravages of deer and rabbits. The other excellent deer- and rabbit-resistant groundcover subjects for shade are the ivies. Many shy away from using them from fear of their invasive and smothering reputation. However, this is very dependent upon the variety chosen. Most of the large-leaved, variegated varieties of *Hedera colchica* are ideal, providing colour and interest throughout the year around deciduous and evergreen shrubs.

Epimediums and *Liriope muscari* under the light shade of
Cornus controversa 'Variegata' at RHS Rosemoor, Devon, UK.

Elaeagnus ×submacrophylla (left) and *Pittosporum tobira* (right) are both well adapted to exposed coastal conditions. Their leathery leaves resist desiccation and pliable branches bend in the wind.

EXPOSED AND COASTAL SITUATIONS

Many plants fail on exposed sites: wind, lack of shade, drought, and salty air can prove challenging conditions for survival. Shrubs that cope with these conditions are the ones that are well adapted, often with tough, reflective, or well-insulated leaves that resist desiccation. They often originate from higher altitudes in arid regions or exposed seashores.

Plants with large, soft leaves are best avoided. Deciduous yellow-leaved shrubs and those with soft green and white variegations often scorch, showing their displeasure with brown leaf edges or brown patches on the most exposed parts of the plants. Purple-leaved shrubs, except Japanese maples, are usually more resilient, the most exposure-tolerant being the purple-leaved berberis varieties.

Shrubs for exposed sites need to be compact or ground hugging to avoid excessive wind resistance. They usually have pliable branches that bend and flex in the wind. Shrubs with brittle stems are to be avoided. The most resilient also have strong, fibrous root systems that anchor the plants well. Plants with fragile roots or wiry tap-root systems are prone to wind rock which breaks new roots and results in poor growth. This is often a problem with fruit trees on dwarfing root stocks and hybrid roses.

A windy site can have its advantages. Diseases are few because fungal spores are blown away by air circulation. Shrubs often need less pruning and stay compact, producing little in the way of lush, vigorous growth. However, wind and sun can be very drying and plants are quickly under stress before roots are well developed to draw water. Even the toughest subjects need good soil preparation and initial irrigation until established.

Often the palette of plants that can be grown on an exposed site can be extended by planting more resilient subjects to break the wind and provide shelter. Shrubs like *Elaeagnus ×submacrophylla* (also available as *Elaeagnus ×ebbingei*) and *Olearia ×haastii* both make excellent hedges that act as effective windbreaks; both are salt tolerant. In milder areas the fast-growing *Olearia traversii* is considered to be the most effective windbreak shrub to cope with salt-laden air.

Brachyglottis (Dunedin Group) 'Sunshine'

90cm × 1.2m (3 × 4 ft.)
UK H4 USDA 8–10

A tough silver foliage shrub that forms a mound of stout silvery stems and grey-green foliage. The leaves become greener on the upper surface as they age, remaining silver and felted underneath. The daisy flowers appear in summer from bunches of grey buds. The blooms are hard yellow and rather coarse in character, so they are often removed before they open. This not only preserves the subtle character of the shrub but also keeps the plant in shape. A drought-tolerant plant that thrives on any well-drained soil, it is also more tolerant of clay and heavy soils than most silver foliage shrubs. Prune as required to maintain shape and size. Mature plants can become leggy and sprawling and are best cut back by half to two thirds in spring to rejuvenate them.

Corokia cotoneaster

1.5 × 1.2m (5 × 4 ft.)
UK H4 USDA 8–10

An interesting shrub, commonly known as wire-netting bush because of its dark, zig-zagging interlaced twigs that form a dense network punctuated by small, leathery dark green leaves, silvery on the undersides. Small, starry, yellow flowers sparkle on the branches in summer, followed by yellow or orange berries in fall. It is not for cold, exposed sites, but excellent for coastal gardens and is best on well-drained soil in full sun. Its form, colour, and character are a useful contrast to most broad-leaved shrubs, and it is a good choice for narrow borders against walls or fences. Pruning is not required, but selective pruning to control shape and size can be carried out in early spring.

Daboecia cantabrica

30 × 45cm (12 × 18 in.)
UK H5 USDA 6–8

Irish heath is a delightful little evergreen shrub that thrives in exposed situations on sea cliffs and moorland. Wiry stems carry tiny, shining, dark green, narrow leaves. The small, often intensely coloured, nodding, urn-shaped flowers are carried on fine stems at the tips of the shoots from late spring right through to late fall. It needs a lime-free soil in an open sunny position to flower well. A number of named varieties have been selected for their compact habit and flower colour from white to deep red-purple. *Daboecia* is an excellent choice to prolong the flowering season of both winter- and summer-flowering heathers and makes a striking planting combination with European gorse. No pruning is required, but a light trim after flowering helps to promote bushy growth.

Elaeagnus ×submacrophylla

3 × 3m (10 × 10 ft.)
UK H5 USDA 7–11

A fast-growing evergreen commonly known as silverberry (also available as *Elaeagnus ×ebbingei*) with strong, upright, then arching stems. The deep green leaves have tiny silvery scales on the undersides, the new shoots covered in a tan-coloured bloom. Tiny, creamy white fragrant flowers appear on the stems in autumn, often going unnoticed apart from their powerful perfume. This is an excellent screening shrub, perfect for windy and coastal situations and at the back of a large border. It grows on any well-drained soil in sun or partial shade. As it responds well to regular cutting, it makes a good hedge and windbreak of 1.2–1.8m (4–6 ft.) in height. It can also be trained onto a frame or trellis to make a narrow screen. Prune to control size and shape at any time, ideally in spring. Hedges may need cutting two or three times in a season.

Escallonia laevis Pink Elle

1.2m × 90cm (4 × 3 ft.)
UK H5 USDA 7–9

An excellent, recently introduced variety of this appealing evergreen shrub. Compact and healthy, it appears more resistant to the leaf spot disease that affects many older varieties. The rounded, leathery, glossy green leaves are the perfect setting for the large heads of sugar-pink flowers that are freely produced from mid- to late summer. Growing on any well-drained fertile soil in full sun, it is tolerant of wind and salt air. It makes an excellent informal low to medium hedge or a good structure shrub among lavenders and sun-loving perennials. No pruning is necessary, but it can be lightly trimmed in early spring to make the habit even more compact.

Griselinia littoralis 'Dixon's Cream'

2.4 × 1.8m (8 × 6 ft.)
UK H5 USDA 6–9

A variegated form of New Zealand broadleaf with upright, then arching green stems and rounded, leathery apple-green leaves splashed with lime green and creamy white. It arose as a sport of *Griselinia littoralis* 'Variegata' and is similarly looser in habit than the plain green-leaved form but equally fresh in appearance. A seashore native, it is tolerant of salt air and is excellent for seaside gardens, although it can be subject to frost damage in inland areas. It likes good drainage, hates waterlogging, and does not succeed on cold, exposed sites. It prefers neutral to acid soil and an open, sunny situation. Prune to control shape and size in early spring or as necessary. Remove plain green reverted shoots as these can quickly take over.

Hebe 'Red Edge'

75 × 75cm (30 × 30 in.)
UK H4 USDA 8–10

A tough hebe with small, leathery, grey-green leaves arranged regularly up short upright stems to form a dense, textural mound. The individual leaves are edged with purple-red, especially at the tips of the shoots. The colouring becomes more intense in winter as it spreads through the foliage. Small spikes of mauve-white flowers, attractive to bees, appear in summer. More drought- and heat-tolerant than many other hebes, it thrives in an open, sunny position on well-drained soil and is tough enough to cope with strong winds and salt air. Hebes often suffer from leaf spot disease in sheltered situations with stagnant air, so windy sites can be an advantage. No pruning is required; however, old plants can be cut back in spring to where new shoots are emerging lower down on the stems, never into bare wood.

Hippophae rhamnoides

3 × 1.8m (10 × 6 ft.)
UK H7 USDA 3–7

Sea buckthorn is a real survivor on windy, coastal sites and in exposed situations. Dark, arching stems carry slender silver leaves. Female plants produce orange-yellow berries crowded on the bare stems in winter, persisting after the leaves have fallen. *Hippophae* is best planted as young bare-root whips in the dormant season. It thrives in full sun on poor, well-drained soils, especially sand. Left to grow naturally, it becomes a tall, rangy shrub, although it can also be trimmed as a dense, twiggy hedge, either for shelter or ornamental purposes, pleasing when sculpted into an undulating cloud effect. Sea buckthorn hedges are easy to maintain and suit contemporary schemes alongside lavender, rosemary, and cistus. The more they are trimmed, the more silver shoots are produced.

Juniperus ×pfitzeriana 'Sulphur Spray'

1.5 × 1.5m (5 × 5 ft.)
UK H7 USDA 4-9

Conifers may not be to everyone's taste, but there is no denying their year-round interest and ability to thrive in cold, exposed situations. Many junipers are loose in habit and easier than other conifers to incorporate with broad-leaved shrubs. 'Sulphur Spray' has strong, ascending but spreading branches with soft pale yellow foliage, creating a light and feathery effect. It is not as large and vigorous as other varieties of Pfitzer juniper, so suits smaller gardens. It grows on most well-drained soils and is excellent on chalk, thriving in sun or semi-shade. Drought tolerant once established, it is ideal on banks and slopes. No pruning is required, but shoots may be cut back selectively at any time to control size and spread.

Phormium cookianum subsp. hookeri 'Tricolor'

1.2 × 1.8m (4 × 6 ft.)
UK H4 USDA 8-10

A big, bold variety of New Zealand flax with long, arching, leathery leaves edged with cream and narrowly margined with red. The habit is broad, mounded, and spreading and makes a strong, evergreen statement in any situation. In summer tall, dark, architectural flower spikes rise above the leaves to a height of 1.8m (6 ft.) or more carrying curious green-yellow tubular flowers. It grows well on any well-drained fertile soil and is drought tolerant but does not take kindly to transplanting once established. Striking for a large pot or container, with rocks and scree, or alongside walls or buildings. Remove old leaves at any time and cut back flower stems in fall. No other pruning is required. Phormiums are not tolerant of extreme cold, but they are very good on windy sites and perfect for coastal situations.

Pinus mugo

1.2 × 1.8m (4 × 6 ft.)
UK H7 USDA 2–8

Mountain pine is very hardy and well adapted to extreme conditions with its needle-like foliage, shrubby habit, and resinous branches. Left to grow naturally, it eventually forms a large shrub of open character, with spreading, then upright branches clothed in dark green needles. The cones appear near the top of the branches in small clusters. It grows on any well-drained soil in full sun and is tolerant of alkaline conditions. An excellent choice for a rocky bank or gravel garden, it is best planted where its form is not overcrowded. Attractive with white-barked birches and shrubs grown for their winter stems and grasses. Size and spread can be restricted by selective pruning at any time; usually branches are best removed to the base of the plant.

Rosa 'Fru Dagmar Hastrup'

1.5 × 1.5m (5 × 5 ft.)
UK H7 USDA 3–9

A disease-resistant rose with pleated, bright green leaves and upright thorny stems. The large, pale pink single blooms resemble dog roses and are produced in flushes from early summer to fall. They are lightly fragrant and followed by red, tomato-like hips which often persist on the stems after the leaves have fallen. Birds enjoy these ripe, vitamin-rich fruits in winter. A cultivar of *Rosa rugosa*, a native of Japanese seashores, it is a rose that grows where others fail and thrives on light sandy soil. Unlike most other roses, it is deer- and rabbit-resistant. It mixes well with other shrubs and perennials and is ideal in an exposed rural or coastal garden grown individually as a shrub or as a hedge.

Spiraea japonica 'Little Princess'

60 × 90 cm (2 × 3 ft.)
UK H7 USDA 4-9

A hardy little shrub forming a low mound of neat mid-green foliage, falling to leave tan-coloured twigs in winter. The tiny deep pink flowers in densely packed heads appear nestled against the foliage in summer; attractive to bees and butterflies, blooms are produced over a long period in an open, sunny situation. It is ideal for small gardens and for planting at the edge of paving or into gravel, and grows easily on any well-drained soil, especially chalk. Its ground-hugging habit means it is well adapted to exposed situations and is drought tolerant once established. No pruning is required, but clipping in winter or early spring to remove old flower heads helps to keep the plant looking good.

Tamarix ramosissima 'Rubra'

3 × 1.8m (10 × 6 ft.)
UK H6 USDA 3-8

Tamarix can be a sprawling, unruly shrub; however, if well maintained it is a lovely subject for its mass of deep pink fluffy flowers in late summer and fall. It flowers on the current season's wood so if trimmed in early spring to promote a compact habit it will produce light, feathery, soft green foliage that blends superbly with the flowers later in the year. It needs an open, sunny situation on well-drained soil with some moisture and is at its best in coastal gardens. It can be planted as an ornamental hedge or windbreak, or grown as a standard to give the effect of a small tree. It combines well with sea buckthorn and rosemary.

Ulex europaeus

1.8 × 1.5m (6 × 5 ft.)
UK H5 USDA 6–8

European gorse is regarded as invasive in some areas because of the amount of seeds it is able to produce which remain viable in the ground for years. Although really deciduous, it appears evergreen because of its dense, prickly, green conifer-like stems. It is a survivor on the most hostile, exposed sites, including sea cliffs and acid moorland. If well managed it is worth considering for difficult situations and naturalistic planting. Masses of bright yellow, coconut-scented pea flowers smother the shrubs in spring and intermittently throughout the year, even in winter in mild weather. An excellent wildlife plant both for nectar and shelter, it grows on any well-drained soil in sun or part shade, preferring acid and neutral conditions. Gorse can be cut back at any time, but pruning after the first flowering season is ideal, before the plants set seed.

OTHER GOOD SHRUBS FOR EXPOSED AND COASTAL SITUATIONS

Cistus ×hybridus

Cornus alba 'Sibirica Variegata'

Euonymus fortunei 'Emerald Gaiety'

Lavandula angustifolia

Mahonia aquifolium 'Apollo'

Olearia ×haastii

Potentilla fruticosa 'Primrose Beauty'

Rhododendron 'Cunningham's White'

Santolina chamaecyparissus

Spiraea japonica 'Goldflame'

PLANTING PARTNERS FOR EXPOSED AND COASTAL SITUATIONS

There is no shortage of plants to combine with shrubs for exposed and coastal situations, but the choice is limited to those of robust constitution that can withstand or bend with the wind. For coastal situations native flora provides the ideal inspiration: plants with tough or narrow leaves, either ground hugging or with strong but flexible stems. Trees may be few in very exposed areas, but some survive, their shape developing with the prevailing wind. Common hawthorn, *Crataegus monogyna*, is among the best, sometimes appearing as a multi-stemmed shrub or frequently a small standard tree, sculpted by the elements. It adapts to both cold, exposed sites as well as those blasted with salt-laden air. In garden situations it adds height among other shrubs and perennials, also contributing valuable shelter.

Grasses are wonderful subjects for open, exposed sites, adding lightness and movement to any planting scheme. Different varieties of miscanthus, sometimes called eulalia, are often used in coastal situations but are hardy enough on exposed sites inland. Those with conspicuous flower heads such as *Miscanthus nepalensis* are particularly lovely when stirred by the breeze. They work well among the rounded mounds of silver foliage shrubs and soften the more rigid lines of conifers.

In bold schemes the dwarf forms of pampas grass form broad mounds of wiry, slender leaves erupting in spectacular displays of creamy plumes in late summer. *Cortaderia selloana* 'Pumila' is strong and compact, growing to around 1.8m (6 ft.) when in flower. It stands up to the wind on exposed sites on the coast and inland and is drought- and wildlife-resistant, even invasive in parts of North America. Some may regard it as dated and old fashioned, but there is no denying its impact against the dark leaves of *Elaeagnus ×submacrophylla* (*Elaeagnus ×ebbingei*) or in combination with *Pinus mugo*.

The dry air of exposed, windy sites is perfect for plants that hate winter wet; covering the surface of the soil with gravel, shingle or stone chips, or larger pebbles also helps. This appears less stark and barren with the addition of low-growing subjects such as thymes and sedums. Cushions of *Armeria maritima*, sea thrift, add yet another texture and flower form as the drumstick flower heads rise above the fine foliage in early summer.

Common hawthorn, *Crataegus monogyna*

above Common honeysuckle, *Lonicera periclymenum*, is extremely hardy and often takes on a shrub-like habit in exposed places.

above The silky plumes of *Miscanthus nepalensis* in late summer bend with the wind.

top The cornflower-like blooms of *Catananche caerulea* are lovely alongside low shrubs at the front of a bed or border.

The delightful, delicate, daisy-flowered *Erigeron karvinskianus* seeds and spreads randomly, filling gaps in paving and wandering between shrubs, often festooning them with fine stems and dainty flowers. It is especially effective with the dense, round mounds of hebes, prolonging the flowering season. Another ground-hugging daisy, *Erigeron glaucus* 'Sea Breeze' is a familiar sight in seaside gardens where it spills over walls and cascades from pots or over the edges of paving. The mauve-pink daisy blooms with golden centres are long lasting and are produced over a long period. They are delightful with *Spiraea japonica* 'Little Princess' and purple sage.

On alkaline soils, hardy yarrow, *Achillea millefolium*, grows well in exposed situations, revelling in sun and dry air. There are many varieties to choose from with finely cut, fern-like grey leaves and flattened heads of flowers that prove attractive to bees and butterflies. The pastel-coloured varieties combine well with hardy (herbaceous)

geraniums and low, sun-loving perennials such as *Catananche caerulea*. Sometimes known as cupid's dart, this is a charming summer-flowering perennial with its wiry stemmed cornflower-like blooms that shine in sunlight and last well when cut. In situations that are exposed but not severely cold in winter, all of these combine well with lavenders and other silver foliage shrubs.

Although it can be rather overpowering when planted with weaker subjects, common honeysuckle, *Lonicera periclymenum*, is an excellent planting partner in exposed situations. Often found rambling around woodlands, in open positions it is normally more compact and bushy. It is often naturalized on sea-cliffs, taking shelter between gorse and heathers. The moving air deters mildew, and the sweetly fragrant blooms are a delight in midsummer. Grow it with gorse and *Rosa rugosa* for a fragrant, nature-friendly planting combination.

Most roses do well on exposed sites and are tolerant of salt air. Those with large soft blooms are best avoided, as are taller varieties. *Rosa* Flower Carpet is a good choice and is available in a range of colours. Most varieties form loose, spreading mounds of reasonably healthy foliage and flower freely from early summer through to fall. They are easily kept in check by pruning with shears in the winter months. The shorter varieties of cluster-flowering or floribunda roses are also worth bearing in mind where a strong block of colour is needed in a planting scheme. They may not be the most refined shrubs, but their flower power is hard to beat.

Erigeron karvinskianus seeds anywhere inhospitable and creates some delightfully informal planting effects, here with *Hebe pinguifolia* 'Sutherlandii'.

Willows, such as the lovely *Salix irrorata*, thrive even on waterlogged soil. Their size can be limited if they are cut back annually in early spring to just above ground level; they make attractive shrubs, especially in winter.

WET AND COMPACTED SOIL, INCLUDING CLAY AND NEW CONSTRUCTION

Clay soils may be fertile, but they are usually heavy and difficult to dig. The tiny mineral particles in the soil pack closely together, excluding air and holding on to water, thereby increasing the weight. In extreme situations the drainage can be poor; water collects in the soil and may even lie on the surface in wet weather. Virtually all air is excluded from the root zone which can cause damage or even death to plants that cannot tolerate these conditions.

Because the clay particles stick together, clay soils easily become compacted, making conditions worse. Excessive foot traffic and infrequent cultivation may be all that is required to cause compaction. Vehicle traffic during construction is particularly damaging, and the soil in gardens of newly built properties is often very compacted even if it does not have a particularly high clay content. In many cases what is left by the builders is little more than subsoil and rubble with a thin layer of topsoil spread over the surface.

This may sound like a rather depressing and limiting growing environment, but it is not all bad news. It is worth emphasizing that these soils are usually fertile. Plants are not deprived of water as often as they are on light, sandy soils. Heavy soils, especially clay, give plants good support and keep them firm in windy, exposed situations. Compacted clay soils can be improved by the addition of copious amounts of organic matter, such as good garden compost and well-rotted manure. Digging in autumn, leaving the surface uneven, and adding horticultural grit allows frost to penetrate and break up the ground.

Many deciduous flowering and foliage shrubs grow well on these soils, some tolerating prolonged waterlogging. Hardy shrubs that tolerate harsh winters are often the ones that also cope with extreme wet. As a general rule most evergreens are less tolerant, and die-back of branches after winter is often a sign that part of the root system has simply drowned. The shrubs that thrive are the ones to choose as the foundation of a planting scheme in a new-construction garden where poor, compacted soil is evident. They will reward from the first season and give long-lasting pleasure.

Cornus alba 'Elegantissima'

1.8 × 1.8m (6 × 6 ft.)
UK H7 USDA 2–8

A vigorous red-barked dogwood with flexible, deep red stems and soft, green and white variegated leaves. Left to grow naturally it soon forms a broad, rounded shrub with long, pliable branches which often put down roots when they touch the ground. Old plants gradually establish large, mounded colonies in ideal growing conditions. If pruned hard every two years, the stems grow vertically and are richer red when the leaves fall in winter. It is extremely hardy and grows on any soil, excelling on wet, heavy ground. It thrives in sun or shade. Prune in late winter to control size and shape. Alternatively the stems can be cut earlier and used for floral decoration.

Deutzia ×hybrida 'Strawberry Fields'

1.8 × 1.5m (6 × 5 ft.)
UK H5 USDA 5–8

Upright, arching stems with peeling tan-coloured bark carry healthy, matt-green, pointed leaves. In midsummer the loose clusters of flowers appear: deep pink buds open to star-shaped mauve-pink blooms, paler towards the centres. The display is long lasting as the flowers open over several weeks. Sadly there is no fragrance, but the beauty of the plant makes up for its absence. An excellent shrub that grows on any soil in sun or partial shade. After the leaves have fallen, the bare stems are not unattractive in winter. Prune after flowering, cutting out some of the stems that have flowered, back to where new shoots are emerging low down on the plants. Resist any inclination to shorten these later in the season as this will spoil the natural, loose habit of the shrub.

Hydrangea macrophylla 'Zorro'

1.2 × 1.2m (4 × 4 ft.)
UK H5 USDA 5–9

An excellent variety of lacecap hydrangea with strong, upright stems, deep green leaves, and firm, filigree flower heads edged with bold sterile florets. The leaves are well-spaced, highlighting the dark stems which are almost black if the plant has sufficient light. The blooms can be vivid blue on acid soil, mauve pink in more alkaline conditions. They give a long-lasting display from late summer, lasting well until the foliage colours richly before the leaves fall. It grows well on most soils, and as the name *hydrangea* suggests, it loves wet conditions. Prune in late winter or early spring, cutting back the faded flower heads to the first pair of healthy fat buds behind the previous year's bloom. On older plants some of the branched tan-coloured stems can be cut back to ground level in winter when the leaves have fallen.

Leycesteria formosa

2.1 × 1.5m (7 × 5 ft.)
UK H5 USDA 7–9

Himalayan honeysuckle or pheasant berry is a fast-growing shrub forming a clump of sea-green, bamboo-like stems that arch towards the tips. The broad, green, pointed leaves are finely edged with purple, the veins often turning purple later in the season. Lantern-like flower clusters hang from the branches in summer, the small white blooms carried between conspicuous red-purple bracts. By late summer the flowers fade and the purple berry fruits appear between the bracts, shining, juicy, and very appealing to birds and wildlife. An ideal shrub for naturalistic settings, on wet or waterlogged soil, in sun or shade. It will seed and is considered invasive in some countries. Prune in winter, cutting out twiggy growth and older branches to enhance the attractive green stems that are displayed when the leaves fall.

Lonicera ×purpusii 'Winter Beauty'

1.8 × 1.8m (6 × 6 ft.)
UK H5 USDA 4–9

Winter-flowering honeysuckle is a vigorous, semi-evergreen shrub with arching tan-coloured stems and oval dark green leaves. It grows quickly and is ideal as a background shrub or to incorporate in a hedge or screen in sun or shade. In winter small, creamy honeysuckle blooms appear in the leaf axils; these have a fragile translucent beauty and a sweet and powerful fragrance. The flowers may be damaged by severe frost and winter wet but are soon followed by more blooms as new buds open. An easy-to-grow shrub that thrives in most conditions, especially on heavy, wet soil. Prune in early spring to control shape and size. Pruning later in the year is at the expense of flowers.

Magnolia ×soulangeana

5 × 5m (16 × 16 ft.)
UK H5 USDA 4–9

A magnificent flowering shrub, eventually a broad, spreading tree. Tulip magnolia is renowned for its goblet-shaped blooms with waxy petals that appear as the leaves begin to unfurl in early spring to mid-season. The flowers are elegantly poised upright on the branches, tulip shaped at first, opening into broad, elegant chalices in warm spring sunshine. The petals are white flushed with pink-purple towards the base, although there are forms with both paler and darker blooms. Sadly they are often damaged by frost, but the risk is worth taking. This magnolia prefers neutral to acid soil and loves clay; it is also more tolerant of other soil conditions than is often portrayed. It loves moist soil and grows well on it in sun or semi-shade. Prune selectively in winter to control size only if really necessary.

Physocarpus opulifolius 'Diablo'

1.8 × 1.2m (6 × 4 ft.)
UK H7 USDA 2–7

The upright, then arching, tan-coloured stems of this variety of ninebark carry deep purple-black maple-like leaves. Clusters of pinkish flowers in early summer mature to jewel-like clusters of deep red fruits. The overall effect is dark and dramatic and a good foil for lighter foliage, especially silver leaves. Plant at the back of a border or as the foundation for planting in a large bed in full sun on any reasonably fertile soil. The foliage colour becomes muddy dark green in shady conditions. Excellent to grow for cutting for floral decoration from midsummer through autumn. Prune in winter, removing some of the older, dark, branched stems. Leave the young lighter-coloured stems to grow naturally.

Rhododendron 'Cunningham's White'

1.5 × 1.8m (5 × 6 ft.)
UK H6 USDA 5–8

One of the hardiest hybrid rhododendrons, it has a sturdy compact habit that withstands a more exposed situation than many others, forming a broad, mounded shrub with dark green leathery leaves. Mauve-tinted buds open to funnel-shaped blooms of icy white flushed with mauve, slightly ruffled and prettily poised in loose heads. The flowers and foliage make a pleasing combination. At its best in semi-shade, it thrives on neutral to acid clay soil and tolerates reasonably wet conditions. No pruning is required, although pruning to shape or rejuvenate old plants can be carried out after flowering. Dead-head, removing just the seedheads if possible, to encourage the new growth.

Rosa gallica var. officinalis

90 × 90cm (3 × 3 ft.)
UK H7 USDA 3–9

Probably the oldest rose in cultivation, the apothecary's rose is among the easiest to grow. It is also relatively disease free and tolerant of situations where other roses fail. Strong, prickly stems carry tough green foliage. The semi-double crimson blooms with golden stamens open from early summer and are freely produced over a few weeks. The flowers are weather resistant and wonderfully fragrant; the petals dry well for pot-pourri, retaining both colour and scent. The perfect rose for heavy, wet clay in full sun but tolerant of some shade, it is good in a mixed border and it makes a lovely, informal hedge. Prune in winter, cutting back by around one third. Lightly prune again after flowering. Feed generously with a rose fertilizer in early spring and again in midsummer.

Salix alba var. vitellina 'Britzensis'

2.4 × 1.5m (8 × 5 ft.)
UK H7 USDA 3–9

Left to grow naturally the red-stemmed form of white willow will make a substantial large tree. However, it can be stooled or pollarded to maintain it as a shrub with upright wand-like stems and slender, silver-backed leaves. The leaves fall to reveal golden orange stems, spectacular in winter sunlight and a wonderful planting partner for red-barked dogwoods. It grows vigorously, rooting easily from hardwood cuttings and thrives in waterlogged and heavy soil conditions. It is extremely hardy and at its best in an open, exposed situation where the winter stems are lit by low sunlight. Prune in late winter, cutting back the stems to the same point every year or two. This can be just above ground level or maintaining a low stem.

Sambucus nigra f. laciniata

2.4 × 2.4m (8 × 8 ft.)
UK H7 USDA 5–7

Cut-leaved elder is a lovely large shrub for country gardens and naturalistic settings. Strong stems carry finely cut, fern-like leaves from spring through to fall. In midsummer large flattened heads of tiny creamy white flowers resembling giant cow parsley are poised on the tops of the branches. These develop into loose drooping clusters of reddish brown berries in late summer. Plant in sun or partial shade on any soil. Like other elders it grows well on clay and chalk and is especially lush and vigorous in wet conditions. It should be pruned hard in late winter in the first two seasons to encourage strong, upright growth. Lighter pruning in subsequent years encourages branching and more flowers.

Spiraea 'Arguta'

1.2 × 1.2m (4 × 4 ft.)
UK H6 USDA 4–8

Commonly known as bridal wreath, this is an enduringly popular shrub for its graceful habit and welcome spring flower power. Arching stems and narrow, soft green leaves form a loose mound. In midspring the branches are crowded with tiny white blooms, creating a foamy, frothy effect, everything a spring-flowering shrub should be. It grows on virtually any soil and thrives on clay and chalk. It tolerates both wet and dry conditions and although the flowering period is relatively brief, the light green foliage and abundant growth make it a useful structure plant. It can be used as an attractive informal hedge if left untrimmed. Prune after flowering, cutting back some of the flowered stems to where new shoots are developing low down in the plant. Avoid light pruning as this robs the plant of its graceful character.

Spiraea japonica 'Anthony Waterer'

90 × 90cm (3 × 3 ft.)
UK H6 USDA 4-9

A delightful Japanese spiraea with upright tan-coloured stems and willow-like mid-green leaves that are often irregularly variegated with cream and pink. In mid- to late summer the pincushion flower heads appear at the tops of the branches. Dark red buds open to crimson-pink flowers that are much appreciated by bees and butterflies. Very easy to grow on most soils, especially on clay and chalk, it tolerates some shade but flowers more profusely in full sun. Because of its light informal habit, it is a useful shrub to mix with perennials, roses, and other shrubs. Prune in late winter, trimming the plant to remove the tips of the stems and faded flower heads. Old plants can be hard pruned to encourage more vigorous growth.

Viburnum opulus 'Roseum'

2.1 × 1.5m (7 × 5 ft.)
UK H7 USDA 3–8

Common snowball is a lovely late spring–flowering shrub. Strong, upright, branched stems carry maple-like green leaves. As the young leaves open the flower clusters develop: spherical heads of green sterile florets gradually expand and turn from green to cream, then white. As they get larger and fuller they hang from the branches before blushing pink as they age. The young greenish flowers are sought after by flower arrangers. No scent, no fall colour, but a ravishing sight when in bloom. Hardy, easy to grow, and an excellent choice for the back of a border and perfect for country and informal gardens. It grows well on heavy clay and is tolerant of wet soil. Prune after flowering, cutting back some of the branches that have bloomed.

Weigela 'Florida Variegata'

1.2 × 1.2m (4 × 4 ft.)
UK H6 USDA 5–8

A variegated shrub with the bonus of beautiful flowers. Compact in habit with soft green leaves edged with creamy white, the plant is highly decorative, even when not in bloom. Clusters of pale pink, trumpet-shaped flowers appear in late spring and early summer, the individual blooms turning darker pink as they age. A second flush of flowers appears in late summer or early fall. There are usually different shades of pink in every flower cluster. This is the ideal weigela for smaller gardens, with interest from early spring to fall. It tolerates tough growing conditions and is perfect for town gardens. Plant in full sun or semi-shade on any soil. Prune after flowering, cutting back some of the branches that have bloomed.

OTHER GOOD SHRUBS FOR
HEAVY, WET SOIL

Amelanchier canadensis

Aronia arbutifolia 'Erecta'

Calycanthus floridus

Cornus sericea 'Bud's Yellow'

Hypericum ×hidcoteense 'Hidcote'

Physocarpus opulifolius 'Dart's Gold'

Salix purpurea 'Gracilis'

Sambucus racemosa 'Sutherland Gold'

Symphoricarpos albus

Viburnum opulus

PLANTING PARTNERS FOR WET AND COMPACTED SOIL

Where soil is permanently moist, perennials that grow with their feet in water will be happy. These include some beautiful subjects for both flowers and foliage and there are plenty to choose from, including rodgersias with their fabulous chestnut-like leaves; *Zantedeschia aethiopica*, arum lily, with exotic foliage and blooms; *Ligularia dentata* 'Desdemona' with spikes of daisy-like blooms in hot orange; and astilbes with their fern-like leaves and feathery plumes. However, the range of shrubs is more limited: willows, dogwoods, elder, and leycesteria being the most tolerant of permanently wet ground.

Where soil is wet in winter and baked hard in summer, many perennials struggle. They put on lush growth in the early part of the year, then wilt when water becomes scarcer. Deciduous shrubs are better equipped to cope. Although some perennials are tougher subjects, there are other factors to consider.

Many perennials need regular lifting and dividing to maintain vigour and the best performance in gardens; however, heavy clay soils make this difficult. Therefore it is important to choose subjects that form neat clumps that do not die out in the centres. These make maintenance easier, and they are less liable to spread and take over. Rampant perennials that spread under the soil are difficult to contain. When you try to dig out unwanted parts of a plant, fragments cling on in the soil and regrow. *Lysimachia ciliata* 'Firecracker' is one such attractive perennial with wine-purple foliage. It grows well on wet clay soils but spreads rampantly via underground rhizomes; once established it is hard to dig out.

The varieties of *Iris sibirica* are good choices. These make clumps of slender upright leaves which stay in good condition throughout the season. The dainty flowers are held above the leaves on slender stems in midsummer. Although best in full sun, they grow in semi-shade and work well with hostas, which also thrive on heavy soils. Although they are troubled by slugs and snails in some gardens, where they can be protected they are so valuable for their decorative rosettes of leaves and late summer flowers. *Hosta* 'So Sweet' is an excellent variety to plant alongside *Hydrangea macrophylla* in wet soil in semi-shade. The delicately variegated leaves brighten the heavy green foliage of the hydrangea and the fragrant flowers of the hosta are a bonus.

Eupatorium purpureum is a tough perennial that is often used with grasses in prairie planting. Growing up to 1.8m (6 ft.) it is ideal at the back of a border or to erupt with its subtle purple-pink fluffy flower heads

Some of the most beautiful perennials thrive in wet conditions. *Rodgersia aesculifolia* has wonderful leaves from spring through to fall; it is an excellent partner for willows and dogwoods grown for their winter stems.

above *Iris sibirica* is a well-behaved clump-forming perennial that needs only occasional lifting and division. It loves wet soil conditions. Blue-flowered varieties are perfect with yellow-leaved shrubs.

opposite top right *Physocarpus opulifolius* 'Diablo' with the green and white striped ribbon leaves of *Miscanthus sinensis* 'Variegatus'.

opposite above right The fiery tail-like flowers of the aptly named *Persicaria amplexicaulis* 'Firetail'. This tough perennial thrives alongside vigorous deciduous shrubs in wet conditions.

opposite right Unlike many other flower bulbs, snake's head fritillary, *Fritillaria meleagris*, likes moist soil and grows well on clay.

in front of heavy foliage. An excellent planting partner for the dark-leaved *Physocarpus opulifolius* 'Diablo', eupatorium grows well on the heaviest soil and, like the shrub, seems to thrive in both wet and dry conditions. Eupatorium is an excellent subject to attract pollinators later in the season. For a lighter more ethereal effect add miscanthus. This lovely clump-forming grass has upright stems and slender leaves, ascending and arching. There are a great number of varieties of different stature, some grown mainly for their leaves, others for their silky long-lasting flower heads. *Miscanthus sinensis* 'Variegatus' has green and white striped leaves which contrast well with dark-leaved shrubs. It is shy to flower, but that is not a disadvantage.

Persicaria amplexicaulis may not be the most refined perennial, but it provides a welcome show of late summer flowers and revels in heavy, wet soil. 'Firetail' is a popular and reliable variety with long-lasting spikes of dark red flowers. Rather lax in habit, it forms a loose mound, but the stems and flowers will grow up through open woody plants such as *Cornus alba*. It works well with both white and golden variegated varieties.

Daylilies are loved for their slender leaves and succession of exotic lily-like blooms from mid- to late summer. Their popularity has led to extensive hybridization and an amazing number of cultivars in a wide spectrum of colours. They make great planting partners for shrubs because of their contrasting texture and leaf form and their showy blooms. Those with hot-coloured flowers work well with dark and golden foliage. The deep pink flowers of *Hemerocallis* 'Summer Wine' set off the soft hues of the summer garden. The pastels are useful to extend the season alongside shrubs such as deutzia and viburnum. Daylilies grow on most soils, including clay; they enjoy moist conditions.

Heavy wet soils are generally not the best environment for flower bulbs. However, the hardier narcissi are the best equipped to cope and do well on heavy soil, as long as it is not too waterlogged in winter. *Fritillaria meleagris*, snake's head fritillary, a native of water meadows, also likes wet conditions as does *Galanthus nivalis*, snowdrop, especially if some organic matter is incorporated into the ground.

English lavender loves a dry alkaline soil.

ALKALINE AND CHALK SOILS

A wide range of evergreen and deciduous shrubs thrive on alkaline soils; that is, those with a pH greater than 7. The only ones that will not tolerate them are ericaceous shrubs such as rhododendrons and pieris and other lime-haters like camellias. There is a complex relationship between the pH of the soil and some plant nutrients that are essential for growth. On alkaline soils, iron, vital for the growth of ericaceous subjects, becomes unavailable to them. As a result growth ceases, the foliage turns yellow, and the plants eventually fail.

It is probably because these few desirable shrubs will not grow on alkaline soils and chalk that they are seen as limiting growing conditions. However, most familiar flowering shrubs including potentilla, deutzia, philadelphus, weigela, and lilac are at their best on chalk soils, which comprise shallow, usually dry soil over white, soft, earthy limestone.

Hardy fuchsias grow well and are useful in shadier spots where sun-loving flowering plants can be poor. Wonderful foliage shrubs such as the black-leaved elders are vigorous and luxuriant on chalk, whereas they can be weak and slow-growing on acid soil. Most popular evergreen shrubs grow well on alkaline soils, especially *Viburnum tinus*, aucuba, and holly. Cherry laurel, *Prunus laurocerasus*, is not so good on chalk, often showing its displeasure with yellowish leaves. Portuguese laurel, *Prunus lusitanica*, is a better choice.

Alkaline soils over chalk can be shallow and dry. These are a little more restrictive as plants that prefer deeper, moister soil may grow poorly. Most subjects that enjoy dry sunny situations are also good choices for dry alkaline soils, especially woody herbs, lavender, and silver foliage shrubs. Popular perennials such as achilleas, geraniums, and penstemons love chalk and make colourful summer additions.

Dry chalk soils can be improved by the addition of copious amounts of organic matter, which is often more acidic. This may lower the pH temporarily, but the alkaline conditions quickly prevail. Sulphur chips are also often recommended as a way of lowering soil pH. These again have a short-lived effect and only really work close to the surface; as plants grow, the roots eventually reach the chalk below the topsoil. If lime-intolerant plants are seen as essential in areas of alkaline soil, grow them in containers or isolated raised beds using lime-free growing media.

Aucuba japonica

1.5 × 1.2m (5 × 4 ft.)
UK H5 USDA 7–10

Spotted laurel is well-known for its large, glossy, dark green leaves, speckled with yellow. Strong growing, with upright stems, it quickly makes an impact and is a wonderful evergreen structure shrub for shady situations. Inconspicuous reddish purple flowers with creamy stamens appear in spring, often going unnoticed among the luxuriant foliage. These develop into showy red berries from midsummer onwards on female plants; these are correctly named *Aucuba japonica* 'Variegata'. An easy-to-grow and reliable shrub, tolerant of pollution and poor soil, spotted laurel also grows well in pots and containers. Very dry conditions can cause shrivelled, blackened growth at the tips of the shoots, often mistaken for frost damage. Prune in late winter or early spring if necessary to control size and shape.

Berberis thunbergii f. *atropurpurea* 'Harlequin'

1.2 × 1.2m (4 × 4 ft.)
UK H7 USDA 4–8

A terrific purple foliage shrub with upright, arching stems and deep red-purple leaves. The tips of the shoots are suffused with salmon-pink, which is more widespread on newer shoots. The foliage colour is best in an open, sunny situation. Small creamy flowers in spring are attractive to bees and are followed by bead-like red fruits in autumn as the foliage turns to flame before it falls. A wonderful shrub for summer and autumn colour that is easy to grow and reliable on any well-drained soil, it is drought tolerant once established. No pruning is necessary, but some old stems can be cut back hard in winter to encourage new shoots from the base of the plant. This variety is not invasive.

Cistus ×hybridus

90 × 90cm (3 × 3 ft.)
UK H5 USDA 7–10

A widely planted, tough, and hardy evergreen sun rose with masses of shining white flowers with golden stamens in midsummer. A few more blooms also appear later on the rounded mound of mid-green foliage. Unlike most other cistus, this one responds well to trimming and light pruning if carried out from an early age. It is a good choice for dry, sunny banks, alongside paving, in coastal gardens, or in mixed borders where it sits well with lavender, woody herbs, and other Mediterranean subjects. Although not particularly long lived, it is easy to grow, quick to establish, and very rewarding, hence its wide use in commercial landscape schemes.

Deutzia ×*elegantissima* 'Rosealind'

75 × 90cm (30 in. × 3 ft.)
UK H5 USDA 6–9

A delightful small shrub with fine, arching stems and slender, pointed dark green leaves, often flushed with purple. The clusters of lightly fragrant, deep pink flowers appear in midsummer, conspicuously displayed against the foliage. Each tiny bloom is perfectly formed, with a tracery of white highlighting the petals towards the centre of the flower. In fall the leaves turn bronze-red before they fall. An ideal shrub for a small garden, 'Rosealind' is more attractive than most large deutzias when not in flower. Easy to grow in full sun on any well-drained soil, it is drought tolerant once established. Prune after flowering, removing some of the flowered stems if necessary. Pruning is not required every year.

Elaeagnus 'Quicksilver'

3 × 2.4m (10 × 8 ft.)
UK H5 USDA 4–9

A lovely form of oleaster with willow-like leaves of silky silver-grey. Arching branches with weeping branchlets create a loose and flowing effect. A deciduous shrub, its foliage is brightest and most reflective through summer when tiny cream flowers fill the garden with their sweet, heavy perfume. The best large silver foliage shrub, it reaches the dimensions given here in five years, perfect at the back of a large bed or border where it provides a lively backdrop for lower-growing subjects. It is stunning planted alongside anything with purple leaves. It grows best in full sun on any reasonable well-drained soil, but will tolerate some shade. Prune in winter to control size and shape. Hard pruning produces vigorous, straight shoots.

Fuchsia 'Riccartonii'

1.8 × 1.2m (6 × 4 ft.)
UK H6 USDA 7–10

Fuchsias are versatile shrubs that grow on most soils in a variety of situations from full sun to shade. *Fuchsia* 'Riccartonii' is a strong-growing variety with upright stems, becoming more spreading with age. It suits mixed borders, grows well against walls and fences, can be grown in containers or even used as an ornamental hedging subject. The pendent crimson and purple-blue flowers hang from the branches throughout summer and autumn; purple-black fruits often follow which are appreciated by wild birds. Although deciduous, the foliage persists on the branches into winter in mild and coastal areas. In harsher climates the stems can be cut to the ground like an herbaceous perennial in winter, to grow again from the base the following year. In all areas prune to control shape and size in early spring.

Hebe 'Spender's Seedling'

75 × 75cm (30 × 30 in.)
UK H5 USDA 7–10

A small, evergreen shrub of light, feathery character with very narrow dark green leaves on slender stems. The narrow flower panicles are equally delicate, pure white and sparkling. The blooms are produced over a long period through summer and autumn, much to the delight of bees and butterflies. Hardier than many other hebes and more tolerant of warm, dry conditions, this is an excellent small shrub for any garden. It combines well with white variegated evergreens in semi-shade and lavenders and silver foliage in sun. It grows on any well-drained soil, but is at its best in alkaline conditions. No pruning is required, but an occasional tidy in early spring keeps the plant in shape.

Lavatera ×clementii

1.5 × 1.2m (5 × 4 ft.)
UK H5 USDA 6-9

The shrubby mallow is not a long-lived plant, but it grows quickly and blooms profusely over a long period from early summer through to fall. Upright stems carry grey-green leaves and funnel-shaped hollyhock-like blooms with tissue-paper petals. The stems tend to become lax and flop under the weight of flowers and leaves later in the season. Usually the habit is better on dry, shallow soil where the plants are also longer lived. There are many similar varieties in varying shades of pink and white. 'Candy Floss' is a good choice for its abundant pale pink blooms. Plant in full sun on any well-drained soil. It is an excellent gap-filler that mixes well with sun-loving shrubs and perennials. Plants are best shortened in fall and then cut back hard in early spring to encourage new shoots to develop from the base. Partial pruning in the growing season helps to keep the plants compact.

Philadelphus 'Belle Étoile'

1.8 × 1.2m (6 × 4 ft.)
UK H7 USDA 5-8

One of the best varieties of mock orange growing to a medium-sized deciduous shrub with arching branches and mid-green leaves. The creamy white single flowers appear along the branches in midsummer, the petals stained purple towards the centre of each flower which is crowded with golden stamens. The sweet orange-blossom fragrance will fill the garden and is a highlight of summer. Although philadelphus bloom only once and the foliage is ordinary, they are easy to grow, tolerant of poor, dry soils, and reliable. Prune after flowering, cutting back some of the flowered stems to where new shoots are emerging low down on the branches. Never trim or snip: maintain that loose, graceful habit.

Potentilla fruticosa 'Primrose Beauty'

90 × 90cm (3 × 3 ft.)
UK H7 USDA 2–8

The shrubby potentillas are among the toughest, most resilient shrubs; easy to grow and with incredible flower power, they bloom from early summer through to late fall. 'Primrose Beauty' forms a rounded, twiggy bush with soft grey-green leaves and profuse soft yellow, buttercup blooms. The gentle colour mixes easily with other shrubs and perennials in full sun or semi-shade. Growing on any well-drained soil, it is often at its best on shallow chalk and poor dry soil. This is a versatile subject, ideal to add summer flowers among plain and variegated evergreens. The dense mass of drab twigs left in winter when the leaves fall should be lightly trimmed in early spring to improve shape and remove the previous season's faded flowers. No other pruning is required.

Prunus lusitanica 'Variegata'

1.8 × 1.5m (6 × 5 ft.)
UK H5 USDA 6–9

The variegated form of Portugal laurel is a most attractive evergreen shrub of loose, conical shape. The softly shining dark green leaves are edged with creamy white, often waved and flushed with pink in winter. The stems are red-brown and the leaf stalks crimson. In early summer short spikes of white flowers appear, although not as freely as on the plain green species. This shrub grows on any well-drained, reasonably fertile soil, including shallow chalk. It is a much better choice for an alkaline soil than *Prunus laurocerasus*, the widely planted cherry laurel, which tends to become yellow and stunted in those conditions. It makes an excellent structure shrub, alternative to a small tree, or hedge. Prune in early spring if necessary to control shape and size; it is considered invasive in parts of North America.

Sambucus nigra f. *porphyrophylla* 'Eva'

1.8 × 1.5m (6 × 5 ft.)
UK H6 USDA 4–8

A wonderful form of elder with strong stems and finely cut purple-black leaves, also available as *Sambucus nigra* 'Black Lace'. At its best the luxuriant foliage resembles the plumage of an exotic bird. Flattened heads of pink flowers appear in early summer, followed by black berries, virtually invisible against the leaves. A striking hardy, deciduous foliage shrub, its light and feathery form makes it a good planting partner for roses, perennials, and other flowering shrubs. The colour is best in full sun and it grows on any well-drained soil; however; it excels on clay and chalk. Prune hard in late winter to encourage vigorous growth of young plants. Prune mature plants lightly for branched growth and more flowers.

Sarcococca confusa

45 × 60cm (18 in. × 2 ft.)
UK H5 USDA 6–9

Sweet box or Christmas box is a useful small evergreen shrub for shade, thriving on most well-drained soils but excelling on chalk. Upright, green, arching stems grow from the ground to form a thick clump. The small, pointed, glossy, dark green leaves are attractively waved and well-spaced along the branches. In late winter tiny white flowers appear in the leaf axils. They may not be showy, but the perfume is sweet and strong and hangs on cold air throughout the winter garden. The tiny blooms are often followed by black berries, sometimes still present on the plants the following flowering season. Plant in shade and avoid sunny situations and pots where the foliage tends to yellow. No pruning is required, but this is an excellent shrub for cutting for floral decoration.

Spiraea japonica 'Firelight'

45 × 90cm (18 in. × 3 ft.)
UK H6 USDA 4–8

Similar in habit to a potentilla, this is the best of the golden-leaved Japanese spiraeas, presenting a changing picture through the seasons. Sparkling flame-coloured new shoots in spring develop into rich golden leaves, orange-red at the tips of the shoots. Clusters of deep pink flowers appear in summer before the foliage turns to red in fall. Even the tan-coloured stems are attractive in winter, especially if the old flower heads and spindly ends of the bare shoots are clipped off when the leaves fall. Drought tolerant, reliable, and thriving on any soil, this is an easy shrub that is at its best in an open, sunny situation. Clip to control shape and size in late winter.

Syringa 'Pink Perfume'

1.2m × 90cm (4 × 3 ft.)
UK H7 USDA 3–7

A pretty dwarf lilac with a bushy growth habit and small, soft leaves. The delicate panicles of mauve-pink flowers appear in midspring, then again in summer through to fall. As most lilacs are a one-season wonder, the repeat flowering of this variety makes it highly desirable for small gardens and cultivation in containers. The blooms are sweetly lilac-scented and freely produced in an open, sunny situation. It grows on any well-drained but sufficiently moist soil and is at its best in alkaline conditions. It is drought tolerant once established, but blooming may cease in hot, dry weather, resuming again when temperatures fall. No pruning is required, but removal of faded flowers will encourage reblooming.

OTHER GOOD SHRUBS FOR ALKALINE AND CHALK SOILS

Brachyglottis (Dunedin Group) 'Sunshine'

Buddleja davidii Buzz Indigo

Cotoneaster franchetii

Daphne odora 'Aureomarginata'

Euonymus europaeus 'Red Cascade'

Hibiscus syriacus 'Hamabo'

Hypericum ×hidcoteense 'Hidcote'

Lonicera ×purpusii 'Winter Beauty'

Photinia ×fraseri 'Red Robin'

Weigela 'Florida Variegata'

PLANTING PARTNERS FOR ALKALINE AND CHALK SOILS

When it comes to choosing planting partners for shrubs on alkaline soil, the gardener will be spoiled for choice. Perennials predominate in gardens on chalk, from early summer right through to fall. Chalk is also associated with another favourite plant group, the clematis, queen of climbers. With so much choice and many new perennial introductions annually, it is the shrubs that have struggled to find space in recent years. However, shrubs and perennials are sociable plants that can share the garden in planting schemes. If clematis are added to the picture they extend the season of interest of flowering shrubs and help to create some exciting colour combinations.

Hardy geraniums are among the most useful mixers in any border, especially the blue-flowering varieties which will associate with any other colour. Easy to grow and trouble free, they are ideal in front of deciduous shrubs and roses where they help to conceal bare stems. Most are at their best in full sun and are happy if the shrubs steal the water. *Geranium* 'Orion' is an excellent tall variety with clear blue flowers for a long period in midsummer. It does require some support so is best planted between low shrubs such as potentillas and spiraeas. *Geranium* Rozanne is the one to grow for continuity of flowering from midsummer right through to fall. Ignore advice to plant in groups of three or more: one plant will produce a spreading mound up to 90cm (3 ft.) across. It can be trimmed midseason or allowed to climb into the base of its woody neighbours.

Alliums are good summer-flowering bulbs to place among geraniums and other low-growing perennials. In all cases the foliage fades as the flowers develop so growing them through leafier subjects helps to conceal this. Drumstick allium, *Allium sphaerocephalon*, is inexpensive to buy and fits in anywhere; it is also later flowering than most. Planted in drifts among dark-leaved sedums in full sun, it is also fabulous with silver foliage shrubs, cistus, and purple-black *Sambucus nigra* f. *porphyrophylla* 'Eva' (*Sambucus nigra* 'Black Lace').

Geums have found a place in more gardens lately with the introduction of many new varieties. They may not be the most flamboyant perennials, but their rounded leaves grow to form useful ground-covering clumps and their buttercup-like blooms add vibrant colour from early summer to midseason. They work well with hardy geraniums at the front of a border. Try the gold-orange–flowered *Geum* 'Totally Tangerine' with *Spiraea japonica* 'Firelight' for a lively early summer cocktail.

Scabious, pincushion flowers, love dry, well-drained soils. They too have enjoyed a surge in popularity, partly

Geranium 'Orion' shown with *Briza maxima* and dark red
astrantias

above *Knautia macedonica* in front of blue geraniums

above *Veronicastrum virginicum* 'Album'

top Drumstick allium, *Allium sphaerocephalon*, provides a contrasting flower form in the summer border. Pictured here with purple sedums and silver eryngiums, it is also excellent with lavenders and silver foliage shrubs.

because of their use as cut flowers and also with the introduction of new varieties that are disease free and easy to grow. *Scabiosa* 'Vivid Violet', for example, is a wonderful colour and exceptionally free flowering when grown in full sun. It is tall enough to add light height and is shown to advantage against the purple-red leaves of *Berberis thunbergii* f. *atropurpurea* 'Harlequin'.

Knautia macedonica is closely related to scabious. It has tall, wiry, branched stems topped with neat, dark red pincushion flowers that move gently in the breeze. On chalk or dry, well-drained soil it seeds itself and drifts through the border, adding a three-dimensional quality to a planting scheme. Superb planted in front of *Elaeagnus* 'Quicksilver'.

For vertical interest try veronicastrum. Tall, slender stems with narrow leaves are topped by fine, pointed spikes of tiny, starry flowers, almost like thick pipe-cleaners. *Veronicastrum*

virginicum 'Album' is pure white and wonderfully delicate in appearance which belies its hardy constitution. Best further back in the border, it is lovely when backlit by sunlight or shown against dark evergreens. The flowers are amazingly attractive to bees. For a more flamboyant tall perennial choose *Campanula lactiflora*: tall stems are topped with clusters of upturned bell-shaped flowers in soft lilac-blue. It is at its best on soil that is not too dry, but is particularly valuable because it blooms well in semi-shade. It is the ideal planting partner for hardy fuchsias.

Early in the year hellebores also enjoy shade and most love alkaline soils, including the Christmas rose, *Helleborus niger*, which is never happy in acid conditions. *Helleborus ×hybridus* may predominate in most gardens, but many are yet to discover some of the evergreen hybrids such as *Helleborus ×ericsmithii*. This has attractive foliage and large clusters of outward-facing blooms that are extremely long lasting.

It is ideal to add early interest alongside both deciduous and evergreen shrubs.

Clematis viticella varieties are the ideal clematis to grow through flowering shrubs to extend the season. Cut back to 15cm (6 in.) above ground level in late winter; the old growth can be easily pulled away from the branches of the shrub, so maintenance is easy. The light, twining stems grow quickly and produce a wonderful display of flowers in late summer and autumn. *Clematis* 'Minuet' planted to grow through *Philadelphus* 'Belle Étoile' adds another flowering period of two months.

Clematis 'Minuet'

The lovely *Rhododendron* 'Daviesii', a deliciously fragrant deciduous azalea that thrives on most acid soils.

ACID SOILS: MOIST AND PEATY, DRY AND SANDY

Acid soils are often the envy of those gardening in alkaline conditions: they offer the opportunity to grow some of the real gems of the woody plant world. Rhododendrons, camellias, pieris, and magnolias are regarded among the most desirable shrubs. However, these conditions can be limiting; many peaty and sandy acid soils are low in fertility. Ericaceous plants are not hungry feeders and are well adapted to a meagre diet; other flowering shrubs that thrive on alkaline soils can be starved and grow weakly.

It is also worth remembering that there are many different types of acidic soil; that is, with a pH of less than 7. Some clay soils are acidic; they are the more fertile ones although drainage can be poor, which is not to the taste of shrubs that dislike wet feet. Peaty soils may look rich and dark, but they too are often wet in winter, very acidic, and very low in plant nutrients. Sandy and stony soils, in contrast, may be dry. Nutrients are soon washed away by rainfall and irrigation and summer heat can quickly put plants under stress. Sandy and stony soils can be improved dramatically by the addition of organic matter such as well-rotted manure, garden compost, or leaf mould. Peaty soils are already high in organic content, but lack mineral particles. They are more challenging to improve.

The term *ericaceous* is often used for any lime-hating plant. It really only refers to members of the family Ericaceae, the heather family. However, from a horticultural point of view it is used more generally to include subjects like camellia and loropetalum.

Many lime-hating shrubs make excellent subjects for pots and containers, which is the way to grow them in areas where the soil is alkaline. A loam-based growing medium is always the best choice; it is longer lasting and does not depend on a wetting agent for water retention. Whether growing in pots or in the open ground, use a specifically formulated fertilizer for lime-hating plants. Standard fertilizers may supply too much nutrient for a lime hater.

In addition, many subjects that grow on dry, alkaline soils also grow on dry acidic soils. Those with moist, peaty growing conditions should make the most of the gems of the plant world that require them.

Calluna vulgaris 'Silver Knight'

30 × 45cm (12 × 18 in.)
UK H7 USDA 4–9

Heather is a hardy little shrub, well adapted to exposure and open, sunny situations on neutral to acid soil. 'Silver Knight' is just one cultivar among many. It has upright stems carrying downy, grey-green foliage in stout spikes. The shining lilac flowers crowd the stems in late summer and early fall; they are very attractive to bees and pollinators. It forms a rounded mat and makes excellent groundcover on well-drained soil. At its best in full sun, it is drought tolerant once established and an excellent subject for dry, sandy soil. In the wild the species is often found growing on sea cliffs and sand dunes. Prune after flowering, clipping back to just below the flowers. This keeps the plants compact and promotes new growth. Plant young, small, pot-grown plants in groups of three or five for best results.

Camellia japonica 'Adolphe Audusson'

1.8 × 1.5m (6 × 5 ft.)
UK H5 USDA 8–9

The varieties of *Camellia japonica* are among the most exotic and elegant flowering shrubs. Of the many varieties to choose from, 'Adolphe Audusson' is an enduring favourite. Bold, deep green, shining evergreen leaves are carried on strong stems. It grows vigorously with an elegant, broad but upright habit. The large, blood-red, semi-double flowers open from fat buds anytime from late winter through to midspring. They are elegantly poised on the branches, long lasting and then gracefully dying, unlike many other varieties. It is at its best in semi-shade but will grow successfully in quite shaded conditions, although it does not flower as well. Avoid situations that catch the early morning sun as this damages frozen flower buds. It needs a reasonably moist but well-drained soil and is excellent in a pot or grown as a wall shrub. Prune only if necessary, after flowering, to control shape and size.

Desfontainia spinosa

1.5 × 1.2m (5 × 4 ft.)
UK H4 USDA 7–10

A choice evergreen shrub of stiff, upright habit with small, emerald green, holly-like leaves, not dissimilar to *Berberis darwinii* at first sight. In summer and early fall the tubular, waxy flowers appear, hanging below the branches; scarlet-orange with yellow mouths, they stand out boldly against the foliage. A native of the Andes it is a delightful plant for a sheltered spot in semi-shade and likes a neutral to acid, well-drained but reasonably moist soil. Perfect for a woodland garden. No pruning is required, but light pruning to control size and shape can be carried out in early spring.

Enkianthus campanulatus

1.8 × 1.2m (6 × 4 ft.)
UK H5 USDA 5–7

The redvein enkianthus is a delightful shrub with ascending red-brown stems and whorls of mid-green leaves. In midspring the delicate bell-shaped flowers hang below the leaves like tiny, pale salmon–coloured Japanese lanterns, intricately veined with dark red. The foliage turns to vibrant shades of dark red and flame before the leaves fall. Upright in habit, becoming broader with age, it is an elegant subject that thrives on a moist, peaty soil in semi-shade. In sun on drier sandy or stony soils the growth is slower and more compact. As a young plant it grows happily in a pot and is a good alternative to a Japanese maple. No pruning is required; however, selective pruning to control shape can be done after flowering.

Fothergilla major Monticola Group

1.2 × 1.2m (4 × 4 ft.)
UK H5 USDA 5–9

Witch alder resembles witch hazel in habit with its spreading grey branches and rounded, lightly ribbed, mid-green leaves. In midspring the bottle-brush flower heads appear like short candles along the branches. Opening as the leaves unfurl, they are fluffy and white, cream towards the centres. Its most spectacular season is autumn when the leaves turn to rich gold and flame before they fall. A hardy native of the U.S., it is at its best in semi-shade on moist, peaty soil but will grow happily in full sun. Eventually it can grow to make a large shrub, but growth is slow and it rarely attains great proportions as a garden plant. No pruning is required.

Gaultheria procumbens

10 × 60cm (4 in. × 2 ft.)
UK H7 USDA 3–8

Creeping wintergreen, or checkerberry as it is sometimes known, is a low groundcover forming an evergreen carpet of small, shining, rounded, deep green leaves on fine reddish stems. It grows in shade or semi-shade, spreading by suckering stems, but is not invasive. Dainty, pinkish white, urn-shaped flowers develop into relatively large, shiny scarlet berries which are nestled among the leaves. In colder weather the upper leaves take on a red-green flush, and both flowers and fruits can appear together in early winter in cultivation. It is ideal on reasonably moist soil under trees and is useful in winter containers. No pruning is required; however, brushing off fallen leaves from overhanging trees and shrubs helps prevent fungal disease.

Hamamelis ×intermedia 'Barmstedt Gold'

1.5 × 1.2m (5 × 4 ft.)
UK H5 USDA 5–8

Witch hazels are remarkable shrubs with the benefit of both fascinating flowers that withstand the winter weather and also good fall foliage colour. 'Barmstedt Gold' is a vigorous shrub with ascending branches, eventually producing a large, vase-shaped plant. The ribbon-petalled, golden yellow blooms are freely produced on the bare branches in midwinter, showy and spicily fragrant. The hazel-like leaves turn to red-orange before they fall. Witch hazel grows on any reasonably moist, neutral to acid soil and is best in semi-shade but with enough sun to ripen the wood to produce flowers. No pruning is required and should be avoided. Because it is a grafted plant, suckers from the rootstock sometimes grow from the base of the plant; remove them as soon as possible.

Kalmia latifolia

1.2 × 1.2m (4 × 4 ft.)
UK H6 USDA 4–9

Mountain laurel or calico bush is a lovely evergreen shrub, similar to a broad-leaved pieris in habit. The shining, deep green leaves form a loose, rounded shrub with red-brown stems. Clusters of dark pink buds that resemble perfectly piped sugar icing open into cup-shaped clear pink flowers in early summer. The blooms are perfectly formed with delicate detail, striking against the dark green leaves. It thrives on acid, peaty soil but can be difficult to establish. In a pot it is unhappy and the roots are unstable; therefore in some areas it is rarely offered for sale. It prefers shelter and is at its best in semi-shade but is remarkably hardy and tolerant in the right growing conditions. No pruning is required.

ACID SOILS

Leucothoe fontanesiana 'Rainbow'

90cm × 1.2m (3 × 4 ft.)
UK H5 USDA 5–8

An attractive evergreen shrub with very arching stems and elegant, pointed shining dark green leaves, heavily streaked and variegated with cream, pink, and deep red. The colour becomes more intense in winter when the foliage flushes with beetroot red if the plant is in an open position. Insignificant, catkin-like flower clusters appear along the branches in late spring, often going unnoticed. An excellent groundcover shrub that is tolerant of fairly dry conditions once established; ideal under the light shade of deciduous trees. It has become a popular landscape plant that brings instant impact to a planting scheme. No pruning is necessary; however, long shoots can be shortened in early spring to keep the plants compact.

Loropetalum chinense var. rubrum 'Fire Dance'

90cm × 1.2m (3 × 4 ft.)
UK H5 USDA 7–10

A gem of a shrub with spreading horizontal branches and neat, softly shining, red-purple leaves. The vibrant pink, witch hazel–like flowers appear mostly in spring but can occur randomly throughout the year. They are a striking contrast against the dark foliage. Regarded as slightly tender, it is widely grown in milder localities but makes an excellent subject for a sheltered spot on any well-drained neutral to acid soil. At its best in semi-shade but with enough direct sunlight to enhance the foliage colour, it grows well in a pot and is a good choice for small town gardens. No pruning is required; however, dead or damaged shoots may need to be removed after winter.

Rhododendron 'Cannon's Double'

1.5 × 1.2m (5 × 4 ft.)
UK H5 USDA 5–8

There are many varieties of deciduous azalea to choose from; 'Cannon's Double' excels in both flower quality and fall foliage colour. Upright, red-brown shoots are topped with deep green leaves, often flushed with dark red. Salmon buds open in late spring to fully double flowers of clotted cream, flushed with deeper yellow and a hint of orange; they are long lasting and beautiful, but sadly without fragrance. The foliage colours brilliantly in fall in shades of crimson and flame. Deciduous azaleas grow in sun or semi-shade on most neutral to acid soils, but growth is slow and sparse in dry conditions. They associate well with birches and Japanese maples and are lovely in a woodland setting. Their open, graceful habit makes them easy to combine with other shrubs. Old plants can be hard pruned after flowering to rejuvenate them.

Rhododendron 'Horizon Monarch'

1.8 × 2.1m (6 × 7 ft.)
UK H5 USDA 5–8

A fine modern hybrid rhododendron with large, leathery, dark green leaves held on copper-brown stems. It grows to form a broad, mounded shrub; an excellent foliage subject, even without the flowers. In midspring the fat orange buds appear in clusters at the tips of the shoots. These burst into large, funnel-shaped blooms, slightly frilled, rich custard yellow flushed with salmon-orange on the reverse. A plant in full flower is a wonderful sight. A hardy rhododendron that grows well in sun or partial shade on any neutral to acid soil, it tolerates quite dry conditions once established. No pruning is required; however, pruning to control shape and size can be carried out after flowering.

ACID SOILS

Rhododendron Loderi Group

2.4 × 1.8m (8 × 6 ft.)
UK H5 USDA 7–9

The Loderi hybrid rhododendrons were raised by Sir Edmund Loder at Leonardslee, Sussex, UK, in the early 1900s. Mature plants make magnificent large shrubs, but even young specimens are quite breath-taking when in bloom. There are several named varieties, although any seedling is worth growing and it will usually bloom from an early age. Open and vigorous in habit with long, lozenge-shaped leaves, they are less dense than most hybrid rhododendrons. Loose trusses of buds open in mid- to late spring into large, trumpet-shaped blooms that resemble small lilies. Delicate waxy petals have a translucent quality and the scent is sweet, strong, and delicious. A shrub for reasonably moist acid soil, rich in leaf mould and organic matter, in semi-shade; a woodland setting is ideal. No pruning required.

Pieris 'Forest Flame'

1.2m × 90cm (4 × 3 ft.)
UK H5 USDA 5–9

The best known variety of lily of the valley bush, with slender, dark green leaves and sprays of creamy bell-shaped flowers opening from bead-like reddish buds in spring. The new growth is bright scarlet and creates a striking effect with the flowers. Flushes of red shoots can appear throughout the year; even if they are knocked back by frost they are soon replaced. This is a lovely shrub for a shaded border with azaleas, rhododendrons, and heathers. Best in semi-shade or shade, on neutral to acid, reasonably moist, fertile soil, it is also excellent in a pot if grown in a lime-free growing medium. Choose a sheltered position to avoid damage to new growth. Prune after flowering in spring, if necessary, to control size and shape.

Viburnum furcatum

1.8 × 1.5m (6 × 5 ft.)
UK H5 USDA 7–9

A very beautiful species of viburnum from Japan and Taiwan with ascending, then spreading branches and large, rounded, strongly veined, deep green leaves, not unlike a witch hazel in appearance. In midspring the large, pure white, lacecap flower heads are held on the ends of the shoots. The fertile florets develop into scarlet fruits that ripen in late summer. The most spectacular season is fall, when the leaves colour in shades of crimson and orange over a period of many weeks before they fall. This shrub needs a neutral to acid, moist, but well-drained soil, ideally in semi-shade. A perfect woodland shrub for a larger garden with rhododendrons and pieris. No pruning is required; it just needs space to grow.

OTHER GOOD SHRUBS FOR ACID SOILS

Acer palmatum

Berberis thunbergii f.
   atropurpurea 'Harlequin'

Cistus ×*hybridus*

Cornus 'Porlock'

Cotoneaster franchetii

Crinodendron hookerianum

Ilex crenata 'Convexa'

Magnolia ×*soulangeana*

Physocarpus opulifolius
   'Diable D'Or'

Pittosporum tenuifolium

PLANTING PARTNERS FOR ACID SOIL

Many ericaceous shrubs grow best in semi-shade, ideally under the light canopy of deciduous trees such as birches; therefore other plants that grow well with them are usually from woodland habitats. However, rhododendrons, azaleas, pieris, and camellias all have dense fibrous roots that form thick mats close to the soil surface which can create a tough environment for other plants to flourish in. Therefore mature ericaceous shrubs are often found surrounded by little more than moss and a few ferns.

Some fern varieties thrive in both moist and dry shaded conditions on acid soil. Their finely cut, filigree fronds may be plain green, but their form and texture is a wonderful contrast to the solid leathery foliage of rhododendrons and camellias. Some are evergreen, others deciduous. The crested male fern, *Dryopteris filix-mas* 'Cristata', is very hardy, perfect for groundcover under trees and large shrubs. It is drought tolerant once established, so copes well with competition. It associates well with hostas, pulmonarias, and dicentras.

The soft shield fern, *Polystichum setiferum* 'Herrenhausen', is striking with feathery filigree fronds in a coppery hue as they unfurl. Old fronds stay evergreen, fading in spring as the new ones emerge. It is the perfect partner to early-flowering narcissus, bronze carex, *Leucothoe fontanesiana* 'Rainbow', and the lovely *Rhododendron* 'Horizon Monarch'.

Hostas grow particularly well on moist, acidic soil. In these conditions they work well with the lower-growing dicentras; those with fern-like grey-green leaves and short stems carrying pendent flowers make the best groundcover. They usually die back in late summer, but if planted with hostas the latter take over for the rest of the season. *Dicentra* 'Stuart Boothman' is a dainty plant with blue-grey foliage, often tinged with bronze. The pendent blooms are deep pink. Once established it is a tough and resilient subject that spreads reliably.

Although more often associated with alkaline soils, blue comfrey, *Symphytum caucasicum*, makes excellent groundcover under mature rhododendrons. The soft green foliage spreads to make large ground-covering mats. Stout stems carry the vibrant blue flowers in midspring, the colour rivalling that of the finest pulmonaria. The flowers are attractive to bees, and this variety is less invasive than some of the other comfreys.

Those gardening on acid soil, rich in organic matter, especially leaf mould, will have the opportunity to grow trilliums, some of the most beautiful woodland flowering plants. Their three-petalled blooms never fail to intrigue and bewitch the plant enthusiast. In the right soil conditions they are easier to grow than many imagine. *Trillium grandiflorum*, American

Symphytum caucasicum

Stokesia laevis

wake-robin, is the more vigorous pure white trillium with conspicuous pure white petals and fresh green foliage. *Trillium cuneatum*, known as sweet Betsy or wood lily, is often sold as *Trillium sessile*. It has dark green, broad, spotted leaves that form a solid collar beneath the dark red–petalled flower. The petals stand upright and maintain a narrow tulip form. A lovely plant to grow with pieris, evergreen azaleas, and spring-flowering bulbs.

Where heathers thrive in a more open, sunny position on dry soil, the delightful *Lithodora diffusa* 'Heavenly Blue' can be allowed to ramble. It starts life as a cushion of small, dark green leaves, becoming more trailing in habit over the years. In late spring the brilliant blue flowers open like tiny stars of lapis lazuli. The colour is exotic and surprising, wonderful against the dark foliage of heathers.

Flame creeper, *Tropaeolum speciosum,* is another surprising planting partner for sheltered gardens on acid soil. The stems climb and scramble, winding their way through the branches of supporting shrubs. From midsummer the vivid vermillion-red nasturtium flowers set the vegetation ablaze. Often seen growing through the mantle of a yew hedge, it is at its best against dark foliage. Although often slow to establish, if it likes its situation it grows freely, festooning all shrubs in fiery garlands.

Most perennials succeed in beds and borders on acid soil if fed with a balanced, slow-release fertilizer once a year. Geranium, peony, penstemon, nepeta, astrantia, and a host of other familiar favourites can be relied upon to perform. Achillea, dianthus, and some other chalk lovers will struggle. Stokes' aster, *Stokesia laevis*, is a perennial that sulks on chalk but loves a well-drained acid soil. It is a valuable late-summer bloomer with its large lilac-blue cornflower flowers and fresh, green foliage.

top *Polystichum setiferum* 'Herrenhausen'

above left *Trillium cuneatum*

left *Lithodora diffusa* 'Heavenly Blue'

Tall and airy *Verbena bonariensis* is a lovely perennial to drift through a planting scheme.

HOT AND DRY CONDITIONS, INCLUDING PROLONGED DROUGHT

Many gardeners are permanently dealing with drought conditions. In some areas rainfall is always low and soil may be thin and free draining. Any moisture quickly disappears and plants have to cope. To create a sustainable landscape that requires little intervention from the gardener, it is important to plant subjects that not only tolerate these conditions, but that thrive: shrubs that originate from regions with similar climatic conditions, often the Mediterranean.

Even in areas where winter is wet and summer is unsettled, drought conditions may prevail at some point. Extremes of weather seem to have become a feature of recent years and we need to plant accordingly. Of course in a garden it may be possible to install a simple irrigation system; many garden owners seem to think it is an essential. However, plants need to fend for themselves in the long term; without irrigation roots go deep in search of water. Many irrigation systems just keep the surface moist, so roots stay there, meaning plants are less likely to survive if the water supply ceases.

Even with drought-resistant plants, good soil preparation ensures that the roots can move through the soil easily in their search for water. Digging in recycled green waste or well-rotted manure is essential to improve the water-holding capacity of the ground. Mulching the soil surface with chipped bark may help to keep the soil cool and retain moisture, but only apply it when the soil is moist, both on level ground and to sufficient depth. Thin layers of bark mulch are totally ineffective.

Most sun-loving, drought-resistant shrubs will be happiest growing through a layer of grit or gravel. This reflects light onto the lower stems and leaves, conserves soil moisture, keeps roots cool and prevents soil splash which is often the downfall of silver-leaved Mediterranean shrubs in winter.

Shrubs that enjoy hot and dry conditions are well adapted. Their leaves are often small and narrow, covered in hairs or with waxy surfaces. Their habit is often compact and their stems very hard and woody. Some have oils in the leaves which help to prevent them from drying out; these are the aromatic woody herbs that are so familiar to us. They are often silver or subtle in colour; lighter colours are more effective at reflecting sunlight as well as being calming and easy to live with.

Those seeking shrubs for hot dry conditions should also explore recommendations for chalk soils and exposed and coastal conditions as these situations include an even wider palette of plants to choose from.

Abelia ×grandiflora

2.4 × 2.4m (8 × 8 ft.)
UK H5 USDA 6–9

This large evergreen or semi-evergreen shrub has the benefits of both a graceful habit and a long flowering season. The small, shining, deep green leaves are carried on elegantly arching tan-coloured stems. The bell-shaped, blush pink flowers appear in clusters at the ends of the shoots from midsummer through to fall. They are pleasingly fragrant and are enhanced by bronze-pink calyces that remain attractive after the flowers have faded. It grows on any well-drained soil in sun or semi-shade, although it flowers more prolifically in sun. It is drought tolerant once established and an excellent choice for the back of a large border or as an informal hedge or screen. The foliage is excellent for cutting for floral decoration. Prune in early spring if necessary to control size and spread.

Artemisia 'Powis Castle'

45 × 60cm (18 in. × 2 ft.)
UK H3 USDA 4–9

Commonly known as wormwood, this is a highly aromatic dwarf shrub with stocky, spreading branches and finely cut silver leaves. It forms a low, loose mound that can become quite sprawling with age. Insignificant yellowish flowers sometimes appear in late summer, but these are best removed. It is a most attractive foliage plant for a dry, sunny situation and is excellent in a pot, very drought tolerant once established and a good choice to plant in gravel or on the edge of paving. Prune in early spring, cutting back to where new growth buds are crowded on the branches. Rather surprisingly it can be prone to aphids (blackfly) in the tips of the shoots. Spray with an organic pest killer at first signs of attack.

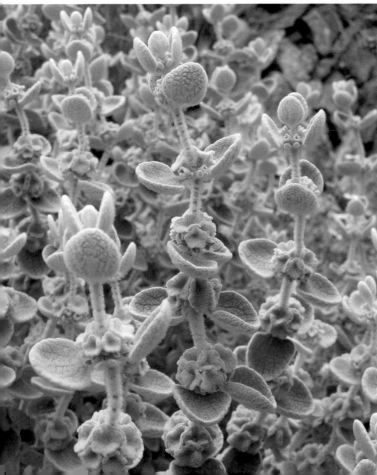

Ballota pseudodictamnus

60 × 60cm (2 × 2 ft.)
UK H4 USDA 7–9

Known as false dittany or Grecian horehound, this soft, felted shrub is well adapted to sunny, dry conditions: upright furry stems carry small, rounded, grey-green woolly leaves. Small pink flowers appear towards the tips of the stems in late summer. The flowers are fairly insignificant, but the shrub is a useful addition to a gravel garden or alongside paving where the foliage will be protected from winter wet. It grows on any well-drained or dry soil and is at its best in full sun. It is drought resistant and makes an attractive contrast to succulents such as dark-leaved aeoniums. Light pruning in spring to remove damaged growth and any dead stems helps to keep the plant in shape.

Buddleja davidii Buzz Series

1.2 × 1.2m (4 × 4 ft.)
UK H6 USDA 5–9

Butterfly bush is one of the most drought-tolerant shrubs, growing successfully on the poorest soil with very little available water. Most varieties grow vigorously and rather too large for small gardens. Therefore the dwarf varieties of buddleja that have been introduced in recent years are particularly welcome. These are also less prone to seeding, which causes the plant to spread and become invasive. The Buzz Series are compact in habit and free flowering. *Buddleja davidii* Buzz Indigo has large panicles of fragrant indigo-blue flowers in late summer which are highly attractive to bees and butterflies. Regular dead-heading prolongs the flowering period which is possible on these compact, smaller plants. Prune hard in late winter, cutting back by half to two thirds.

Callistemon citrinus 'Splendens'

2.4 × 1.8m (8 × 6 ft.)
UK H3 USDA 8–11

The crimson bottlebrush, an Australian native, is surprisingly hardy and happily thrives outdoors in milder areas and coastal situations. Supple, arching stems carry narrow, leathery leaves of dull, olive-green. The vivid scarlet bottlebrush blooms open from midsummer through to fall, appearing to be threaded onto the stems. As the flowers fade they leave behind woody, beaded seed clusters. Growth continues from the ends of the flower clusters, leading to very elongated branches. The secret of success is to prune straight after flowers have faded, cutting back to just behind each faded flower head. This results in branching and avoids straggly growth. Callistemon needs full sun and well-drained soil. It is extremely drought tolerant and often looks best when grown against a wall or fence.

Cistus ×pulverulentus 'Sunset'

75 × 75cm (30 × 30 in.)
UK H4 USDA 8–10

A lovely evergreen rock rose that hates wet conditions but is perfect for hot, dry situations. Forming a low, mounded shrub with soft grey-green, felted leaves, it mixes well with silver foliage shrubs and lavenders. The silky tissue-paper blooms open from midsummer, vivid cerise with yellow stamens and striking against the velvety foliage. Unlike many other cistus, it produces blooms throughout summer. It grows on any well-drained soil but is at its best on chalk or dry alkaline soils and needs full sun to succeed. It is ideal for the gravel garden, alongside paving, and perfect for seaside gardens. No pruning is required, but any dead or damaged shoots should be removed after winter. Cistus are not long-lived shrubs and may need replacing every few years.

Convolvulus cneorum

45 × 45cm (18 × 18 in.)
UK H4 USDA 8–10

A charming little shrub with straight stems and narrow, shining silver leaves, hence the common name, silverbush. From early summer the funnel-shaped flowers unfurl from scrolled maroon-pink buds. They are pure white, flushed yellow in the centre and stained with purple-pink on the outside. Blooms appear throughout summer and into fall. It grows on any well-drained soil and loves hot, dry conditions in full sun. Although it will tolerate some shade, it does not flower as freely. Neat and compact in habit, it is ideal for pots and small gardens as well as in narrow borders alongside paving. No pruning is necessary, but older plants can be cut back by half in early spring to promote bushy growth.

Lavandula angustifolia 'Hidcote'

60 × 60cm (2 × 2 ft.)
UK H5 USDA 5–9

Deservedly popular for its reliability, enduring performance, and habit. Compact in growth with narrow grey-green aromatic leaves, it forms a dense, bushy plant. The spikes of deep, violet-blue, fragrant flowers open from midsummer, creating a velvety haze over the plant. A plant in bloom is a magnet for bees and butterflies. This excellent variety makes a superb low hedge or addition to any sunny border on well-drained soil. In the right conditions it is long lived. On heavy soils, mulching under and around the plant with grit or gravel helps to extend its life. Prune immediately after flowering, cutting back to just below the base of the flower stems. This keeps the plants compact and prevents soggy faded flowers from collapsing onto the foliage.

Olearia ×scilloniensis

1.2 × 1.2m (4 × 4 ft.)
UK H3 USDA 8–10

This tender evergreen shrub has ascending branches with narrow, dark green, leathery leaves, silver on the undersides. The leaf axils are crowded with felted green buds in early spring, bursting into neat clusters of delicate, small white daisy blooms with yellow centres in late spring. The appearance is rather like that of Michaelmas daisies, the abundance of flowers totally obscuring the foliage. A lovely choice for a sheltered situation in full sun, although it will tolerate some shade. Plant on any well-drained soil. An excellent plant for mild, coastal gardens. Prune after flowering if necessary, cutting out some of the older, flowered stems. Various olearias are sold under this name and nomenclature and hardiness information is confused. Buy a pot-grown plant in bloom if possible.

Perovskia Lacey Blue

45 × 45cm (18 × 18 in.)
UK H5 USDA 4–10

A recently introduced Russian sage that is more compact in habit, hardier, and extremely drought and heat tolerant. Silver-grey upright stems carry aromatic grey-green leaves. The silver flower stems rise above the foliage, smothered with tiny, vivid blue flowers from late summer through fall; these are very attractive to bees and butterflies. In dry conditions the white stems remain attractive into winter long after the flowers have faded. A lovely shrub for the front of a sunny border where it provides light height. This variety needs no support and grows on any well-drained soil in full sun. Prune in early spring, cutting back to where tiny, grey-green growth buds are crowded on the lower parts of the stems.

Phlomis fruticosa

1.2 × 1.2m (4 × 4 ft.)
UK H4 USDA 6–10

Jerusalem sage is a surprisingly hardy, drought-resistant shrub hailing from the Mediterranean. The specific name *fruticosa* means shrubby which is an apt description for its growth habit. Upright, then sprawling, square stems carry soft, slightly hairy, heart-shaped, grey-green leaves arranged in pairs. From early summer, whorls of yellow nettle-like flowers open in the leaf axils. These fall to leave small conical brown calyces that persist on the stems. It grows on any well-drained soil and withstands tough, dry conditions. In milder climates it is evergreen; in harsher conditions the branches may be knocked back in winter, allowing the shrub to regenerate from the base. Prune as required in spring, to control size and shape and to remove faded flower stems.

Rosmarinus officinalis

1.2 × 1.2m (4 × 4 ft.)
UK H4 USDA 6–10

Common rosemary is often underestimated as an excellent evergreen shrub that thrives in an open, sunny position on poor soil. In these conditions the foliage is at its most aromatic, full of oils that make the plant drought resistant. Upright stems are clothed in very narrow grey-green leaves, a valuable contrast in texture to most broad-leaved evergreens. In spring small sky-blue flowers light up the plant for several weeks. Rosemary mixes well with silver foliage subjects, other woody herbs, and lavender. It grows on any well-drained soil and thrives in coastal gardens. Prune in spring to control size and shape as necessary. The cut foliage is long lasting, fragrant, and excellent for floral decoration. The variety *Rosmarinus officinalis* 'Arp' is reputedly hardier than the species.

Salvia 'Hot Lips'

75 × 75cm (30 × 30 in.)
UK H4 USDA 8–10

Also available as *Salvia ×jamensis* 'Hot Lips', this woody salvia is remarkable for its strikingly coloured flowers and the length of the flowering period. Fine, straight stems grow to form a bushy plant with small green, aromatic leaves. The small blooms with their narrow upper and broad lower petals can be bright scarlet or white at first, becoming bicoloured as the season progresses, flowering from midsummer to late fall. It grows on any well-drained soil in full sun and loves a hot, dry border by a wall or terrace. The stems are brittle and easily damaged, so exposed windy sites are best avoided. From midwinter the stems are bare and slender, showing no signs of life until buds burst in spring. Prune in early spring, cutting back by one third to maintain a bushy habit.

Salvia officinalis 'Purpurascens'

45 × 75cm (18 × 30 in.)
UK H5 USDA 4–9

Purple sage is far more than a culinary herb: it is a highly useful small foliage shrub. Forming a low-spreading mound of purple-green leaves, purple-grey in winter, it grows quickly, soon making an impact. It is perfect for the front of a border, spilling over the edge of paving, growing through gravel, or in a pot. In early summer the spikes of royal blue flowers are loved by bees and pollinating insects. Purple sage loves a sunny spot on well-drained soil. It hates winter wet, so mulching under the plant with grit or gravel really helps. To enhance the foliage, cut back the flower stems when the blooms have faded. Prune in early spring to control shape and size.

Santolina chamaecyparissus

45 × 60cm (18 in. × 2 ft.)
UK H5 USDA 7–9

Cotton lavender is among the most reliable of silver-leaved shrubs with dense conifer-like, aromatic, woolly grey foliage that is resistant to drought and desiccation by wind. In summer masses of grey buds open to button-like yellow flowers that are not to everyone's taste. It grows on any well-drained soil in full sun and is tolerant of some shade, perfect to soften paving and to grow with lavenders and other silver foliage subjects. As plants get older the branches tend to open up, so regular trimming is essential to keep the plants in shape. Cutting back to just below the flower stalks when the plants are in bud maintains the silver effect. Harder pruning can be done in early spring, cutting back to where small shoots are visible on the lower stems. This is not a long-lived shrub and is best replaced every few years.

HOT AND DRY CONDITIONS

OTHER GOOD SHRUBS FOR HOT, DRY CONDITIONS

Brachyglottis (Dunedin Group) 'Sunshine'

Ceanothus thyrsiflorus var. *repens*

Erysimum 'Bowles's Mauve'

Helianthemum 'The Bride'

Helichrysum italicum 'Korma'

Phlomis italica

Teucrium fruticans

Thymus 'Silver Queen'

Vitex agnus-castus

Yucca flaccida 'Golden Sword'

PLANTING PARTNERS FOR HOT AND DRY CONDITIONS

Many shrubs that thrive in hot, dry conditions share similar characteristics, so they combine easily in plantings. The silver or felted leaves, which protect them from desiccation, are subtle in colour, and most are of similar size and habit; few grow to very large proportions. In this environment shrubs predominate; their woody stems and tough leaves are more resistant to drought than the soft growth of perennials. However, some herbaceous subjects and grasses have adapted and make valuable planting partners.

Eryngium, sea holly, has tough stems and holly-like leaves. Some varieties, natives of seashores, prefer soil with some moisture. Others, natives of arid landscapes, have adapted to dry conditions by growing when water is available, then flowering, setting seed, and dying back when the landscape becomes baked in the height of summer. The biennial *Eryngium giganteum*, native of Iran and the Caucasus, grows in this way. Often known as Miss Willmott's ghost, after the famous horticulturist who carried its seeds in her handbag and planted them in the gardens of fellow gardeners, it has the ability to seed and pop up anywhere when the conditions are right. Delightful surrounded by blue lavender or soft grasses.

Verbena bonariensis is another wonderful drifter that is very drought tolerant once established. It also attracts bees and butterflies. In mild areas it seeds freely, producing clumps of dark green foliage that give rise to tall, slender flower stems topped with tiny vivid purple flowers with orange eyes. In dry conditions it is not usually quite as tall, growing to 90cm (3 ft.) or so. An excellent contrast to the round mounds of most shrubs, it is good further forward in the border to add light height. It is also a delight with the ethereal flower spikes of perovskia, Russian sage.

California poppy, *Eschscholzia californica*, is a sun-loving annual that thrives on poor dry soil, especially in coastal and gravel gardens. Fine cut blue-green foliage and vivid orange funnel-shaped blooms are a lively contrast to the subtle shades of sun-loving shrubs. Fabulous in mid- to late summer with deep blue buddleja.

Plants that grow at the beginning of the season, bloom, and then wither can leave gaps in a border. However, when combined with shrubs they can add an amazing display before they disappear. Oriental poppies, varieties of *Papaver orientalis*, produce some of the most spectacular blooms in the summer border, but they retreat beneath the ground soon after flowering. Their ancestors are from Turkey and the Caucasus, so they like plenty of sun from the beginning of the season. They dislike being smothered by their neighbours. The woody salvias, such as *Salvia* 'Hot Lips', make great planting partners for oriental poppies. These shrubs are late into leaf and light and open in habit. Planted in front of the poppies, they perform later in

The steely flowers and foliage of *Eryngium giganteum*, known
as Miss Willmott's ghost, make a striking contrast to soft foliage
shrubs such as lavender and santolina.

Sedum 'Red Cauli', an excellent variety for late summer interest with sun-loving shrubs.

the season, filling the gaps after the poppies have bloomed.

Many flower bulbs are also very useful to add seasonal colour in hot, dry conditions. The more robust varieties of tulip will often establish as long-lasting spring subjects, whereas they would perish on heavy, wet soil. Species tulips, such as *Tulipa tarda*, are particularly successful and can add a real blast of colour early in the season. Alliums are an excellent choice among lavender, santolina, helichrysum, and cistus. Allium leaves start to wither

as soon as the flowers develop; the shrubs help to conceal the fading foliage. Later in the summer the sparkling, chandelier-like flowers of *Allium cernuum* are a delight growing through the foliage of wispy *Stipa tenuissima*. This delicate grass, with its soft, waving "hair," seeds freely and wafts like mist among low, sun-loving shrubs.

Of course the other group of plants that are well adapted to hot, dry conditions are those with fleshy leaves and stems, developed for the storage of water reserves. Those gardening in warmer climes will be able to grow cacti and succulents, some of which are surprisingly hardy and are increasingly popular in temperate regions.

Sedums have even wider appeal, from the small creeping varieties used on green roofs to the clump-forming perennials that make bold statements in the summer border. They have a long season: the fleshy stems and foliage are attractive from late spring, the flattened summer flower heads are loved by bees and butterflies, and the faded flower heads remain attractive into winter. *Sedum* (or *Hylotelephium*) 'Herbstfreude', with its ice-green foliage and large pink flower heads, is widely grown; *Sedum* 'Red Cauli' is a newer variety with grey-purple leaves and crimson-red flower clusters, superb with the silky, silver leaves of *Convolvulus cneorum*.

above *Allium cernuum* is a dainty allium, delightful growing in a haze of *Stipa tenuissima*.

above left Species tulips, such as *Tulipa tarda*, are ideal in hot, dry conditions where they provide vibrant colour at the beginning of the year.

left The vibrant orange trumpet flowers of California poppy, *Eschscholzia californica*, shine in hot sunshine.

Cornus sanguinea 'Midwinter Fire' puts on a show regardless of the weather.

HARSH WINTERS

Those gardening in colder climates have a more limited palette of plants to choose from. The broad-leaved evergreens and Mediterranean natives that abound in mild, temperate gardens are out of the question. Instead conifers and hardy heathers provide evergreen interest, while hardy deciduous shrubs contribute foliage interest and summer flowers. However, the shrubs that survive severe winter weather are not ones to confine to gardens in the coldest climates. Many are extremely ornamental and among the most popular hardy garden plants.

Harsh winter weather is very drying, which is why deciduous shrubs have a better chance of survival. If the leaves and stem of a plant thaw and start to transpire, the plant cannot draw water from the ground if it is frozen. As a result the foliage and stems shrivel and die. This is common in temperate zones after severe freezing conditions; often the damage caused by frost does not show until the weather becomes warmer.

Where there is heavy snowfall some less hardy subjects may survive severe weather if protected under a blanket of snow. *Euonymus fortunei* varieties are a good example. These low-growing evergreens such as 'Emerald 'n' Gold' are able to survive colder conditions than their hardiness rating suggests if winter snow protects them from the drying effects of icy winds. Even if some of the foliage is damaged, the stems survive and regrow in spring.

Many hybrid roses survive harsh weather conditions by growing new stems from the base of the plant if the older stems are killed by hard frost. Varieties that regenerate in this way are recommended by breeders for cultivation in the colder zones of the United States and Northern Europe. One big advantage is lack of disease, as spores of fungal disease do not have the opportunity to remain on the plants and reinfect during the following season.

As with all challenging growing conditions, the gardener tries to push the boundaries. Of course hardiness is affected by other factors than climatic zone. Soil conditions, exposure, microclimates, and the availability of winter protection will influence what survives and what perishes. Hardiness ratings can never be regarded as definitive, so it is always worth experimenting with plants that you really want to grow.

Amelanchier canadensis

2.4 × 1.5m (8 × 5 ft.)
UK H7 USDA 3–7

A native of North America, serviceberry is a large, suckering shrub with upright branches and small oval green leaves. In early spring upright panicles of starry white flowers light up the branches as the new, copper-tinged leaves begin to unfurl. The flowers are followed by purple-black berry fruits in late summer which are quickly taken by birds. In an open, sunny position the foliage often turns to rich shades of flame and gold in fall. A very hardy shrub that grows on most soils, especially in wet conditions. It tolerates some shade but is at its best in full sun. It is an ideal subject for naturalistic settings and country gardens. Prune to control shape and size straight after flowering, although this is rarely necessary in the right situation.

Cornus alba 'Sibirica'

1.8 × 1.2m (6 × 4 ft.)
UK H7 USDA 2–8

Among the best of the red-barked dogwoods, this variety produces the most intensely coloured winter stems with glowing scarlet winter bark on vigorous upright shoots. The leaves are plain dark green and quite large. In an open, sunny situation the autumn colour of the foliage is superb: long-lasting shades of red and flame, amazing when backlit by low sunlight. Small white flowers appear at the top of the stems on unpruned plants; these develop into white, blue-flushed berries. The cultivar 'Baton Rouge' supposedly has superior coloured bark, but most would find it difficult to tell the difference. A vigorous, easy-to-grow shrub that thrives on any soil, especially heavy, wet clay. For the best winter stems, cut back hard to near ground level in early spring. This promotes strong, upright growth and richly coloured bark.

Cornus sericea 'Bud's Yellow'

1.5 × 1.2m (5 × 4 ft.)
UK H7 USDA 2–8

A good variety of yellowtwig dogwood, also known as 'Budd's Yellow', with more richly coloured stems than the widely planted *Cornus sericea* 'Flaviramea'. A strong, suckering shrub, it grows quickly to form a clump of upright stems with soft green leaves. The shoots are yellow-green, becoming richer gold in winter when the leaves fall. Very effective when planted with red-stemmed cornus varieties and good with gold and green variegated evergreens in milder areas. It is very hardy and grows easily on any moist soil; it thrives on wet clay. Cut back hard in early spring to just above the ground to promote vigorous, upright shoots which have the best bark colour.

Erica carnea f. alba 'Winter Snow'

15 × 30cm (6 × 12 in.)
UK H7 USDA 4–7

The winter heaths are some of the hardiest dwarf evergreen shrubs, with the added bonus of winter and early spring flowers. They are ideal for small gardens and containers and under the light shade of trees. They grow on any reasonable soil and tolerate alkaline conditions as well as acid ones. They survive extreme cold, especially when covered with a blanket of snow. 'Winter Snow' forms a neat cushion of bright green foliage. The abundant white flowers with conspicuous brown stamens open from late winter through to midspring. They are highly attractive to early-flying bumble bees in search of pollen and nectar. Clip after flowering to remove faded flowers and promote bushy growth.

Euonymus alatus 'Compactus'

1.2 × 1.2m (4 × 4 ft.)
UK H6 USDA 4–9

The dwarf winged euonymus is an unassuming shrub for most of the year but among the showiest for autumn colour. Stiff, straight, spreading branches carry light green leaves through summer and tiny yellow-green flowers in spring. The fall foliage colour is truly spectacular: vibrant shades of crimson-pink will light up the garden. 'Bladerunner' is an excellent form with more pronounced winged stems and an even more compact habit. In parts of North America the species is regarded as invasive; known locally as "burning bush" it is widespread in some areas at the cost of native species. However, elsewhere it is a hardy, useful shrub that grows on most soils in full sun. No pruning is required, although selective pruning to control shape may be done in winter.

Hydrangea arborescens 'Annabelle'

30cm × 1.2m (1 × 4 ft.)
UK H7 USDA 3–9

A graceful hydrangea with slender, upright stems and soft, pale green leaves. From midsummer the large heads of tiny florets develop through pale green, then cream, eventually pure white and spectacular, often weighing down the stems at their peak. A shade-tolerant shrub, it is at its best in full sun or semi-shade on any reasonable well-drained soil. It is useful to grow under the light shade of deciduous trees, such as birches, as long as the ground is not too dry. Easy to grow and reliable, 'Annabelle' is popular across Northern Europe and North America despite its rather lax habit when in flower. Few very hardy flowering shrubs give such a flamboyant display. Prune hard in late winter, cutting to 15cm (6 in.) above ground level to encourage vigorous growth and strong stems.

Hydrangea paniculata 'Limelight'

1.5 × 1.2m (5 × 4 ft.)
UK H6 USDA 3–9

A widely planted variety of *Hydrangea paniculata*, remarkable for a relatively recent introduction. Strong upright stems carry soft green leaves; in late summer the shoots are topped by densely packed conical heads of sterile florets. These start green, becoming pale green and cream as they mature, eventually white, then flushed pink. In dry conditions the flower heads turn parchment and remain attractive through winter. A hardy shrub that grows in sun or semi-shade on most soils, it is especially effective under the light shade of deciduous trees and at the back of perennial borders. Where space allows it makes a glorious informal hedge. The mature flowers are excellent for cutting. Prune hard in early spring, cutting back to 60–90cm (2–3 ft.) above the ground. This promotes vigorous upright stems that need no support under the weight of the flowers.

Physocarpus opulifolius 'Dart's Gold'

1.2 × 1.2m (4 × 4 ft.)
UK H7 USDA 3–7

A compact form of ninebark with neat, maple-like leaves of bright gold, vivid in spring and retaining a good colour through the season. Small clusters of white flowers appear in early summer, but these are insignificant against the foliage. This shrub grows almost anywhere but is at its best in semi-shade on moist soil. The colour is brasher in full sun; although fairly scorch-resistant, leaves will have some browning of the edges on very dry soil. 'Dart's Gold' is extremely hardy and among the best small yellow-leaved shrubs, an excellent contrast to purple foliage subjects. Prune in winter, if necessary, to control shape and size, cutting out some of the older, darker stems.

Pinus mugo 'Carsten'

60 × 60cm (2 × 2 ft.)
UK H7 USDA 2–7

A dwarf mountain pine also known as 'Carsten's Wintergold', it is similar to 'Wintergold' but slower growing, so a better choice for smaller gardens. With its fine, needle-like leaves, stocky growth, and strong branches, this compact pine is well-equipped to survive the cold. The foliage is olive green through the summer months, turning warm golden yellow as the weather turns colder. 'Carsten' makes a good planting partner for dogwoods grown for their winter stems and grows on any well-drained soil. Unlike many other pines, it thrives in alkaline conditions and is a great choice for gravel and scree gardens. No pruning is required. If necessary to control size, whole branches should be removed to ground level to avoid ruining the architectural form of the plant.

Potentilla fruticosa 'Pink Beauty'

90 × 90cm (3 × 3 ft.)
UK H7 USDA 2–7

Potentillas are perhaps the longest blooming of all the flowering shrubs. Opening their first buttercup-blooms in early summer, they continue right into fall. 'Pink Beauty' has soft, pale pink, single and semi-double flowers with golden stamens set against bright green foliage. Originally raised in Canada, this is a very hardy variety with a long flowering period. It thrives in an open, sunny situation on well-drained soil, especially on sandy and chalky soil, and is very drought tolerant. This is a great choice for a small garden and is among the easiest shrubs to grow. Winter is not the most attractive season: little more than a tangle of brown stems and faded flowers. Trim in late winter to remove the old blooms and ends of shoots to promote vigorous growth and a bushy habit.

Rhododendron 'Northern Hi-Lights'

1.5 × 1.2m (5 × 4 ft.)
UK H7 USDA 3–7

The Northern Lights series is a hardy group of deciduous azaleas originally developed by the University of Minnesota. With the characteristic open, rounded form of deciduous azaleas, they are elegant shrubs with soft green leaves that turn rich shades of red and flame before they fall. 'Northern Hi-Lights' is free flowering, with clusters of soft yellow buds in late spring, opening to creamy white blooms flashed with brighter yellow on the upper petals of the flowers. The fragrance is sweet and strong, reminiscent of honeysuckle. Like all in this genus, it needs an acid soil with adequate moisture, but with good drainage. Perfect in semi-shade, it is happy in full sun if there is adequate soil moisture. No pruning is necessary, but older plants can be cut back after flowering to rejuvenate them.

Rhus typhina Tiger Eyes

1.5 × 1.2m (5 × 4 ft.)
UK H7 USDA 3–8

A lovely cut-leaf sumac, a form of the American native, introduced by Bailey Nurseries of Portland, Oregon. More compact than the species but with the same felted, stags-horn stems, Tiger Eyes is more suited to smaller gardens. The fern-like leaves emerge pale green-yellow, soon becoming clear yellow, elegant and lacy in appearance. The foliage turns to rich shades of amber gold before the leaves fall. The characteristic felted, rust-coloured seedheads are few, but appear in late summer. Some report the same suckering habit as the species, but generally the problem is less common. A lovely shrub for naturalistic settings and to take the place of a small tree, it grows on any reasonable soil although leaves fall quickly in dry conditions. It tolerates some shade, but the leaf colour is best in an open, sunny position. No pruning is required.

Sambucus racemosa 'Sutherland Gold'

1.8 × 1.5m (6 × 5 ft.)
UK H7 USDA 3–8

A lovely golden-leaved form of European red elder with finely cut, fern-like foliage of bright golden yellow, tinged with bronze on the young shoots. Unlike *Sambucus racemosa* 'Plumosa Aurea', it does not scorch in full sun but is a more pleasing shade of yellow-green in light shade. It is also more vigorous and makes an impressive plant more quickly. It grows on any soil and excels on clay and in wet conditions. The small white flowers in early summer are insignificant, as are any berries that develop; this is a shrub to grow for the foliage. Prune in late winter, cutting back hard in the first couple of years to promote vigorous shoots. Prune lightly in subsequent years to maintain a branch framework.

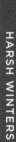

Sorbaria sorbifolia 'Sem'

1.2 × 1.2m (4 × 4 ft.)
UK H7 USDA 2–11

A compact form of false spiraea forming a clump of upright tan-coloured stems with neat fern-like foliage. The new leaves are vivid pink to orange-red at the tips of the shoots, yellow-green as they mature. Later in summer the foliage changes to mid-green, bronze at the tips, and often colours red before the leaves fall. In late spring crowded spikes of whitish flowers appear at the tips of the shoots; these soon go brown and are best removed as they fade. It grows on most moist soils and is an excellent shrub for heavy soil and wet conditions. The foliage colour is brighter in full sun, but 'Sem' grows well in semi-shade and is effective when grown in a pot. Prune in winter if necessary to control size and shape, cutting back some of the older stems.

Spiraea nipponica 'Snowmound'

1.5 × 1.5m (5 × 5 ft.)
UK H7 USDA 3–8

Nippon spiraea is a native of Japan. A loose, mounded shrub with small, dark green leaves, it blooms in late spring. The white flowers are carried in clusters all along the branches, in a good year smothering the shrub like snow. The flowers attract bees and pollinators. Very hardy, easy to grow on any soil in full sun or partial shade, it is useful on banks and slopes. On fertile soil it can make a most attractive informal hedge and is deer resistant. Descriptions of the size of this shrub vary, undoubtedly depending on growing conditions, but it is easily controlled if it grows too large. Little pruning is required, but some of the flowered stems can be cut back straight after flowering.

OTHER GOOD SHRUBS THAT SURVIVE HARSH WINTERS

Calluna vulgaris

Clethra alnifolia

Elaeagnus 'Quicksilver'

Hippophae rhamnoides

Prunus ×cistena

Salix alba var. *vitellina* 'Britzensis'

Symphoricarpos albus

Syringa vulgaris

Ulex europaeus

Viburnum opulus

PLANTING PARTNERS FOR HARSH WINTERS

Deciduous herbaceous perennials are well equipped to survive harsh winters. They die down and take refuge beneath the soil during the coldest months, ready to re-emerge in spring; hardy flower bulbs adopt a similar approach. The ones that succeed are those that originate from cold climates, whereas those from warmer regions may need protection if frost goes deep. Hardy annuals grow quickly as soon as warmth and water permit, completing their life cycle during the growing season and over-wintering as seeds. All of these make excellent planting partners for hardy shrubs, adding colour and different plant forms to planting combinations.

Low-growing perennials are partic-ularly useful under large deciduous shrubs. During the growing season they provide valuable groundcover and help to suppress weeds. *Alchemi-lla mollis*, lady's mantle, is among the most vigorous, almost too successful in some situations. The soft, velvety green leaves are lovely in their own right. The foam of lime green flowers in early summer is a wonderful foil for other colours. As time moves on they develop a less attractive yellow-green hue before setting seed, which they do profusely. Alchemilla is usually grown at the front of a border, but it tends to flop and smother its neighbours. It is far better further back under shrubs such as *Hydrangea paniculata*, physocarpus, and elder where it adds early interest and an effective lower layer. Cut off the flowers as soon as they start to fade to prevent unwanted seeding.

Tiarella cordifolia, foam flower, is a charming low-growing perennial that thrives in shade alongside pulmonar-ias. Clumps of heart-shaped leaves emerge in spring, soon followed by short spikes of tiny starry white flow-ers on pink stems. It grows well under *Hydrangea paniculata* in the light shade of deciduous trees such as birches.

Really a creeping shrub, *Cornus canadensis*, known as bunchberry, is a highly desirable gem with very short upright stems topped with small mid-green leaves, forming a collar around the creamy early summer bracts. The blooms are miniature versions of those of the flowering dogwoods, beautifully set against the low foliage. Berry-like fruits follow the blooms in fall. A native of the woodland floor, it makes an excellent groundcover around hardy deciduous azaleas.

Plants that naturally seed and spread through beds and borders soften planting schemes using shrubs. They add light height, which gives a garden depth and vertical interest. *Aquilegia vulgaris*, columbine, is a very hardy perennial, overwintering by means of its wiry tap-roots. The attractive divided leaves emerge in spring, soon followed by bonnet-shaped blooms elegantly poised on tall, slender stems. There are many named varieties, but they hybridize readily and seed freely, giving rise to various subtle-coloured offspring. Even if the plants die out, the seed survives and plants appear randomly. It is an excellent mixer,

Alchemilla mollis, lady's mantle, adds a froth of fresh lime-green under established shrubs.

above The steely blue flowers of globe thistle, *Echinops ritro*, are very attractive to bees.

above Solomon's seal, *Polygonatum ×hybridum*, is a lovely perennial, thriving in shade and perfect with hardy shrubs.

top Purple coneflower, *Echinacea purpurea*, mixes well with grasses and dark-leaved shrubs; for example, purple-leaved berberis and *Physocarpus opulifolius* 'Diablo'.

lovely with hardy hostas and Solomon's seal, *Polygonatum ×hybridum*, in shade or among hardy geraniums in sun.

Purple coneflower, *Echinacea purpurea*, is a very hardy perennial that thrives in an open, sunny situation. It associates well with hardy grasses such as calamagrostis and panicum and produces its striking blooms with reflexed petals in late summer. The cone-shaped seedheads remain attractive after the petals have fallen and may stand right into winter, poking through snow to provide seeds for foraging birds.

Globe thistle, *Echinops ritro*, is equally hardy. Blue-green spiny leaves emerge in spring, giving rise to strong blue-grey stems topped with steely globe-shaped flowers in late summer. It grows almost anywhere and

is a great contrast in form to the soft shapes of shrubs. In a sunny spot it works well with potentillas and spiraeas.

Dogwoods grown for their winter stems always look better growing through evergreen groundcover. In the coldest areas this may not be possible; however, where vincas and the less vigorous ivies will survive, they provide a green carpet beneath colourful stems, enjoying the shade in summer when the cornus are in full leaf. Early-flowering hardy flower bulbs work brilliantly beneath the winter stems, producing flowers before the leaves unfurl and pruning takes place. On moist soil the common snowdrop, *Galanthus nivalis*, is unbeatable once established. It can be transplanted in leaf in spring or as dry bulbs in early fall. In this case plant as soon as bulbs

become available; they quickly lose viability out of the ground.

Deciduous clematis are a wonderful way to add another season of interest to shrubs. *Clematis alpina*, with its dainty nodding blooms, requires little pruning and maintenance and can be planted to ramble through the branches of shrubs that can be left to grow with little pruning. A blue-flowered variety would work well with *Physocarpus opulifolius* 'Dart's Gold'. *Clematis viticella* blooms from late summer to fall. It can be cut back to within 15cm (6 in.) of the ground in early spring so is ideal to grow through vigorous shrubs that require a similar pruning regime. Although not quite as hardy as *C. alpina*, it usually survives if planted deep in the shelter of a large shrub.

Common snowdrop, *Galanthus nivalis*, is a welcome sight in late winter when planted under deciduous shrubs before their leaves unfurl.

Shrubs for Restricted Planting Spaces

Phormium, pittosporum, berberis, and other shrubs form the foundation of the planting on this terrace with heucheras and the seasonal addition of well-chosen tulips.

Hydrangea paniculata Bobo, a compact form of paniculate hydrangea with long-lasting flowers in late summer, is perfect for a pot.

POTS AND CONTAINERS

For some gardeners planting in the ground is not an option. Those with paved courtyard gardens or balconies have to grow their plants in containers. These garden spaces need greenery and year-round plant interest even more than larger gardens do. In all gardens, growing in containers offers the opportunity to bring the garden closer to the house—onto the patio or doorstep where these plantings bring life to hard landscaping. With specially formulated growing media, growing in pots also enables the gardener to grow plants that would not thrive on their soil such as rhododendrons and camellias in areas where the soil is alkaline.

Through years of habit most gardeners see pots and containers as the place to grow seasonal bedding plants and bulbs. These may deliver a great show of colour, but the effect is short lived and plantings need to be replaced once or twice a year to maintain interest. The down time between peaks is a big disadvantage, periods when the pots are empty or recently replanted. Also, most seasonal bedding plants are needy, requiring regular watering, feeding, dead-heading, and grooming to keep them looking good.

Why not plant more permanently? Many shrubs are perfect for pots and deliver interest for more than one season, year after year. They improve with age, rather than just fading away after a few weeks. Many are more resilient and cope without such frequent watering and pampering, especially if planted in the right growing medium. In pots that are grouped together, shrubs, especially evergreens, become the foundation of enduring planting combinations. Seasonal bedding plants and bulbs still have their place: as temporary enhancements in the same way that they work in the open ground.

Gardeners may resist growing in pots through the misconception that pots are hard work. They do need regular watering, but this can be reduced by using loam-based growing media and choosing larger containers in the first place. Grouping pots together not only looks good, but it makes watering easier and shades the sides of containers, helping to keep them cool, reducing water loss. Feeding with a slow-release fertilizer at the beginning of the growing season reduces the need for regular feeding with a liquid or soluble fertilizer for the rest of the year.

Growing in pots is more than just a means of cultivation. A planted container is a permanent feature, a piece of garden art, a living sculpture. Therefore a shrub is a natural choice, an opportunity to create an eye-catching combination of pot and container that enhances a particular garden setting.

Acer palmatum 'Jerre Schwartz'

1.2m × 90cm (4 × 3 ft.)
UK H5 USDA 6–9

A compact Japanese maple, ideal for small gardens and containers. Dense and upright in habit, it forms a stout, broad column with neat leaves composed of slender, pointed leaflets. The foliage is purple-red through summer, turning bright scarlet in fall in an open, sunny position. It is less sensitive to dry conditions than most maples but should ideally grow in a loam-based growing medium and be kept well-watered. Position where there is shelter from strong winds, but avoid the baking effect of a sunny wall. Contrary to popular belief Japanese maples are very hardy and they do tolerate lime in the soil; ericaceous compost is not necessary. No pruning is required and should be avoided, especially in winter. Good drainage is essential.

Berberis thunbergii f. atropurpurea 'Admiration'

45 × 45cm (18 × 18 in.)
UK H6 USDA 4–9

A superb little shrub with a long season of interest from early spring through to fall. It forms a compact, domed plant that sits beautifully in a pot. The small, rounded leaves emerge orange-red in spring, becoming wine red, delicately edged with gold through summer. The foliage develops vibrant scarlet-flame shades before the leaves fall, leaving a tangle of dark stems and small, shining, scarlet berries. Tiny cream flowers in spring are not unattractive but often go unnoticed among the leaves; however, they are attractive to early bees in search of nectar. At its best in full sun, it is a tolerant shrub that withstands dry conditions and exposed situations. It requires no pruning and is happy in a pot for several years. In ground the species is invasive in parts of North America.

Buxus sempervirens 'Elegantissima'

90 × 90cm (3 × 3 ft.)
UK H6 USDA 5–8

Common box is a natural for pots and containers. Usually trimmed into balls, cones, or even spirals, it graces many a window box, balcony, and doorstep. The variegated form is less often seen, although it too can be trimmed and trained as topiary. It is slower growing than common box and is lovely if left to grow naturally as a small shrub of compact but loose habit. The stiff branches carry tiny, leathery dark green leaves broadly edged with cream giving the plant a lighter effect than plain evergreens. It grows in sun or shade and is remarkably drought tolerant. It also copes with more exposed situations and urban environments. It can be trimmed or pruned to control shape and size, ideally in midsummer. The foliage is good to cut for floral decoration.

Coprosma repens 'Tequila Sunrise'

90 × 90cm (3 × 3 ft.)
UK H3 USDA 8–11

The mirror plant is aptly named for its small, oval, leathery leaves which are intensely glossy and reflective, a quality that only enhances the wonderful colours of the foliage. 'Tequila Sunrise' is an upright and spreading small shrub with emerald green and gold variegated foliage with hints of orange. The leaves become more orange in summer and then turn burgundy and brown in winter. It is best in sun or semi-shade for foliage colour but will tolerate shade. It is perfect for sheltered town gardens or in mild areas as it is not the hardiest of shrubs. Small plants are ideal for window boxes where they are sheltered. Larger ones are best in containers near the walls of the house. Prune in early spring to control shape and size and promote bushy growth.

Hydrangea paniculata Bobo

75 × 75cm (30 × 30 in.)
UK H7 USDA 3–8

A wonderful dwarf variety of *Hydrangea paniculata*, from the same breeder as the popular Pinky-Winky, forming a mounded shrub with strong stems and mid-green leaves. The rounded conical flower heads are freely produced in late summer, first pale green, then creamy white, flushing pink as they age. The blooms last for many weeks, eventually turning parchment as the leaves colour red-burgundy before they fall. It grows in sun or semi-shade and the flower colour is unaffected by the pH of the growing medium. It is perfect for small gardens, both in the open ground and in pots and containers. Prune hard, cutting back to 20cm (8 in.) in late winter to encourage strong new growth which blooms the following summer.

Leucothoe axillaris 'Curly Red'

45 × 60cm (18 in. × 2 ft.)
UK H6 USDA 5-8

An unusual dwarf evergreen shrub with wiry stems and reflexed, curled, leathery, small shining leaves. The foliage is deep green flushed with red through summer, becoming deep red as winter progresses and the days get colder. A highly effective winter container plant that is at its best in a dark glazed container where it creates a distinctly Japanese effect, 'Curly Red' is excellent for maintaining winter interest alongside Japanese maples. It is best in semi-shade but needs enough direct light for good foliage colour. Grow in a loam-based, lime-free growing medium or on a neutral to acid soil in the open ground. No pruning is required apart from the removal of dead or damaged shoots.

Leucothoe Scarletta

45 × 60cm (18 in. × 2 ft.)
UK H6 USDA 5-8

This dwarf evergreen shrub has become a popular winter container plant, but few appreciate that it is an excellent long-term subject. Short, upright arching stems carry leathery, arrow-head leaves of deep, shining green often flushed with dark red. In winter they gradually turn to bright scarlet, the colour developing through the entire plant. It thrives in semi-shade and can be grown as a groundcover subject on neutral to acid soils. In a pot it requires a lime-free growing medium. In a mixed container it makes a good planting partner for small skimmias and heucheras. No pruning is required, but older plants may need straggly shoots removed to promote compact growth.

Lophomyrtus ×ralphii 'Magic Dragon'

90 × 60cm (3 × 2 ft.)
UK H3 USDA 9–11

This may not be the hardiest evergreen, but it is a striking foliage shrub. Fine, dark stems carry the small rounded leaves on a light, bushy plant. Each leaf is a mix of pink, cream, and burgundy with little green, a contrast to most other garden plants. It grows quite quickly during spring and summer when pinkish flowers appear in the leaf axils. These often go unnoticed against the leaves. It needs a sheltered spot in sun but only overwinters outdoors in the mildest areas. Elsewhere it may need the protection of a cold greenhouse or conservatory. It can be lightly pruned at any time in the growing season to control shape and size.

Nandina domestica Obsessed

60 × 45cm (2 ft. × 18 in.)
UK H4 USDA 6–11

This dwarf variety of sacred bamboo is unsurpassed as an evergreen shrub for all-year interest in a pot. The elegant fern-like leaves radiate from stout upright stems. They are more tightly packed together than they are on the species, creating an altogether more compact and bushy plant, ideal for a small garden or a container. The lower leaves are olive green, coral towards the top of the plant. In winter the upper leaves gradually turn rich crimson, the colour progressing further down through the foliage. The colour persists well through spring. A versatile shrub that mixes well with other plants and suits all styles of garden. It needs a sheltered spot in sun or semi-shade and regular watering. No pruning is required.

Phormium 'Crimson Devil'

90 × 90cm (3 × 3 ft.)
UK H4 USDA 8–11

There are many varieties of New Zealand flax ranging from giant to modest in size and habit. Generally those with more colourful foliage are more suited to pots and small gardens because they are smaller and less vigorous. 'Crimson Devil' is a striking plant with arching strap-like leaves of bright red-pink with darker stripes and dark green edges. This variety rarely flowers. It grows fairly slowly but makes an eye-catching focal point from an early age with its vibrant colour. Some may consider it rather exotic for a traditional setting, but combined with other shrubs in pots, heucheras, aeoniums, and seasonal colour, it contributes a contrasting leaf shape and sharper form. At its best in full sun, it tolerates some shade in a sheltered position. Hardy only in milder regions, it needs winter protection from hard frost. No pruning is required, apart from the removal of dead leaves which need to be cut at the base.

Pieris japonica 'Little Heath'

75 × 75cm (30 × 30 in.)
UK H5 USDA 6–9

A compact lily of the valley bush, grown more for its leaves than the flowers. Dense and bushy in habit, it has dainty, small, narrow leaves of soft green, edged with white. The new growth is delicate salmon-pink, a colour that persists in the young leaves. Small sprays of brown-pink buds open to white-pink lily of the valley flowers in early spring; although pretty they are not freely produced. Although it does not excel in production of flowers or the colourful quality of the new growth, it is a wonderful foliage shrub that makes an excellent choice for a pot. It requires a lime-free growing medium and a position in semi-shade or shade, sheltered from frosts which can damage the new growth. No pruning is required.

Pittosporum tenuifolium 'Golf Ball'

75 × 75cm (30 × 30 in.)
UK H4 USDA 8–11

In milder climates and sunny situations 'Golf Ball' is an excellent alternative to the ubiquitous box ball. Fine black stems and oval, rounded, shining bright green leaves grow naturally to produce a globe-shaped shrub. It can be left to grow loosely or trimmed for a more compact effect. The shining quality of the foliage and bright colour of the leaves make it a more cheerful alternative to many other evergreens. It is best in full sun but tolerates some shade and is ideal for sheltered town gardens. In colder areas it may need winter protection, especially when young. The tender new growth in spring can be very vulnerable to late frosts, but damaged shoots are easily clipped. Prune in spring if necessary.

Pittosporum tobira 'Variegatum'

1.2m × 90cm (4 × 3 ft.)
UK H4 USDA 8–11

The variegated Japanese mock orange is a slow-growing shrub with whorls of evergreen leaves with rounded tips and margins that tend to curl downward. The leaves are soft sage green with paler marbling, conspicuously edged with creamy white. The cream flowers, which yellow with age, appear in clusters at the tips of the shoots in summer; they are deliciously orange blossom–scented, hence the common name mock orange. Although regarded as slightly tender, it is surprisingly tough and excellent for sheltered town and coastal gardens. It flowers more freely in full sun, but the foliage is usually at its best in semi-shade. Pot in a lime-free growing medium for best results. It is fairly drought resistant once established and responds well to pruning, hence its frequent use as a hedge in Mediterranean regions.

Skimmia japonica 'Magic Marlot'

45 × 45cm (18 × 18 in.)
UK H5 USDA 6–9

A compact little skimmia forming a low, domed shrub with attractive soft green leaves edged with cream. An evergreen with year-round appeal, it flowers freely, producing clusters of cream-pink buds at the tips of the shoots in early winter. These gradually change to crimson-pink as the weather gets colder, remaining attractive until they burst into tiny, white-pink fragrant flowers in spring. It grows on any well-drained soil but is at its best in a pot with loam-based growing medium. A reliable small shrub, 'Magic Marlot' is more tolerant of sun than most skimmias but still prefers semi-shade. No pruning is required apart from the removal of faded flowers and any dead foliage.

Ugni molinae 'Flambeau'

60 × 60cm (2 × 2 ft.)
UK H3 USDA 8–11

This variegated variety of Chilean guava is a charming little shrub forming a tangle of arching, wiry branches and small, leathery, narrow leaves which tend to trail and flow over the edge of a container. The foliage is a charming mixture of cream, green, and pink, the colours becoming more intense in full sun. Small pink, bell-shaped, fragrant flowers can develop into red-brown edible berries, but these are not freely produced on this variegated form. Best in full sun or partial shade in a sheltered position, it enjoys good drainage and is drought tolerant. Ideal for small gardens, it is attractive in a pot on its own or as part of a planting combination. Pruning may be necessary to control shape and size and to remove dead or damaged growth in spring.

OTHER GOOD SHRUBS FOR CONTAINERS

Acer palmatum 'Katsura'

Astelia 'Silver Shadow'

Camellia ×*williamsii* 'Jury's Yellow'

Convolvulus cneorum

Erica carnea

Euonymus japonicus 'Microphyllus Albovariegatus'

Pittosporum tenuifolium 'Tom Thumb'

Rhododendron yakushimanum

Skimmia ×*confusa* 'Kew Green'

Viburnum davidii

PLANTING PARTNERS FOR POTS AND CONTAINERS

Just as shrubs are a permanent solution to planting in pots, their planting companions can also be long-term subjects that last from year to year. Perennials grown for their foliage are particularly useful as they usually add a different leaf form, and at a lower level, thereby creating layers in the planting picture when pots are grouped together.

Hostas make excellent pot subjects, offering an amazing variety of foliage form and colour. Some prefer semi-shade and are ideal under larger shrubs such as Japanese maples. Many, especially those with tougher leaves, are happy in the sun, so can be used in more open situations where they also add flowers later in summer. There is a practical advantage to growing hostas in pots: it is far easier to protect them from attack by slugs and snails, either with copper tape just below the rim of the pot, or an organic slug deterrent mulch over the surface of the growing medium in spring. These methods are successful, but care is needed later in the year when the leaves grow out and form bridges with other plants: the molluscs then soon move in.

There are a great many varieties of hosta to choose from, so recommendations are difficult. *Hosta* 'Patriot' is an excellent green and white variegated variety with bold leaves. *Hosta* (Tardiana Group) 'June' is soft yellow and blue-green, one of the loveliest. Blue-leaved hostas tend to be more slug resistant. Both 'Halcyon' and 'Blue Wedgwood' are favourites; both grow well in full sun.

Heucheras and heucherellas are enduringly popular perennials, unsurpassable for their variety of leaf colour. Heucheras are better in sun, heucherellas in shade. They both have the advantage that they look good through fall and early winter, holding onto their foliage throughout the year. New leaves emerge in spring and that is the time for a tidy-up. In recent years the fungal disease heuchera rust has been an issue, they also often succumb to vine weevil: the larvae devour the roots. However, they are easy to replace and quick to make an impact.

Purple-leaved heucheras are the toughest of their kind. They work best in sun and can even be used in containers alongside, or even combined with, sun lovers such as lavender and *Convolvulus cneorum*. The rich wine foliage of *Heuchera* 'Plum Pudding' is lovely with delicately variegated *Ugni molinae* 'Flambeau'.

The copper-leaved heucheras and heucherellas often look out of place in the border but wonderful in pots. *Heucherella* 'Brass Lantern' is an excellent variety that works well in containers alongside flame-leaved phormiums and *Nandina domestica* Obsessed. In a sheltered town garden it would make a striking combination with *Coprosma repens* 'Tequila Sunrise'. For those who prefer a more subtle subject, ×*Heucherella* 'Tapestry' is a good mixer with the benefit of pretty pink flowers

Hosta 'Patriot' makes a strong statement against a backdrop of *Acer shirasawanum* 'Aureum' and *Buxus sempervirens* 'Elegantissima', the permanent subjects in this grouping.

Heucherella 'Brass Lantern' is tough and reliable and looks wonderful through-out winter.

from late spring. The finely patterned foliage looks good alongside plain evergreens or the subtly variegated *Buxus sempervirens* 'Elegantissima'.

For shadier situations ferns are a good choice and sit well with pieris, camellias, and rhododendrons. Ferns thrive on neglect, requiring little in the way of feeding. Some may regard them as rather dull; however, they offer a different texture and can be used in conjunction with flower bulbs to add a shot of seasonal colour, especially in situations where they get more light early in the year.

Flower bulbs are an ideal way to add seasonal colour alongside shrubs in pots. They are inexpensive to buy, offer great variety, and are easily removed when the flowers fade. In beds and borders the foliage can become unsightly after flowering as it gradually dies down; in pots the problem can be removed.

Tulips are perfect in pots, especially as they rarely make good long-term garden plants. The bulbs are best replaced every year, making it possible to create different colour combinations. The secret of success is to plant good quality bulbs, plant them deep enough (at least three times the depth of the bulb), and never plant before late fall. Early planting can lead to disease and disappointment. Keep the

pots sheltered over winter, under the eaves of the house. Then move them into position when they are in growth in spring.

We all crave colour, hence the appeal of seasonal bedding plants. As shrubs maintain the interest throughout the year, a few pots can be given over to annual or short-term seasonal plants such as violas and primroses for spring and a host of other subjects for summer. The tendency is often to mix seasonal plants together in a pot. However, when grouped with shrubs and perennials, they often look better planted as one variety in a pot. Simplicity has more impact and is a more certain way of finding the right planting partner.

above A pot of red-flowered cosmos adds a seasonal shot of colour alongside *Phormium* 'Crimson Devil'; simple planting with great impact.

above left ×*Heucherella* 'Tapestry', a more subtle variety for sophisticated planting combinations.

left 'Honey Bee' viola adds a little spring colour among newly planted woody herbs.

Larger shrubs have their place in a small garden, providing they contribute year-round interest and fill that middle layer in the planting picture.

SMALL GARDENS

Gardens are getting smaller, especially in more densely populated parts of the world. Small gardens have their challenges. Access can be restricted and difficult. Shade from neighbouring buildings has an impact on the growing environment. The disposal of garden waste can prove a problem. Often there is no hiding place; every aspect of the garden is in full view all of the time.

Easy-care shrubs are the perfect plants for small gardens: they can deliver colour and interest throughout the year. The secret of success is to choose shrubs with a long, or more than one, season of interest, hard-working shrubs that suit the situation. Many popular flowering shrubs such as the larger-growing philadelphus, lilac, weigela, and buddleja have a short flowering period and ordinary foliage. They may not be the best choice, even if the period of interest is extended by the introduction of climbers. These shrubs also require regular pruning, which may mean taking bulky prunings through the house and the challenge of disposal.

Large deciduous shrubs also result in copious leaf fall, but they do offer a changing element in the planting picture. Evergreens, however, maintain their impact through the seasons, shedding their old leaves gradually. The ideal is to have a combination of manageable deciduous shrubs and interesting evergreens of varying height and shape.

It is a mistake to choose all small, compact plants for a small garden. Even small spaces need height to make them three dimensional, otherwise they become flat if all the planting is confined below eye level. If the space is too small for a tree, a tall, slender shrub can often fulfil the role, even if it is grown in a pot.

Shrubs with attractive foliage should always make up the majority of the planting. Flowers can be added with well-behaved perennials, flower bulbs, and seasonal bedding plants, even if these are all grown in pots.

A gardener who downsizes from a large garden to a small one, perhaps to make life easier, often finds his or her new garden very restricting. The secret of success is to see it as an opportunity to garden differently. Avoid the plants that could easily be accommodated on a large plot and concentrate on a more detailed approach. With the right shrubs a small garden can be every bit as rewarding as a large one.

Abelia ×grandiflora Confetti

75 × 75cm (30 × 30 in.)
UK H5 USDA 7–9

A delightful semi-evergreen shrub with arching stems and small leaves, growing to form a loose, rounded dome. The leaves are shining, narrow, and dark green, edged with creamy white; they flush pink in winter. Fragrant, funnel-shaped flowers appear in fall, surrounded by pink calyces which remain in clusters at the tips of the branches after the flowers have fallen. A shrub with year-round interest for a sheltered spot, perfect for a small garden, it thrives in sun or semi-shade on any well-drained soil and is ideal in a large pot. No pruning is required, except the occasional removal of upright shoots that detract from the shape.

Acer palmatum 'Beni-maiko'

1.5 × 1.2m (5 × 4 ft.)
UK H6 USDA 5–9

A lovely, bushy Japanese maple with horizontally spreading, slender branches and delicate foliage. The leaves unfold crimson-pink in spring, changing through pink to reddish green as summer progresses. In fall the leaves take on shades of orange, red, and gold before they fall. From spring to autumn the foliage maintains a translucent quality and is a wonderful contrast to the heavier foliage of other shrubs. It grows best in a sheltered garden away from strong winds in semi-shade. Although tolerant of alkaline conditions, it is best on moist but well-drained fertile soil with plenty of organic matter. Avoid hot, dry situations. Use a loam-based growing medium in a pot. No pruning is required and is best avoided, but if necessary to shape, pruning must be done when the plant is in leaf to avoid die-back and disease.

Choisya ×dewitteana White Dazzler

90 × 90cm (3 × 3 ft.)
UK H5 USDA 7–9

This compact evergreen Mexican orange is a much better choice for smaller gardens than the widely planted *Choisya ternata* or *Choisya ×dewitteana* 'Aztec Pearl'. Rounded and bushy in habit, it has abundant dark green leaves with slender leaflets. The fragrant white flowers appear in small clusters in spring and again in late summer or fall, starry and sparkling against the dark leaves. It grows in sun or semi-shade on any well-drained soil and is a good choice for a large pot. A good planting partner for white and green variegated evergreens, it makes an excellent structure shrub with the benefit of flowers. No pruning is necessary, but light pruning to control shape and size can be carried out after the first flush of flowers.

Cornus alba 'Sibirica Variegata'

90 × 90cm (3 × 3 ft.)
UK H7 USDA 3–7

The most versatile of the red-twigged dogwoods, remaining fairly compact in habit and perfect for smaller gardens. The soft green and white variegated leaves mix beautifully with other shrubs and roses. In a sunny situation they flush purple pink from midsummer, gradually turning pink and crimson before they fall to reveal dark red winter stems. Small clusters of white flowers in early summer often develop into bluish white berries by fall. A dogwood that grows on any soil, including heavy, wet clay and quite dry chalk in sun or semi-shade. Ideal to plant with perennials where its strong stems will lend support. Only occasional pruning is required to control shape and size. Old plants can be hard pruned in early spring to stimulate new growth.

Daphne ×transatlantica Eternal Fragrance

60 × 60cm (2 × 2 ft.)
UK H5 USDA 6–9

A wonderful little daphne with a long flowering season. Compact in habit, it forms a rounded shrub with straight stems and narrow mid-green leaves in a whorled arrangement around the stems. The small flower clusters are freely produced both at the tips and occasionally along the stems, mainly in spring, but then intermittently to fall and often in midwinter in milder areas. The blooms are pale pink with yellow stamens, sweetly fragrant and often followed by red berries. The shrub is evergreen in sheltered gardens and semi-evergreen in colder areas. It likes a well-drained, fertile soil and often succeeds best in alkaline conditions. Once planted it resents disturbance and is not the best choice for a pot. No pruning is required.

Hebe pinguifolia 'Sutherlandii'

60 × 60cm (2 × 2 ft.)
UK H5 USDA 6–11

A very useful hebe growing to form a regular mound of grey-green foliage. The tiny leaves, crowded on the stems, give the plant a different texture to most other evergreen shrubs. In summer small spikes of white flowers, attractive to bees, appear at the tips of the shoots. An easy hebe to grow, it is ideal in gravel or at the edge of paving. It combines well with trimmed boxwood and other hebes of similar habit. Preferring full sun, it is more tolerant of hot, dry conditions than many hebes and grows on most well-drained soils. No pruning is required. Old plants may become more open in habit; they sometimes respond to pruning, cutting back to where new shoots are growing lower down on the stems.

Hebe 'Silver Dollar'

60 × 60cm (2 × 2 ft.)
UK H5 USDA 6–9

A sport of *Hebe* 'Red Edge', 'Silver Dollar' is similar in habit with upright stems and regularly arranged small, leathery leaves forming a neat, domed shrub. The foliage is pewter grey, each leaf edged with creamy white, sometimes pink. The tips of the shoots flush red-purple in winter. Short spikes of tiny, pure-white flowers appear near the tips of the shoots in summer; these are very popular with bees and butterflies. It grows in full sun on any well-drained, fertile soil. Like 'Red Edge' it is more tolerant of hot, dry conditions and freezing temperatures than hebes with large, soft leaves. No pruning is required. If plants become untidy they can be cut back to wherever new shoots are present lower down on the stems.

Luma apiculata 'Glanleam Gold'

1.2m × 90cm (4 × 3 ft.)
UK H3 USDA 9–11

A slow-growing evergreen shrub, taller than broad, with ascending branches and small, rounded, softly shining leaves crowded on the stems. Like the common myrtle, it develops characteristic cinnamon-coloured bark on mature specimens. The tiny dark green leaves are conspicuously margined with cream, giving the whole plant a creamy yellow appearance, tinged with pink at the tips of the shoots. Small white flowers with fluffy stamens appear on the branches in summer, sometimes followed by red-black fruits. A native of Chile, it likes a sheltered situation in full sun on any well-drained fertile soil and is a good choice for a pot or against a wall or fence. No pruning is necessary, although selective pruning to control shape and size can be done in spring.

Magnolia stellata 'Water Lily'

1.5 × 1.2m (5 × 4 ft.)
UK H6 USDA 4–9

The best magnolia for small gardens, growing slowly to form an elegant shrub with layered branches and medium soft-green leaves. Silky, soft grey winter buds, conspicuous in sunlight, burst in spring into starry open blooms of pure white with ribbon-like petals and a sweet fragrance. The delicate flowers are surprisingly weather resistant and do not suffer frost damage as badly as larger-flowered varieties do. Flowering continues over several weeks in a sheltered garden, much longer than many other flowering shrubs and trees. It grows well on most well-drained soils, is tolerant of alkaline conditions and chalk, and loves clay. It likes an open sunny position but tolerates some shade. Any pruning should be done when the plant is in full leaf, as soon as possible after flowering.

Nandina domestica 'Fire Power'

60 × 60cm (2 × 2 ft.)
UK H4 USDA 6–11

A dwarf form of sacred bamboo, growing to form a loose mound of olive green foliage, turning rich shades of flame and scarlet from fall through winter. The leaves, which resemble branches, are made up of a number of slightly curled and puckered leaflets, giving the plant an interesting texture. Although it prefers a sheltered situation, a breeze easily ruffles the foliage, making the sound of a bamboo. Plant it either as single specimens or as small groups with groundcover subjects such as ajuga, ericas, ivy, or vinca. Nandina grows on any reasonably fertile, well-drained soil in sun or semi-shade. It dislikes cold, exposed situations and acid, wet soil. No pruning is necessary, apart from the removal of dead or damaged leaves.

Osmanthus heterophyllus 'Goshiki'

90 × 75cm (3 ft. × 30 in.)
UK H5 USDA 6–9

Sometimes called false holly, *Osmanthus heterophyllus* has leathery evergreen leaves with spiny margins, very similar to small holly leaves. The foliage of 'Goshiki', which means "five colours," is dark green, marbled with cream. The new shoots are copper-coloured, warm, and conspicuous. It grows slowly to form a dense, rounded shrub that makes an excellent structure plant in any garden. Tiny white flowers produced in the leaf axils in autumn often go unnoticed, apart from the sweet scent that wafts through the garden. It grows on any well-drained soil in sun or shade; the foliage colour is richer in sun. A good subject for a pot. No pruning is required.

Pittosporum tenuifolium 'Irene Paterson'

1.5m × 90cm (5 × 3 ft.)
UK H4 USDA 8–11

An eye-catching evergreen with small, waved, pale green leaves heavily marbled with soft white, giving the plant an overall light and bright appearance. Compact and narrowly conical in habit, it has well-branched black stems and abundant foliage. The small, dark purple flowers often go unnoticed hidden among the leaves in early summer. Their honey fragrance gives them away on warm days. Best in full sun but tolerant of some shade, it grows on any well-drained soil and prefers a sheltered situation. No pruning is necessary, but it responds well to light trimming in spring to promote a more compact habit. The foliage of unpruned plants is lovely for cutting.

Prunus incisa 'Kojo-no-mai'

1.2m × 90cm (4 × 3 ft.)
UK H6 USDA 6–9

A dwarf form of Fuji cherry, eventually a medium-sized shrub with zig-zag twigs and small, neat, dark green leaves. It has a mature appearance from an early age, often giving the impression of an aged bonsai, rather than a newly planted hardy shrub. Round buds on the bare winter branches burst into showers of white, pink-flushed blossoms in early spring, the flowers blushing deeper pink as they age. 'Kojo-no-mai' means "flight of butterflies," a descriptive name for the plant in flower. Green summer foliage turns to crimson flame in fall. A hardy shrub that grows on any well-drained soil in a sunny position, often at its best on clay or chalk. An excellent shrub for a pot. Any pruning to control shape and size must be done in summer when the plant is in leaf.

Rhododendron yakushimanum

90cm × 1.2m (3 × 4 ft.)
UK H5 USDA 6–9

There are many hybrids of *Rhododendron yakushimanum* that have inherited its compact, domed shape, making them ideal rhododendrons for small gardens. The evergreen leaves are shining, dark green above, felted russet or grey on the undersides. The new shoots are covered in grey felt for protection. The species produces dense heads of funnel-shaped, apple-blossom pink flowers in late spring; these open from darker pink buds. The petals have a fragile transparency, beautiful against the solid, dark foliage. A shrub for reasonably moist acid soil, ideally in semi-shade. Although it is exceptionally hardy, the blooms can be damaged by hard frost, so the shelter of a small, enclosed garden is perfect. No pruning is required.

Sarcococca hookeriana Winter Gem

30 × 60cm (1 × 2 ft.)
UK H5 USDA 7–9

A short, stocky variety of sweet or Christmas box with upright tan-coloured stems and pointed, elliptical leaves, reminiscent of those of a camellia. The evergreen foliage is shiny and dark green; the stems form a dense clump that never suckers and spreads unwanted shoots. The tiny pinkish white flowers appear in the leaf axils in mid- to late winter; they may not be showy, but they are wonderfully fragrant. An excellent small shrub for a shady corner on any well-drained fertile soil, it is good on clay and chalk. Unlike other sarcococcas, it grows well in a pot. Avoid open, sunny situations as this can cause yellowing of the foliage. No pruning is necessary.

OTHER GOOD SHRUBS
FOR SMALL GARDENS

The recommendations for pots and containers and for narrow beds and borders are also particularly appropriate for small gardens.

Abelia parvifolia 'Bumblebee'

Buddleja davidii Buzz Series

Convolvulus cneorum

Daphne odora 'Aureomarginata'

Erysimum 'Bowles's Mauve'

Hebe 'Youngii'

Lavandula angustifolia 'Hidcote'

Myrtus communis

Photinia ×fraseri 'Little Red Robin'

Spiraea japonica 'Little Princess'

PLANTING PARTNERS
FOR SMALL GARDENS

Most small gardens are surrounded by walls and fences. Left bare, these structures really define the boundaries of the space; however, used as a planting opportunity they can more than double the planting space of the garden. The most important thing to remember is to use those climbers as part of the planting—never think of them in isolation. They should work with the shrubs planted alongside to create interesting and enduring planting combinations.

When it comes to evergreen climbers, the choice may seem limited, especially if ivies are avoided. Many consider a large- or small-leaved hedera as a dangerous planting decision, concerned that it might take over or cause damage to the supporting structure. Although they cling by aerial roots, if the wall or fence is sound any damage should be negligible and they are easily kept in check. They are easy to grow, cope with heavy shade, and reward with a year-round living wall. It is hard to think of a good reason not to like them. The popular *Hedera algeriensis* 'Gloire de Marengo', with its green and white marbled and variegated leaves, makes a wonderful backdrop for *Pittosporum tenuifolium* 'Irene Paterson' and the dark green foliage and starry white flowers of *Choisya ×dewitteana* White Dazzler. Add *Sarcococca hookeriana* Winter Gem and *Euonymus fortunei* 'Emerald Gaiety' and you have the perfect combination for a shady border in a small garden.

Trachelospermum jasminoides is among the most popular climbing plants because it has evergreen foliage and fragrant jasmine-like flowers. It needs some sun to flower well and something to climb on. The least obvious means of support for climbers on walls and fences is to use vine eyes: these are threaded eyelets which are screwed into the wall; then galvanized wires are stretched between them. The wires must be held at least 4cm (1.6 in.) away from the wall to enable the stems of the climber to twine around them.

Walls and fences are not the only places for climbers; shrubs are also an excellent means of support. Clematis may be beautiful in summer when in bloom, but the deciduous varieties are nothing but a tangle of dead stems in winter. By growing them through supporting shrubs you see them at their best and they disappear in winter. Breeding has produced some excellent compact varieties that flower freely from summer to fall; these are perfect to grow through small and medium-sized shrubs or in pots that can be moved into position in summer. *Clematis* The Countess of Wessex is an excellent large-flowered clematis

Trachelospermum jasminoides is the most popular evergreen climber with sweetly fragrant jasmine-like flowers in summer. In a sunny situation the foliage flushes red in winter.

Large-flowered *Clematis* The Countess of Wessex is excellent for the small garden.

Gaura lindheimeri 'The Bride'

growing to 90cm–1.2m (3–4 ft.). It is free flowering and grows in sun or shade, perfect for the small garden. All stems can be cut back to 15cm (6 in.) in winter.

Just as taller shrubs have their place in small gardens, so do taller perennials, especially those of light airy character. These are particularly useful in the foreground, where they veil the view of the rest of the garden, increasing the perspective and making the space look larger. *Linaria purpurea* 'Canon Went' is a good example. This delightful form of purple toadflax grows up to 75cm (30 in.) or more with fine, grey-green stems topped with tiny soft pink snapdragon flowers. It fits in well with low shrubs and perennials in a sunny or lightly shaded spot. It is invasive in parts of North America.

Later in the year gaura is unbeatable with its wiry stems and dancing flowers. There is a tendency towards the more compact varieties, but taller ones are more graceful and add another dimension to the planting. *Gaura lindheimeri* 'Whirling Butterflies' and *Gaura lindheimeri* 'The Bride' are two of the best; plant where the breeze can bring the flowers to life.

Flower bulbs fit in anywhere, but remember that you need to leave the foliage to die down naturally if they are to perform the following year. The dying foliage of larger narcissi is not attractive, so it is best to choose varieties with finer leaves that die down quickly. Early bulbs such as galanthus, crocus, chionodoxa, and fritillaria are never a problem. For later in the season alliums are an inspired addition because the leaves die down as the flowers develop. These are easily hidden if you grow them among low shrubs and perennials. The wonderful rounded heads are such a different flower form and a total contrast to anything else in the early summer garden.

Allium cristophii sparkles with lilac starry flowers held on strong stems. The seedheads that follow are equally attractive and last into fall. It seems to adjust its height according to what it has to grow through. *Allium atropurpureum* is taller but with smaller flower heads the colour of crushed blackcurrants, fabulous growing through grey-green hebes and silver foliage shrubs.

Hardy geraniums are among the most popular perennials and many are perfect at the front of borders where they can spill over paving, or to fill the space under shrubs. *Geranium* Rozanne is a marvellous plant for its long flowering period; however, it does grow large and many small garden owners find it rather overpowering. Breeding has produced similar varieties with long flowering periods that are more manageable. *Geranium* 'Azure Rush' is a good example.

Allium cristophii is among the easiest alliums to grow, perfect growing through light-coloured foliage, here with *Cornus alba* 'Sibirica Variegata'. The fading foliage of the allium is concealed by the cornus.

left *Geranium* 'Azure Rush' flowers from midsummer to late autumn, a hard-working perennial that sits well with shrubs.

The climbing *Hydrangea anomala* subsp. *petiolaris* produces its lacy white blooms in midsummer.

NARROW BEDS AND BORDERS

Narrow beds and borders are common features in gardens of all sizes and present a real planting challenge. Often backed by a fence or wall, plants have only one way to grow if they are not going to encroach on lawn, path, or patio. The width of planting areas may be limited by space, especially in small gardens. A narrow bed along a boundary may be the only planting possibility in a passageway or other restricted space. However, some spaces are narrow by design, often from the belief that an area of lawn is easier to maintain than a bed. If widening the planting area is a possibility, this is always worth considering. Larger beds and borders offer far greater planting possibilities and avoid the need for regular pruning and trimming to keep plants within bounds. This often happens when the wrong subjects are chosen.

Many perennials have a tendency to spread over time. They need lifting and dividing to maintain performance and vigour. Even if they are upright in habit, these are not the best choices for narrow borders. Deciduous varieties that die down in winter leave the space empty, presenting a depressing picture during winter if backed by a wall or fence. Shrubs, in contrast, can bring the area more depth and interest throughout the year. The secret is to choose shrubs that grow up rather than out.

In narrow borders around paved areas or alongside paths, neat, compact shrubs are the ones to choose. If there is room to spill over the edge of hard surfaces, they have a softening effect and help to join hard and soft landscape areas together. However, if they spill over the edge of grass, this is an obstacle when mowing and is likely to cause problems for the grass and the plants. Planting position in the border may overcome this, or again widening the planting area at the outset may solve the problem.

The most difficult thing to achieve in a narrow bed is a planting scheme that holds together, rather than a disparate row of plants that fail to relate. In long borders, repetition of some subjects helps to give the scheme rhythm and unity. Limiting the planting palette and colour scheme also helps. If the border is backed by a wall or fence, then climbers can work with the shrubs to hold the scheme together, especially if they are evergreens.

Berberis thunbergii 'Orange Ice'

75 × 30cm (30 × 12 in.)
UK H7 USDA 4-9

A colourful new variety of barberry, upright in habit and compact, healthy, and perfect for small gardens. The ascending stems carry characteristic, rounded leaves that are coral orange in spring, becoming copper flushed with orange and turning to vibrant orange-red later in the season. Small yellow fragrant flowers appear on the stems in spring and are favourites with bees and pollinators. Small red fruits may follow the flowers in autumn. It thrives on any soil that is not waterlogged and is a good choice for clay or chalk as well as for containers in restricted spaces. The foliage colour is best in full sun, but it tolerates some shade. *Berberis thunbergii* 'Orange Rocket' is similar, a little larger and well established as a popular garden shrub. No pruning is required, apart from the removal of any branches that stray from the columnar shape and spoil the line of the shrub. The species is invasive in parts of North America.

Camellia ×williamsii 'Jury's Yellow'

1.5m × 75cm (5 ft. × 30 in.)
UK H5 USDA 7–9

There are many camellias of upright habit, but this is among the best and most free flowering. Narrow and upright, it forms a column of dark green, glossy foliage and remains compact as it grows. Creamy yellow blooms, freely produced and beautiful against the dark green leaves, open from fat buds in spring. Each double bloom has a ring of larger outer petals, the centre packed with plentiful smaller ones. The flowers mostly fall away as they fade, keeping the plant looking good through a long flowering period. An ideal shrub for a sheltered courtyard in shade or semi-shade. Avoid a situation that catches the early morning sun. Camellias grow on well-drained but moist neutral to acid soil; in a pot, use a lime-free growing medium. No pruning required.

Caryopteris ×clandonensis 'Heavenly Blue'

75 × 75cm (30 × 30 in.)
UK H4 USDA 5–9

Commonly known as bluebeard, caryopteris is a useful late-flowering shrub for a sunny position. 'Heavenly Blue' has upright stems and grey-green serrated leaves; the foliage is slightly aromatic. In late summer and early fall, grey buds in the leaf axils open to bristling sapphire blue flowers that are very attractive to bees and late pollinators. The flowering season is not long, but welcome late in the year. An easy shrub to grow in full sun on well-drained soil, all selections prefer alkaline conditions and mix well with lavender, woody herbs, and silver foliage shrubs. Prune in late winter, cutting back by two thirds or more to where grey buds are present on the stems.

Ceratostigma willmottianum

75 × 60cm (30 in. × 2 ft.)
UK H4 USDA 6–9

Hardy Chinese plumbago is a useful little shrub for narrow planting spaces. Tan-coloured stems grow upwards with small mid-green leaves that often colour well in fall if the plant is grown in a sunny position. The sapphire blue, plumbago-like flowers appear from late summer and continue into autumn; they are carried in small clusters at the tips of the shoots. Left to grow against a wall or fence, it gets taller, sometimes using the wall for support as well as protection. In cold areas it can be cut back to ground level in winter, rather like a fuchsia. This keeps the plant more compact and encourages upright growth. Ceratostigma grows on any well-drained soil and thrives on clay and chalk. Either prune in late winter to tidy or cut back to regrow from the base.

Deutzia setchuenensis var. *corymbiflora*

1.2m × 75cm (4 ft. × 30 in.)
UK H5 USDA 4–9

A dainty little deutzia, perfect for small gardens and narrow spaces. Upright in habit, it grows slowly with tan-coloured stems and tough green leaves, grey-green on the reverse. The lacy flower heads appear from mid- to late summer, tiny starry white blooms resembling gypsophila in finely branched clusters at the tips of the shoots. It flowers for several weeks in sun or partial shade and grows on any reasonable soil including clay and chalk. A shrub that deserves wider planting but that requires patience to reach any size. Lightly prune in early spring to remove faded flower heads and some older stems on mature plants.

Euonymus fortunei 'Emerald Gaiety'

60 × 90cm (2 × 3 ft.)
UK H5 USDA 5–9

A wonderfully versatile evergreen shrub that has
so many uses in the garden. Left to grow naturally
in the open ground, it forms a loose bushy mound
of whitish stems and small dark green and white
variegated leaves that often flush pink in cold winter
weather. The stems can become quite trailing, hence
the common name wintercreeper, making it an
excellent groundcover plant, especially when grown
in groups. Planted in a narrow border against a wall
or fence, it will cling and climb, making an excellent
evergreen short climber for a shady situation. Growing on any well-drained soil in sun or shade, it is
ideal under the light shade of deciduous trees. It sits
well alongside paving or gravel and is a good choice
for pots and containers. No pruning is necessary,
except to control shape and spread.

Euonymus japonicus 'Chollipo'

1.5m × 75cm (5 ft. × 30 in.)
UK H5 USDA 6–9

A superb green and gold variegated evergreen shrub
with upright stems and a bushy habit. The leaves
are shining and leathery, rounded, dark green in the
centre, broadly margined with bright golden yellow.
Originally from the Chollipo Arboretum in South
Korea and introduced to the U.S. in the mid-1980s,
it is a much better choice than the widely planted
Euonymus japonicus 'Ovatus Aureus' and far less
likely to revert. Growing in sun or shade, it is a tolerant shrub, particularly useful in town and coastal
gardens. It grows on any well-drained soil and is
ideal for a narrow border alongside a wall or fence.
In very restricted situations it can be trained to grow
vertically on a trellis. Pruning is unnecessary if space
allows, although it responds well to pruning and
trimming which are best carried out in spring.

Euonymus japonicus 'Green Spire'

1.5m × 60cm (5 × 2 ft.)
UK H5 USDA 6–9

A striking evergreen shrub with very upright stems and a compact, columnar habit, becoming broader as it matures. The rounded, glossy, dark green leaves are closely packed on the ascending stems giving the plant a bold, architectural appearance. With year-round appeal this is a good choice for courtyards, balconies, small spaces, and very narrow borders. It can be planted individually or as a narrow hedge. It grows in sun or shade and is a good choice under trees and in coastal gardens on any reasonably fertile well-drained soil. *Euonymus japonicus* 'Green Rocket' is similar, but smaller in stature. No pruning is required, apart from the removal of any lax stems that could spoil the shape.

Euonymus japonicus 'Microphyllus Albovariegatus'

60 × 45cm (2 ft. × 18 in.)
UK H5 USDA 6–9

The varieties of *Euonymus japonicus* with tiny leaves are excellent alternatives to common box and are frequently used where box blight is a problem. *Euonymus japonicus* 'Microphyllus Albovariegatus' has upright green stems, forming a compact, evergreen bush. The small, shining, narrow leaves pack the stems, giving the plants a dense, structural appearance. The leaves are dark green, conspicuously variegated with white. A shrub that grows in sun or shade and is ideal for town gardens, it is also ideal by the coast. Any well-drained growing medium works well, and it is drought tolerant once established. No pruning is required, but plants can be shaped before new growth commences in spring.

Hydrangea paniculata Confetti

1.2m × 75cm (4 ft. × 30 in.)
UK H5 USDA 4–7

A superb new hydrangea, perfect for the narrow border. Compact and upright in habit the stems are topped by lilac-like heads of sterile and fertile florets from midsummer through to fall. The green buds open to pure white flowers, blushing pink as they age; flower heads are often mixed shades of pink and white giving a pretty, lacy effect. The flowers are delicately fragrant, unusual for a hydrangea. A hardy shrub, it grows on any reasonably moist but well-drained soil in sun or partial shade. It is ideal for a pot or container and a great variety for small gardens. The flower heads turn to parchment in winter, remaining attractive if the weather is dry. Prune in late winter, cutting back by half or two thirds just above a pair of buds. This promotes strong, straight stems and well-displayed flowers.

Ilex crenata (Fastigiata Group) 'Fastigiata'

1.8m × 60cm (6 × 2 ft.)
UK H6 USDA 5–9

A fastigiate form of Japanese holly with very upright stems forming a dense column of small, dark evergreen leaves, easily mistaken for box. It can become wider with age and reach a greater height, but growth in most situations is slow. Tiny white flowers are followed by black berries which are easily missed against the dark foliage. An excellent structure shrub that fits into the smallest space, 'Fastigiata' adds height to narrow borders and is also effective in a pot. 'Sky Pencil' is a very columnar all-female form introduced by the U.S. National Arboretum in Washington DC. *Ilex crenata* grows on any well-drained soil but is very slow growing in extremely dry conditions. Although recommended for sunny situations, it will tolerate some shade. No pruning is necessary apart from the removal of any stray branches.

Juniperus communis 'Hibernica'

1.8m × 60cm (6 × 2 ft.)
UK H7 USDA 2–7

Irish juniper is a very hardy coniferous shrub with vertical shoots forming a dense column of fine grey-green aromatic foliage. The leaves are needle-like with a slightly prickly texture and may cause skin irritation if handled. The rounded berry-like fruits are used in cooking and flavouring gin. Growth remains compact and slender, and the plant has a strong presence in a planting scheme from an early age. It can eventually reach greater heights and is often used in place of the Italian cypress in colder gardens. Growing on any well-drained soil, it thrives on chalk soils and poor ground; best in full sun or partial shade, it tolerates wind and exposure. No pruning is required.

Nandina domestica

1.5m × 90cm (5 × 3 ft.)
UK H5 USDA 6–9

Sacred bamboo forms a clump of cane-like stems with stiff, fern-like leaves, mid-green through summer, flushing red and flame in fall. Sprays of small white flowers at the tops of the stems in summer produce loose clusters of round, red berries in autumn in a sunny situation. *Nandina domestica* 'Richmond' is good to grow for flowers and fruit. The shrub can eventually form a broader, bushier clump, but it consists of a group of three or four canes in a garden situation. Narrow beds restrict its growth and the upright habit makes it ideal for tight spaces. It grows on any well-drained soil and prefers a sheltered situation in sun or semi-shade. In temperate areas it is evergreen, sometimes losing its foliage in colder winters. No pruning is required apart from the removal of stray stems and dead or damaged growth.

Rosa Queen of Sweden

90 × 60cm (3 × 2 ft.)
UK H6 USDA 6–9

An English rose bred by David Austin, this is an excellent small flowering shrub for a restricted space. Very upright and compact in habit with strong stems and healthy mid-green foliage, it is easy to grow and reliable. The cupped, double, shell-pink flowers are exceptionally beautiful with an upward-facing habit, unusual for an English rose. Flowering from early summer to midseason, it repeats well and is excellent for cutting. The blooms are only delicately fragrant, but they are weather resistant and perfectly formed. Like most roses it thrives on heavy, fertile soil with adequate moisture. Flowering is most prolific in full sun, but it will tolerate some shade. Prune after flowering to remove faded blooms and promote branching. Prune again in mid- to late winter, cutting back by no more than one third. Feeding with rose fertilizer in spring and again in midsummer promotes flowering and helps disease resistance.

Taxus baccata 'Fastigiata Aureomarginata'

1.8m × 90cm (6 × 3 ft.)
UK H6 USDA 4–8

Golden Irish yew is an imposing evergreen columnar shrub with vertical stems densely clothed in narrow leaves, deep green in the centres, margined with rich gold. Even a small specimen makes an impressive focal point or exclamation mark in a planting scheme. Ultimately it can grow much larger than stated here, but growth is slow and the shape remains compact. It grows on any well-drained soil and is particularly happy on clay and chalk. It is tolerant of exposure, sun, and shade. A pair of golden Irish yews are a good choice to frame an entrance; their compact form prevents them from invading the space. No pruning is required, although it can be clipped regularly across the top of the stems to maintain a specific height. This results in a broader plant which makes a strong architectural statement.

OTHER GOOD SHRUBS FOR
NARROW BEDS AND BORDERS

Berberis thunbergii f.
  atropurpurea 'Admiration'

Berberis thunbergii f.
  atropurpurea 'Helmond
  Pillar'

Chaenomeles speciosa

Euonymus japonicus 'Bravo'

Juniperus communis
  'Compressa'

Luma apiculata
  'Glanleam Gold'

Perovskia 'Blue Spire'

Pittosporum tenuifolium 'Irene
  Paterson'

Rosmarinus officinalis

Sarcococca confusa

PLANTING PARTNERS FOR
NARROW BEDS AND BORDERS

Often a narrow garden area is backed by a wall or fence, making climbing plants an obvious choice. These extend the planting space and the possibilities of interesting planting combinations. Some popular evergreen climbers, including ivies, are highlighted in the section on small gardens; these work particularly well when planted with *Euonymus fortunei* varieties in narrow, shady borders.

For sunnier situations, blue passion flower, *Passiflora caerulea*, is a fast-growing semi-evergreen climber with attractive lobed leaves and exotic creamy white blooms, each one crowned with a halo of blue and brown filaments and golden stamens. Golden yellow fruits follow the flowers, hanging on the stems well into fall. It climbs by means of tendrils, so requires wires or trellis for support.

Climbing hydrangea, *Hydrangea anomala* subsp. *petiolaris*, is self-clinging, using short roots, similar to those of ivy. It is deciduous; however, the tracery of tan-coloured stems left when the leaves fall is very attractive. Lacecap creamy white flower heads are produced from midsummer, delightful against the abundant green foliage, making a wonderful backdrop to *Hydrangea paniculata* or green and white variegated shrubs.

If the soil is not too dry, Japanese anemones can add both height and late flowers. Taller varieties such as the lovely *Anemone ×hybrida* 'Honorine Jobert' multiplies and spreads in fertile soil with some shade. Tall, upright stems carry pure white, cupped blooms with golden stamens from late summer into autumn. The attractive dark green leaves make good groundcover.

Warm, sun-baked narrow borders may be challenging for many plants, but they are perfect for nerines. Planted with the necks above ground and left undisturbed, the bulbs send up slender naked stems in fall to be crowned with elegant, narrow-petalled blooms. *Nerine bowdenii* is vibrant pink, a surprise alongside the flame and gold of fall foliage. It hates competition from other plants but sits well alongside aromatics such as lavender, sage, rosemary, and sun-loving caryopteris.

Lily of the Nile, agapanthus, is a good perennial to use in a narrow, sunny space. There are many varieties to choose from, varying in stature and hardiness. In cooler regions, choose a suitable variety that will grow and flower well; some need warmer conditions to perform. *Agapanthus* 'Northern Star' is considered one of the best hardy varieties, free flowering with deep blue blooms. *Agapanthus* Headbourne hybrids are still the best known garden varieties and are widely grown and available. Both bloom in late summer, a welcome addition at a time when colour can be lacking.

Graceful nerines love a hot, sunny border at the base of a wall;
their delicate blooms open in autumn.

Lily of the Nile or African blue lily, aga-panthus, forms clumps of narrow leaves beneath sparkling heads of sapphire blooms in late summer.

Penstemons are shrubby in character and most are compact and upright. Evergreen in milder areas, if they are not cut back hard in spring they start to bloom early and are often still in flower in late fall. With flowers in a wide range of colours, penstemons are available to suit most planting combi-nations and are ideal with roses and hebes.

Most euphorbias are woody-based perennials that retain their stems and foliage over winter. Those of upright bushy habit fulfil the role of shrubs and sit well with them in restricted spaces. *Euphorbia ×martini* 'Ascot Rainbow' is a tough, resilient plant with year-round appeal. Stocky in character, it has strong rhubarb-coloured stems carry-ing narrow leaves of olive green edged with old gold. The tips of the shoots are flushed with orange from late winter, gradually giving rise to loose heads of bright, lime green flowers. It grows in sun or semi-shade on any well-drained soil. Planted with *Berberis thunbergii* 'Orange Ice' and *Cera-tostigma willmottianum*, it would make a colourful combination, maintaining evergreen interest through winter and early spring.

Helleborus ×hybridus is another useful perennial to add winter and spring colour to narrow borders in sun or partial shade. In long, narrow beds it works well planted with hemerocallis and compact evergreen shrubs. The daylilies and hellebores have opposite seasons and the shrubs contribute the structure. Hellebores also work well with sarcococca and euonymus and even under roses.

above Penstemons flower for months, so give great value in small spaces. *Penstemon* 'Raven' has deliciously dark flowers on slender spikes.

above left *Helleborus ×hybridus* is useful for adding seasonal colour between compact shrubs.

left With its shrub-like, compact habit *Euphorbia ×martini* 'Ascot Rainbow' is ideal in narrow beds and borders.

The graceful, spreading branches of *Juniperus squamata* 'Blue Carpet' cascade down a steep slope.

STEEP SLOPES AND BANKS

Steep slopes and banks can be some of the most challenging situations in any garden. Just from a practical point of view, working on them can be extremely difficult. If you grass them over, there will be the challenge of mowing them. If you want to add planting, you need to keep the soil in place while groundcover plants fill in; rainfall may cause quick soil erosion. Soil conditioning and cultivation prior to planting is virtually impossible.

On very steep inclines just the task of planting can be really tricky. Also if you choose taller subjects you need to plant at the right angle to keep them vertical. This usually means cutting back into the bank and planting each one in a depression to make watering possible. Often conditions are drier at the top of the slope than at the bottom, which may influence your plant choice.

One thing is certain: after planting, maintenance needs to be kept to a minimum. That is why shrubs are the perfect plants for slopes. Deciduous perennials need to be cut back on an annual basis, which will be awkward and will leave the ground bare for some of the year. The shrubs you plant also need to achieve successful groundcover to suppress weeds.

Perennial weeds need to be eradicated prior to planting, best achieved with a non-residual herbicide. You could install a weed-control membrane and plant through it. However, on a slope it is impossible to cover this with chipped bark or any other mulch; it will simply slip off. Exposed weed control membrane looks unsightly and will do until complete groundcover is achieved, if it ever is.

Obviously evergreen subjects are preferable, although there are many deciduous shrubs that give good groundcover because of their dense and branching habit. These are particularly useful if they are fast growing and keep close to the ground. The plants you use do not all need to be completely flat; they can be mounded. Just as variation in height is important in beds and borders, so it is on a slope.

Slopes and banks can be very visible planting areas. The angle of the ground can make the planting an important feature in the garden, especially if the ground slopes towards the house. A pleasing planting combination can make a slope a noteworthy feature rather than an obstacle to be dealt with.

Ceanothus thyrsiflorus var. repens

90cm × 1.8m (3 × 6 ft.)
UK H4 USDA 7–9

The widely grown prostrate form of California lilac, commonly known as creeping blue blossom, is a fast-growing evergreen shrub, making excellent groundcover with year-round appeal. The strong stems grow horizontally across the ground, becoming more arching as the mounds of foliage build up. The small, dark green leaves are very glossy and healthy, even on the poorest soil. In late spring the flower buds appear on short stalks, opening into tight, fluffy clusters of pale blue flowers that are highly attractive to bees and pollinators. It needs full sun to flower well and likes a well-drained soil, preferring neutral to alkaline conditions. Where space allows no pruning is necessary; however, this groundcover can be controlled by light pruning, cutting back only into green stems with leaves, never into old wood.

Cotoneaster atropurpureus 'Variegatus'

60 × 90cm (2 × 3 ft.)
UK H6 USDA 6–8

The variegated form of herringbone cotoneaster is an attractive low-growing shrub with spreading branches and tiny white and green variegated leaves. The tiny pinkish flowers, much loved by bees, appear in late spring. These are followed by red berries that stud the branches in fall when the foliage turns to rich crimson and pink before falling to leave a dark skeleton of straight twigs. Its prostrate habit makes it ideal at the front of a shaded border where it is a good planting partner for evergreen groundcover subjects such as ivy, pachysandra, and vinca. It is also ideal on exposed banks and slopes or at the base of walls or fences. It grows on any well-drained soil in sun or shade. No pruning is required.

Cotoneaster dammeri

30cm × 1.5m (1 × 5 ft.)
UK H6 USDA 5–8

Bearberry cotoneaster is a ground-hugging shrub with creeping, dark tan–coloured stems and small, shining, deep green leaves. An evergreen with year-round appeal, it has the added bonus of small, solitary white flowers in spring, followed by shining scarlet berries in fall. On this excellent wildlife plant, the tiny single blossoms are a rich source of nectar for insects, and the berries provide early winter food for wild birds. Growing on any well-drained soil, it thrives in sun or shade, making it particularly useful for slopes under trees. The stiff but prostrate stems can reach considerable length and will cascade over rocks or walls. No pruning is necessary, but selective pruning to control spread can be carried out in spring.

Cotoneaster salicifolius 'Gnom'

45cm × 1.5m (18 in. × 5 ft.)
UK H6 USDA 5–8

An elegant low-growing evergreen groundcover shrub with long, trailing, and arching branched stems. The bark is dark, shining brown, and the leaves small, narrow, leathery, and deep green. With a spreading and cascading habit, 'Gnom' and others of this species are lighter in character than many other groundcover shrubs, perfect to grow on a steep bank or over a wall. In spring small clusters of two or three tiny white flowers are sprinkled over the branches, developing into shining orange-red berries that persist well into winter. It grows on any well-drained soil in sun or semi-shade but flowers and fruits more prolifically in a sunny situation. In spring prune only to control size and spread. However, cutting back some of the current year's growth in late fall reveals the berry-bearing branches that otherwise may be concealed beneath.

Helianthemum 'Rhodanthe Carneum'

30 × 45cm (12 × 18 in.)
UK H4 USDA 5-8

Rock roses are charming dwarf shrubs with fine, lax stems and narrow leaves. Despite their rather fragile appearance they are remarkably robust and ideal for sunny sites where their shining blooms light up the garden in early summer. There are a large number of varieties in colours ranging from palest pastels to vibrant hot shades. *Helianthemum* 'Rhodanthe Carneum' has pink flowers with orange centres which are freely produced in early summer on plants with silver-grey stems and foliage. Helianthemums need full sun and well-drained soil, preferring alkaline conditions. They thrive on chalk and struggle on peaty soil. They make good planting partners for closely related cistus and woody herbs such as sage, rosemary, and thyme. Prune after flowering, clipping over the plants to remove the stems of faded flowers and any straggly growth. This ensures branching and better groundcover.

Juniperus squamata 'Blue Carpet'

30cm × 1.5m (1 × 5 ft.)
UK H7 USDA 3-9

Among the most popular ground-hugging varieties of flaky juniper with long, lax branches that follow the contours to cascade down banks or over walls. The foliage is steely blue-grey, arranged in abundant tufted clumps, occasionally revealing the tan-coloured flaking bark of the stems beneath. It grows in sun or partial shade on any well-drained soil and is extremely hardy, perfect for cold, exposed situations. 'Blue Carpet' is an excellent groundcover plant that associates well with stone, also perfect for rocky banks and low walls. It is a vigorous grower that needs space. No pruning is necessary except to control size and spread. The aromatic foliage can cause skin irritation: wear gloves when handling it.

Lonicera nitida 'Maigrün'

75 × 90cm (30 in. × 3 ft.)
UK H6 USDA 6–9

Commonly known as boxleaf honeysuckle or poor man's box, this low-growing shrub is widely used in commercial landscape planting for good reason. It is an adaptable evergreen that covers the ground efficiently and makes a good planting partner for shrubs with larger leaves and variegations. Straight stems that grow almost horizontally carry small, shining green leaves, creating an attractive layered effect in a planting scheme. Growing on virtually any soil that is not waterlogged, it tolerates dry conditions and deep shade. It adapts well to contours in the ground, making it a useful choice on slopes and under trees. No pruning is necessary, but it can be trimmed with shears which promotes branching and denser growth.

Microbiota decussata

30cm × 1.5m (1 × 5 ft.)
UK H7 USDA 2–7

Commonly known as Siberian cypress or Russian arbor-vitae, this groundcover conifer is as hardy as its name implies. Resembling a juniper in habit, it forms a low mat of feathery evergreen foliage, the fine stems covered in small green scale-like leaves. In cold winter weather the shrub changes colour to a pleasing shade of bronze-purple. The small, berry-like fruits are inconspicuous and barely noticeable against the foliage. Growing on any well-drained soil that is not too dry, it prefers a situation in semi-shade where it makes excellent groundcover. The feathery layered effect is all the more pleasing on a slope. No pruning is necessary.

Rosa Flower Carpet White

60 × 90cm (2 × 3 ft.)
UK H6 USDA 4-10

A wonderful Flower Carpet rose forming a mound of arching green stems and healthy semi-evergreen, dark green, shining leaves. The semi-double, cupped, pure white flowers with golden stamens are freely produced from early summer through to fall. Carried in small clusters, they are slightly fragrant and very weather resistant. Flower Carpet roses vary in vigour and habit, but this is among the most consistent, giving excellent groundcover with its dense, bushy habit. It grows on any well-drained fertile soil with adequate moisture and loves clay. Perfect for banks and slopes with evergreen groundcover shrubs, it adds summer flowers. Flowering is most prolific in an open, sunny position, but it tolerates some shade. Prune in late winter, cutting back weak and damaged shoots and removing faded flower stems; this can be done with shears.

Rosmarinus officinalis Prostratus Group

30cm × 1.2m (1 × 4 ft.)
UK H4 USDA 8-11

Creeping rosemary is the perfect shrub for banks and slopes in hot, sunny situations. The prostrate branches will follow the contours of the ground, sweeping up at the tips and cascading over walls and rocks. The narrow silver-green leaves are evergreen and highly aromatic; the small, pale blue flowers appear in the leaf axils in late spring and early summer and are highly attractive to bees. Drought resistant, it needs well-drained soil in an open sunny position and hates winter wet; mulching the soil surface with grit or gravel helps. Perfect for coastal situations in milder areas, it will not tolerate severe cold, but in ideal conditions it grows vigorously once established. No pruning is required except to remove dead and damaged shoots.

Rubus tricolor

45cm × 2.4m (18 in. × 8 ft.)
UK H5 USDA 6–9

A vigorous and rampant groundcover shrub, Chinese bramble is shunned by some and embraced by others. The long, prostrate stems grow quickly; green with soft, chestnut bristles they appear redder at the tips of the shoots. The dark green leaves are shining on the upper surface, evergreen, healthy, and abundant, giving excellent groundcover. Small, white bramble flowers develop into red, blackberry-like, edible fruits in summer. It grows on any soil, tolerating the heaviest clay and the poorest ground. Aspect is unimportant, but it thrives in shade, making it useful on difficult slopes and banks and in dry shade under trees. It is vigorous, so occasional shearing to control size and spread is necessary. This is best done in spring and summer to give plants time to recover before winter.

Stephanandra incisa 'Crispa'

30 × 90cm (1 × 3 ft.)
UK H5 USDA 3–7

Commonly known as lace shrub, this hardy, easy-to-grow plant deserves wider use. It is extremely tough and tolerant of exposure. Arching tan-coloured stems form low, spreading mounds that will cascade attractively down slopes and steep banks. The small, lobed leaves are toothed and waved, fresh green when they unfurl in spring, colouring rich gold and flame in fall. The stems are not unattractive in winter. Tiny cream-coloured flowers decorate the shrub in early summer, appearing like fine lace just above the foliage. It grows on any well-drained soil in sun or semi-shade and makes very effective groundcover. Prune occasionally in early spring to keep the plants tidy.

Symphoricarpos ×chenaultii 'Hancock'

90cm × 1.2m (3 × 4 ft.)
UK H7 USDA 5–7

Snowberry may not be the most exciting or showy garden plant, but it is tough and versatile, adapting to most growing conditions, apart from hot and dry. From midspring slender arching stems carry neat green leaves arranged in pairs along the straight twigs. The plants have a spreading habit, forming layered branches and effective groundcover. Small white summer flowers, usually at the tips of the shoots, develop into white berries speckled with red and pink. They are not particularly showy, but the fruit is not the main feature of this plant. It grows on most soils, including damp and waterlogged clay in sun or shade. Plant as bare-root whips in winter. No pruning is required, but cut back if necessary in spring.

Vinca major 'Variegata'

45cm × 1.2m (18 in. × 4 ft.)
UK H6 USDA 4–9

Common periwinkle is a vigorous shrub with long, slender trailing stems that arch, touch the ground, take root, and form more plants. The evergreen leaves are relatively large, shining, and dark green edged with creamy yellow. Large blue flowers appear intermittently from spring through summer, an attractive combination with the foliage. The shrub has an open, airy habit so that a solitary plant rarely gives effective groundcover. However, it grows anywhere in sun or shade on any soil and provides a welcome addition among other tolerant ground-cover subjects. Ideal on difficult banks or slopes, it thrives under trees. Prune only to control spread, ideally in late winter before the new growth emerges. At this stage it can be sheared to ground level if necessary.

Vinca minor 'Bowles's Variety'

15 × 60cm (6 in. × 2 ft.)
UK H6 USDA 4–10

An excellent variety of the lesser periwinkle, forming dense mats of fine, prostrate stems and neat emerald green leaves. The clear blue flowers, more freely produced than on many other varieties, stud the plants from early spring through to summer. More compact in habit than other periwinkles, it is less straggly and invasive and a much better ground-cover plant for small gardens. Ideal on slopes and banks, under trees, or at the front of shady borders, it grows on any soil that is not too dry in sun or shade although flowering is more prolific in a sunny position. No pruning is necessary, but an occasional crop with a pair of shears in late winter rejuvenates the plants.

OTHER GOOD SHRUBS FOR STEEP SLOPES AND BANKS

Calluna vulgaris

Cistus ×dansereaui 'Decumbens'

Cornus canadensis

Cotoneaster horizontalis

Erica carnea

Euonymus fortunei 'Emerald Gaiety'

Gaultheria procumbens

Mahonia aquifolium 'Apollo'

Pachysandra terminalis

Salvia officinalis 'Purpurascens'

PLANTING PARTNERS FOR STEEP SLOPES AND BANKS

Among the most important functions of planting on slopes and banks is to stabilize the ground; therefore plants with good ground-covering ability are the ideal choice. Shrubs such as *Rubus tricolor*, *Vinca major*, and *Vinca minor* all have rooting stems; these effectively make a colony of plants with widespread roots that hold the soil and prevent erosion. Some climbers also grow successfully in this way: they are naturally adapted to scrambling across the ground when no support is available to climb upon. These can be very effective when planted with shrubs to create a more varied and undulating scheme.

Ivy is the most natural groundcover plant for slopes and banks, which is how it is often found in the wild. On banks it provides important wildlife habitat, offering shelter to a wide variety of species. It is also an effective insulation of the ground beneath. Common ivy, *Hedera helix*, can be very rampant and quickly gets out of hand; however, there are many less vigorous

varieties. *Hedera helix* 'Green Ripple' is a bushier form with attractive, shining, cut leaves and arching stems. A good choice to plant with variegated shrubs such as *Cotoneaster atropurpureus* 'Variegatus'; the hedera maintains its foliage interest in winter.

Large-leaved ivies are also worth considering, the variegated ones a great way of adding colour. *Hedera colchica* 'Sulphur Heart', with its large gold and green heart-shaped leaves, combines well with winter-flowering *Jasminium nudiflorum*. This untidy climber comes into its own cascading down a slope. The straight green stems are self-rooting and fast growing, although they can look sparse. The hedera can add evergreen winter interest, and the gold variegation accentuates the flowers of the jasmine.

Muehlenbeckia complexa, commonly known as wire vine or maidenhair vine, is a charming, if rather rampant, climber that grows virtually anywhere if the climate is mild. Ideal for

town and coastal gardens, it thrives in sun or shade and is salt- and pollution-tolerant. The dark wiry stems and tiny round leaves make a tangled mat, perfect on a dry slope with large-leaved evergreen shrubs. It grows well in containers and seems to need very little soil. Cut back to the ground in severe weather, it regrows from the base. This means that it can be sheared back to keep it in check. The tiny green flowers and white fruits usually go unnoticed but may become more obvious in fall.

Banks and slopes are often shaded by trees. Balm-leaved red deadnettle, *Lamium orvala*, is an attractive perennial to establish in this situation. It spreads by underground stems to make fleshy red clumps that emerge in spring clothed in soft green nettle-leaves and crushed strawberry–pink flowers. Growing to a height of 30cm (12 in.) or less, it is not too tall and shows to advantage on sloping ground. It makes an attractive planting partner for primroses, *Primula vulgaris*.

The shining, colourful leaves of *Hedera colchica* 'Sulphur Heart' add year-round interest when used as groundcover under deciduous shrubs and on steep slopes and banks.

Lamium orvala, a delightful deadnettle of early spring interest under trees and on shaded banks.

Aubrieta deltoidea, often called purple rock cress, adds a blast of colour in full sun on dry, alkaline soil.

This modest little perennial is often overlooked in gardens in favour of the more colourful hybrids. However, the species self-seeds, spreads, is hardy, and flowers for weeks, even months. Planted with a blue-flowered vinca, it is the essence of spring and perfect for a bank.

Because most woody plants that work on slopes and banks are horizontal in habit, it is good to have some vertical interest. Foxgloves, digitalis, are well adapted to growing on sloping ground. Common foxglove, *Digitalis purpurea*, is a biennial. If forms a rosette of leaves in year one, then flowers, sets seed, and dies in year two. So it has the whole first season to establish before it needs to support a flower spike. It grows on poor soil in sun or shade and is good at finding spaces between other plants. Encouraged to self-seed in naturalistic settings, it adds welcome early summer colour. It also replants itself each year, an added bonus.

Planting partners for sunny slopes and banks are more difficult to find. On chalk soils aubrieta is a joy in late spring if it likes you. The simple vibrant blooms are wonderfully attractive to bees. Low-growing perennial wallflowers like the same conditions. Recent years have seen the introduction of many new named varieties of perennial erysimum. These should be treated as short-term plants as few survive more than a year or two.

Woody herbs work well on dry, sunny slopes, creating a landscape resembling a Mediterranean hillside. Prostrate rosemary combines well with sage, shorter varieties of lavender, and thyme. Creeping thyme, *Thymus serpyllum*, can be particularly useful for its ground-covering habit and mass of flowers in summer. All of these also combine well with ceanothus, cistus, and helianthemum.

One final piece of advice about planting on slopes or banks: plant small. Avoid larger specimens of shrubs and planting partners; smaller stock is easier to plant, and a larger number of small plants gives quicker, more successful groundcover than a few large specimens would achieve.

above *Erysimum* 'Apricot Twist', just one of many perennial wallflowers with a long flowering period on poor, alkaline soil.

left The summer flowers of creeping thyme, *Thymus serpyllum*, are a magnet for bees.

Mature evergreen *Magnolia grandiflora* beautifully trained against a high wall. Few climbers will give this much impact throughout the year.

WALL SHRUBS, ALTERNATIVES TO CLIMBERS

Many shrubs make excellent alternatives to climbers on walls and fences. A shrub does not require the support that a vine needs, which can be an advantage where installing wires or a trellis is not possible, as on the fence of a neighbouring property. Shrubs also broaden the choice, especially when it comes to evergreens; relatively few climbers are more than bare stems in winter.

A wall or fence may provide sufficient warmth and shelter to enable more tender subjects to thrive, ones that would fail in more open positions. If the site is sunny a wall can store and radiate considerable heat, even in the winter months, creating a microclimate within the garden. A wall or fence normally creates a rain shadow, meaning that the ground is drier. This can be an advantage on heavy soils, but it can also limit growth on well-drained sites. Whatever the conditions, it is really important not to plant too close, certainly no closer than 45cm (18 in.). At first the plant may seem a long way out from the support, but not as soon it starts to grow.

Wall shrubs grow out from their support more than most climbers. They are not a good choice in a narrow area, alongside a driveway, for example. A ceanothus could grow out from a wall by 1.2m (4 ft.) or more, but attempting to restrict it will limit its foliage and flowers.

Some wall shrubs are best grown as completely free-standing specimens, pruned only to keep them within bounds. Others, such as pyracantha, can be trained, much in the same way as fruit trees can be trained as espaliers or cordons. Grown in immaculately trained columns, pyracantha transforms a bare wall with foliage, flowers, and fruit. Even deciduous shrubs grown in this way can change the character of a wall or fence in winter.

Wall shrubs are an excellent way of achieving height in a small garden. In a shady corner an itea or garrya could fulfil the role of a small tree, also adding valuable evergreen structure. In a garden surrounded by a high wall or fence, wall shrubs help to break up the boundaries and increase the planting area by using the vertical space.

Abutilon 'Souvenir de Bonn'

1.8 × 1.2m (6 × 4 ft.)
UK H2 USDA 9–11

A stunning flowering maple: large leaves with pointed lobes are soft green, conspicuously edged with rich cream. In ideal conditions it is completely evergreen, but it can be cut back, protected, and overwintered in a semi-dormant state in colder areas. The lantern-like flowers are carried on drooping stalks from spring through to autumn, or even in winter in warmer zones. The apricot petals are delicately veined in dark red and are shown to perfection against the striking foliage. It grows quickly on any well-drained soil in a sheltered sunny position. In cooler regions it is ideal for a conservatory or in a pot outside in summer, overwintered in a greenhouse. Prune as necessary to control shape and size, ideally in early spring, depending on flowering.

Argyrocytisus battandieri

3 × 1.8m (10 × 6 ft.)
UK H5 USDA 7–10

Moroccan or pineapple broom is a vigorous, fast-growing, tall shrub with flexible silver stems and laburnum-like leaves of silver grey. The cone-like clusters of rich yellow flowers appear in midsummer, mostly at the tips of the shoots. The blooms are long lasting and pineapple scented, hence the common name. A fairly hardy shrub, it likes a warm sunny wall and poor, free-draining soil to flower well. On rich, moist soil it grows too vigorously, producing leaf and stem instead of flowers. It needs a high wall, such as the gable end of a house, for maximum support. It can also be grown as a free-standing specimen but can be unstable on exposed sites. Prune lightly after flowering to control size and shape and to encourage branching, which results in more flowers. Hard pruning results in vigorous, upright growth.

Ceanothus 'Italian Skies'

1.8 × 1.5m (6 × 5 ft.)
UK H4 USDA 8–10

A glorious variety of California lilac with a light, airy habit, slender green stems, and small, dark, evergreen leaves. The arching, spreading branches lean and drape elegantly. Flower buds all along the branches explode into fluffy, deep sapphire blue flowers in late spring or early summer. The perfect ceanothus to shower over a wall or fence and a lovely planting companion for later-flowering roses and clematis. Plant in full sun on any well-drained soil; however, it is never at its best on shallow chalk soils. Like other ceanothus, it grows quickly but is not long lived. Can be pruned lightly at an early age to encourage bushier growth, but this should be avoided as the plant matures.

Chaenomeles speciosa 'Moerloosei'

1.8 × 1.2m (6 × 4 ft.)
UK H6 USDA 5–9

Japanese quince, sometimes called japonica, is a spreading, sprawling shrub which is best grown against a wall or fence for support. The flexible stems are branched, often at random angles. Small, glossy green leaves are well-spaced along the stems from spring to fall. Fat, round buds appear on the bare branches from late winter, opening to clusters of apple-blossom flowers in early spring. Occasionally quince-like fruits follow the flowers late in the year, remaining on the branches into winter. A shrub for any reasonable soil including clay and chalk, it grows in sun or shade and is a good choice with ivies on a partially shaded wall. Prune as necessary after flowering to control spread. Chaenomeles is best trained onto wires or a trellis if it is to grow closely against a wall.

Coronilla valentina subsp. *glauca*

90 × 60cm (3 × 2 ft.)
UK H4 USDA 7–11

Commonly known as scorpion vetch, this is a delightful small evergreen shrub with lax, almost trailing, blue-green stems and small, clover-like leaves of a similar hue. The bright yellow pea-like flowers appear in clusters in midspring in profusion, then intermittently throughout the year. The blooms are peach and lemon scented. Unsupported it forms a loose, mounded shrub or cascades over a rock or onto paving. Against a wall it achieves greater height but rarely more than 1.2m (4 ft.). It likes a well-drained soil in a sunny, sheltered position. In cooler regions it is ideal for a cool conservatory or a summer patio container, protected in the greenhouse over winter. Prune lightly after the main flush of flowers and remove any stray, dead, or damaged shoots as necessary.

Crinodendron hookerianum

2.4 × 1.5m (8 × 5 ft.)
UK H4 USDA 9-11

Chilean lantern tree is a stunning large shrub with straight branches and very dark evergreen pointed leaves. Often grown as a large, free-standing, bushy plant in a woodland setting, it is an excellent choice for a sheltered wall. The stiff pendent buds can appear on the branches anytime from late winter. These develop into crimson lantern flowers that hang all along the branches in late spring and early summer. A choice shrub, it is an arresting sight in full bloom that is certain to attract attention. It needs a well-drained but reasonably moist, fertile, neutral to acid soil and is best in semi-shade. Cold winds and exposure can cause scorching of the foliage, especially at the tips of the leaves, so a sheltered site is essential. Pruning is only necessary to control shape and size and is best done straight after flowering; avoid spring pruning.

Drimys winteri

4.8 × 2.4m (16 × 8 ft.)
UK H4 USDA 7-10

Winter's bark is a handsome large, evergreen shrub of open habit. In its native Chile and Argentina, it reaches tree proportions and was considered a symbol of peace by indigenous peoples. The large, elongated, leathery leaves are blue-green beneath and aromatic when crushed. Mature plants develop attractive mahogany-coloured bark. The fragrant white flowers are produced in loose clusters in late spring, sparkling against the dark green leaves. Drimys likes a moist, fertile soil that is never too dry and a sheltered position in full sun or partial shade. It will not tolerate an open, exposed situation. More compact forms are offered, but part of the charm of the plant is its elegant, open habit. It is a shrub to plant for the long term. No pruning is necessary.

×*Fatshedera lizei*

1.2m × 90cm (4 × 3 ft.)
UK H3 USDA 8–11

Tree ivy is a hybrid between hedera and fatsia, with characteristics from both. The lax, sprawling stems are never self-supporting, but it will form a scrambling mound without something to lean upon. Against a wall, fence, or tree trunk it will lean and climb. The evergreen leaves are small versions of those of the false castor-oil plant, the habit more like a compact ivy. Mature plants produce small heads of creamy white flowers in autumn. It grows on any soil in semi-shade or shade and is particularly useful on a low, shady wall or fence, or over a tree stump. It is ideal for town and coastal gardens and can also be grown indoors as a houseplant, perfect for cool, shady hallways and porches. No pruning is necessary, although old plants can be cut back hard to rejuvenate them.

Garrya elliptica 'James Roof'

2.4 × 1.2m (8 × 4 ft.)
UK H4 USDA 7–9

The common name silk tassel is obvious when the shrub is draped with silky, silver catkins in late winter. A bushy, dark, evergreen shrub, it can achieve a considerable height when grown against a suitable wall. The large, leathery leaves are broad and oval, packed on stout branches; their matt surface makes them seem even darker than they are. A native of coastal regions of the United States from Oregon to California, it likes a sheltered situation on any well-drained soil. The foliage can be damaged by harsh winter weather. It grows best in shade or semi-shade and thrives in town and coastal gardens. 'James Roof' is stunning in flower, but it can be rather drab for the rest of the year so is best planted with green and white variegated evergreens. Prune only to control size and shape once the catkins have faded.

Genista 'Porlock'

1.8 × 1.2m (6 × 4 ft.)
UK H3 USDA 7–9

A large, bushy evergreen broom with straight green twigs and clover-like green leaves. It grows quickly in the right situation and rewards with a magnificent spring display of flowers and an encore in autumn, or even winter in the mildest locations. The bright yellow pea-like flowers, carried in small clusters, smother the branches and are wonderfully citrus fragrant. Although the colour may not be to everyone's taste, there is no denying the impact of a shrub in full bloom. Growing on any well-drained soil, it is tolerant of chalk. It prefers a situation in full sun and, although fairly hardy, needs the protection of a wall or fence. In colder areas it can be grown in a cold conservatory. Prune after spring flowering to control size and promote bushy growth.

Itea ilicifolia

1.8 × 1.8m (6 × 6 ft.)
UK H5 USDA 5–9

A lax, spreading, evergreen shrub with green twigs and olive green, holly-like leaves. Sometimes called holly-leaved sweet spire, it is a wonderful sight in late summer when it is draped by long greenish white catkin-like flowers with a pleasing fragrance. It can be grown as a free-standing specimen but is best with the support of a sunny or partially shaded wall or fence. A native of Western China, it needs shelter and grows on any fertile soil that is not too dry. It is often slow when first planted, growing more quickly once established. Prune in early spring to remove any flower remains or damaged growth and to promote a bushier habit.

Magnolia grandiflora

4.8 × 2.4m (16 × 8 ft.)
UK H5 USDA 6–10

Left to grow naturally as a free-standing specimen, bull bay is a large, stately evergreen tree. Although hardy it enjoys the warmth and shelter of growing as a wall shrub, a restricted environment that often promotes more prolific flowering. There are many named cultivars, often selected for flowering earlier in the tree's life or for more compact growth or hardiness. All have large, glossy, evergreen leaves, usually chestnut and felted on the undersides. The summer blooms are waxy, creamy white, magnificent, and deliciously lemon-scented, if not individually long lived. It grows on most well-drained fertile soils and is lime tolerant, enjoying sun or partial shade. Do not plant too deeply as this can inhibit growth. Prune in early spring to control size and shape. It can be trained more formally against a wall providing this is done from an early age.

Pyracantha Saphyr Rouge

2.4 × 1.8m (8 × 6 ft.)
UK H6 USDA 5–8

An excellent firethorn of bushy habit with stiff, branched, thorny stems and small, glossy, dark evergreen leaves. Resistant to fireblight and canker, which affect many varieties of pyracantha, it can be grown as a hedge or free-standing specimen, or trained against a wall or fence. Clusters of white hawthorn-like flowers in spring are attractive to bees, followed in fall by bold clusters of plump red berries which wild birds appreciate when ripe. It grows on any soil that is not waterlogged, in sun or shade, and therefore is ideal for shady walls. Prune after flowering to control size and shape, cutting back any long shoots to just above the faded flower clusters. Prune again in late summer, cutting back the current season's shoots to just above the fruit; this displays the berries to advantage.

Solanum crispum 'Glasnevin'

3.6 × 1.8m (12 × 6 ft.)
UK H4 USDA 9–11

Often classified as a climber, this vigorous, sprawling shrub is a member of the potato family. The long, lax, green stems carrying narrow, pointed semi-evergreen leaves can be trained onto a support or allowed to scramble. Large clusters of round buds burst into purple, potato plant–like flowers with golden yellow beaks in late summer. The blooms are slightly fragrant and are freely produced in a sunny situation; they are often followed by small, insignificant white berries. It grows on any well-drained soil but is at its best on chalk in full sun. Prune after flowering or in early spring before growth commences, cutting back the bushy growth and reducing the main stems by a third or more.

Sophora Sun King

2.1 × 2.4m (7 × 8 ft.)
UK H4 USDA 8–11

An unusual evergreen shrub with straight but sprawling stems carrying pretty dark green leaves, each one composed of many small leaflets in a ladder-like arrangement. In spring golden yellow bell-shaped flowers hang from the branches in loose clusters, a stunning contrast against the dark foliage. Left to grow as a free-standing subject, Sun King makes a large but rather bony shrub. However, it is ideal to train against a sunny wall or fence, making it suitable for gardens of all sizes. It grows in sun or semi-shade on any reasonable well-drained soil and is hardier than often stated, although severe winter weather may result in leaf drop. It combines well with green and gold ivies and *Euonymus fortunei* cultivars. Prune after flowering to control shape and size. The flower buds form on the new growth produced after pruning, so avoid pruning later in the year.

OTHER GOOD WALL SHRUBS

Abeliophyllum distichum

Abutilon 'Kentish Belle'

Azara microphylla

Camellia japonica

Ceanothus ×delileanus 'Gloire de Versailles'

Chimonanthus praecox

Euonymus fortunei 'Silver Queen'

Forsythia suspensa

Ribes laurifolium

Rosa ×odorata 'Mutabilis'

PLANTING PARTNERS FOR WALL SHRUBS

Of course the obvious planting partners for wall shrubs are climbers, and in many cases the two are difficult to differentiate. Roses really fall into both categories. Many so-called climbing roses are just tall-growing selections of bush varieties. The roses that really climb are the ramblers. These produce long shoots with thorns like grappling hooks which enable them to scramble up into trees or over pergolas, walls, and buildings. In many instances rambler roses are too vigorous to grow on walls and fences and are overpowering companions for wall shrubs.

The climbing English roses are excellent alongside wall shrubs: they are not too vigorous and they repeat flower. The well-known *Rosa* Gertrude Jekyll is a good example. Strong-growing and upright in habit, she produces abundant velvety blooms with a strong and delicious old rose fragrance. Gertrude Jekyll is also a good planting partner for a blue ceanothus or solanum.

English roses offer a variety of colours, including some excellent yellows, such as *Rosa* The Pilgrim, a good choice for a shaded wall. Although climbing roses prefer sunny walls, most will flower well as long as they get four or more hours of direct sunlight a day through the growing season.

Rosa 'Compassion' is a different type of climber, upright, with dark, glossy leaves; its habit and flower shape are more akin to those of a hybrid tea rose. The copper-pink blooms are produced almost continuously, fragrant and long lasting. Its compact habit makes it ideal for small gardens, and it does not require the support of wires and associated training that many climbing roses need.

Clematis rank alongside climbing roses as the most popular climbers. Most are deciduous and little more than a tangle of dormant stems in winter, although there are a few evergreen varieties for milder areas. The

fern-leaved, winter *Clematis cirrhosa* and all its cultivars make good planting partners for wall shrubs, extending the season with their delicate pendent flowers. However, the large-flowered clematis are the show stealers in the summer garden, producing a profusion of blooms, most with an encore later in the year. Growth habit and vigour vary, so it is important to choose ones that suit the stature of their planting companions.

The pale blue *Clematis* 'Perle d'Azur', for example, grows vigorously, producing long shoots with well-spaced leaves. It is ideal to grow through a large, well-branched wall shrub or climbing rose. Its delicate colour makes it an excellent planting companion for a wide variety of subjects. It produces a breath-taking display of pale, pure blue flowers in midsummer. *Clematis* 'Princess Diana', in contrast, has slender, ascending stems and small tulip-shaped blooms of vivid pink later in summer. It is ideal to grow

above Clematis steal the show in the late summer garden but are less appealing in winter. Growing them alongside evergreen wall shrubs makes their off-season shortcomings less evident.

left An old variety that has stood the test of time, *Rosa* 'Compassion' is upright in habit, disease resistant, and free flowering.

Clematis 'Princess Diana' is upright in habit, perfect to grow up through a shrub or short climbing rose.

up through a shorter shrub or climbing rose and an excellent choice to extend the flowering season.

On a shady wall the twining climber *Akebia quinata* is a good choice. The semi-evergreen foliage is light in character, each leaf a whorl of perfect leaflets. The pendent blooms can be anything from white to rich plum-purple and are often deliciously chocolate scented, hence the common name chocolate vine. It grows

vigorously and is ideal where there is space to cover. It does require wires or a framework for support.

Actinidia kolomikta is a highly useful climber for long-lasting impact. It does not rely upon flowers for colour; the broad, soft green leaves are variously banded and tipped with white and pink, just as if they have been painted. It makes an excellent planting companion for shrubs and roses in a sunny situation; the colour is never as good in shade.

Wall shrubs also include those more tender shrubs that enjoy the

protection of a wall. These are useful to combine with climbers and taller wall shrubs to produce a more interesting border. *Leptospermum scoparium*, tea-tree, can grow to make a substantial shrub or small tree; however, it is too tender for all but the most favoured climates. *Leptospermum scoparium* 'Red Damask' is more compact in habit than the species and perfect to grow against a sheltered wall. Here it produces its double, deep-red, long-lasting flowers in summer, delightful with the silvery leaves of Moroccan broom or under-planted with lavender.

above Chocolate vine, *Akebia quinata*, is an attractive climber for a shaded wall.

left The "painted" foliage of *Actinidia kolomikta* gives a long-lasting colourful display.

215

Shrubs with Desirable Characteristics

The fruits of *Cornus* 'Porlock' ripen in early fall. They make a spectacular display hanging like ripe strawberries along the branches.

The striking foliage of *Tetrapanax papyrifer* 'Rex' is reflected in a formal, black pool at RHS Wisley, Surrey, UK.

ARCHITECTURAL AND DRAMATIC FOLIAGE EFFECTS

When it comes to long-lasting impact from dramatic foliage in temperate gardens, shrubs reign supreme. Some bulbs and perennials may have impressive leaves, but most are deciduous; evergreen perennials with bold foliage are confined to tropical regions.

Shrubs with architectural foliage have many different uses in gardens. In a small courtyard or on a balcony, a single specimen in a pot makes a statement, its scale all the more impressive in a small space. As single specimens, subjects like phormiums and yuccas make strong focal points in a garden. They can be used to draw the eye and to highlight features.

Used together with exotic perennials and strong colours, shrubs with bold foliage can create a tropical effect in a temperate garden. Tender subjects such as musa, canna, ricinus, and colocasia may make a stunning display in a warm sheltered situation, but usually they come into their best in late summer and need protection as soon as the first frost arrives. Hardy shrubs, however, maintain the effect throughout the year.

These dramatic subjects suit contemporary planting schemes where their forms are strong enough to balance the bold lines of modern buildings and other structures. Big leaves look good reflected in glass and water and against plain walls or a background of dark foliage.

Shrubs with architectural foliage also have a place in more traditional planting schemes. Bold leaves are a contrast to the foliage of most flowers and perennials, so using them helps to create more interesting and eye-catching combinations. The big hand-shaped leaves of fatsia or the rigid spine-tipped leaves of mahonia add drama among the rounded, softer forms of other shrubs.

Most shrubs with big, bold leaves need more sheltered situations where wind will not tear and damage their foliage. The majority are not for cold gardens: in these situations the structural forms and interesting textures of conifers are usually better choices.

Aralia elata 'Variegata'

3 × 3m (10 × 10 ft.)
UK H5 USDA 4–8

Japanese angelica tree is usually a large, suckering shrub with curious straight, spiny stems that stand as surreal bare poles in winter. The leaves, which are branched with many leaflets, are carried in whorls at the tops of the stems, totally changing the appearance of the plant through summer. This variegated form has attractive green leaflets edged with creamy white. They colour crimson in fall, at the same time as the heads of small white flowers appear. It is best in shade or semi-shade and has the potential to reach much larger proportions, but growth is slow. It grows on most well-drained fertile soils and prefers a sheltered situation. No pruning is required, except the removal of faded flower stems.

Catalpa ×erubescens 'Purpurea'

3 × 3m (10 × 10 ft.)
UK H6 USDA 5–9

Purple catalpa is a hybrid of the Indian bean tree. It has the same stags-horn silhouette and light, beige-brown bark when the leaves fall in winter. The shoots are dark purple and the new leaves flushed with purple becoming dark green as they age. The mature leaves are large, soft with a light sheen and an angled margin. Spikes of small, balsam-like, pink flowers appear in late summer. It grows on any well-drained soil and likes a sheltered situation to avoid damage to the leaves. The colour is best in full sun, but 'Purpurea' will tolerate some shade. Left to grow naturally it will form a substantial, spreading tree. However, it is best hard pruned as this stimulates vigorous shoots and more impressive foliage. It can either be pollarded by cutting back to a similar level each year or stooled by cutting back to 30cm (12 in.) or so to grow as a shrub.

Clerodendrum bungei 'Pink Diamond'

1.5 × 1.5m (5 × 5 ft.)
UK H4 USDA 7–11

Sometimes known as glory flower or Mexican hydrangea, this is a suckering shrub with straight, upright, dark stems forming a spreading clump. The leaves are broad, in pairs, soft grey-green and irregularly edged with cream. Heads of fragrant pink flowers appear at the tops of the stems in early fall; these are long lasting and attractive to insects. A shrub for semi-shade in a situation where it can be allowed to spread, it grows on any well-drained fertile soil and is a good choice where deer and rabbits are a problem. No pruning is essential, except the removal of faded flower heads.

Cordyline australis 'Torbay Dazzler'

1.8m × 90cm (6 × 3 ft.)
UK H3 USDA 8–11

This variegated cabbage palm is a striking architectural evergreen with green and cream striped, strap-like, pointed leaves, forming a rounded crown, eventually on a stem. A fountain of architectural foliage when young, it will eventually make a statuesque shrub or even a small tree in a warm and sheltered garden. Large, conical, branched heads of small creamy white flowers with a powerful, tropical fragrance sometimes appear in early summer. Best in full sun or semi-shade, it needs protection from extreme cold which can damage the growing point. It grows on any well-drained fertile soil and is ideal for a large pot or a seaside garden. No pruning is required, except the removal of dead and damaged leaves as necessary.

Eriobotrya japonica

3 × 4m (10 × 13 ft.)
UK H4 USDA 7-11

The loquat is grown for its edible fruits in warmer countries. In temperate gardens it is cultivated as a large, architectural shrub, often against a wall. The massive, corrugated, dark green leaves can be 30cm (12 in.) long and are gathered at the ends of the spreading branches. They are usually velvety beneath, shining on the upper surface. In a warm year clusters of fragrant, hawthorn-like flowers appear in winter, and these may develop into the pear-shaped yellow fruits. It grows on any well-drained soil and is drought tolerant. It is evergreen but needs a sheltered position in full sun or partial shade to avoid damage to the leaves which may be shed in a cold winter. No pruning is necessary, except to control shape and size.

Euphorbia mellifera

1.5 × 1.5m (5 × 5 ft.)
UK H3 USDA 8-10

Canary spurge is often considered an evergreen perennial even though it has the constitution and character of a shrub. The straight green, solid branches grow to form a large, rounded mound of fresh green, narrow, very uniform leaves arranged regularly up the stems. In late spring clusters of honey-scented copper-brown flowers appear at the tops of the stems. These are followed later in the year by green capsule-like fruits. A tender shrub from Madeira and the Canary Islands, it needs a warm, sheltered spot in full sun or partial shade. It grows on any well-drained soil when it is protected from excess winter wet. A drought-tolerant plant, it is ideal for a rocky slope or the base of a wall. No pruning is necessary apart from the removal of damaged or dead shoots. Take care when handling: the milky sap is aggressively irritant.

Fatsia japonica 'Murakumo-nishiki'

1.8 × 1.2m (6 × 4 ft.)
UK H4 USDA 7–10

A stunning but rarely seen form of the false castor oil plant, sometimes known as the camouflage fatsia, with magnificent evergreen foliage of tropical appearance. The name 'Murakumo-nishiki' means "gathering clouds brocade," referring to the large, exotic leaves that are richly patterned in gold and yellow with irregular dark green borders. They are carried towards the top of the strong, upright stems which become irregularly branched with age. In late fall the stems are topped with branched flower spikes of creamy white, occasionally followed by rounded greenish black fruits. At its best in shade or semi-shade, it grows on any soil that is not waterlogged and is ideal for a large container in a sheltered urban garden. No pruning is required; however, old plants can be hard pruned in spring to rejuvenate them.

Hydrangea quercifolia

1.2 × 1.5m (4 × 5 ft.)
UK H5 USDA 6–9

Oak-leaved hydrangea is a deciduous shrub of loose, open habit. The sparse stems usually grow upright and arching and are irregularly branched, weighted down in summer by the heavy foliage and flower heads. The magnificent, large, textured leaves are shaped like those of an oak, dark green above and paler beneath. They colour richly in fall with long-lasting shades of crimson and flame. Conical heads of large, creamy white sterile florets appear at the ends of the branches in late summer. It grows on any reasonably moist, fertile soil in sun or shade, ideally in semi-shade for the best foliage through summer and reasonable autumn colour. No pruning is needed; however, light pruning can be carried out in spring to removed weak, lax stems.

Mahonia japonica

1.5 × 1.2m (5 × 4 ft.)
UK H5 USDA 5–8

Strong, upright stems carry whorls of striking architectural leaves with holly-like leaflets. The foliage is leathery, evergreen, and drought resistant. Long sprays of lily of the valley–scented, pale yellow flowers appear in late winter. These are carried in loose whorls at the tips of the stems and are often followed by green berries that turn blue-black as they mature. A tough plant that grows on any well-drained soil in sun or shade, it tolerates dry shade and is a good subject to grow under trees, even conifers. Prune in spring after flowering, if necessary. Old plants can be hard pruned to stimulate new growth, cutting back to just above a joint or a whorl of leaves.

Melianthus major

1.5 × 1.5m (5 × 5 ft.)
UK H3 USDA 7–11

A striking architectural shrub with ascending stems carrying steely blue-green leaves with deeply toothed leaflets. Every leaf is surreally perfect and neatly folded as it emerges. Slender conical heads of deep crimson tubular flowers appear at the tips of the stems in late summer in a warm year; the blooms are honey scented, hence the common name honey flower. It needs a warm, sheltered position in sun but tolerates some shade. Not the hardiest of plants, it is soon hit by frost and can be knocked back to the ground like a fuchsia in cold weather. New shoots normally emerge again in spring, growing quickly to regain normal height in a year. A shrub for any well-drained soil; ideal in a pot. Prune in early spring to control growth and remove dead and damaged stems.

Phormium 'Yellow Wave'

1.2 × 1.5m (4 × 5 ft.)
UK H4 USDA 7–11

A colourful form of New Zealand flax with arching, sword-shaped leaves of soft yellow, edged and thinly striped with green. Architectural and striking, it is also graceful and elegant in form, making a wonderful focal point in a planting scheme or on the patio. In most years dark, almost black flower stems emerge in summer, rising to a height of 1.5m (5 ft.) topped with short angular branches carrying tubular ochre flowers. At its best in full sun, it tolerates some shade and grows on any well-drained fertile soil. Excellent in pots and containers, it is ideal for coastal gardens and sheltered situations where there is protection from extreme cold. Established phormiums in the open ground rarely respond well to lifting and moving. No pruning is required. Remove old and damaged leaves and flower stems at any time as required.

Rhododendron macabeanum

3 × 4m (10 × 13 ft.)
UK H4 USDA 8–10

Although more limited in its use than other architectural shrubs, in the right conditions *Rhododendron macabeanum* is worth growing for the foliage rather than the flowers. Even as a young plant it is impressive with its massive dark green leaves, shining green above, silver and tomentose beneath. Each one can be 30cm (12 in.) long. As the leaves emerge the protective red sheaths fold back, remaining for a time around the base of the leaf stalks. Mature specimens produce trusses of bell-shaped, pale yellow flowers, often blotched with purple. They are not as showy or flamboyant as many rhododendron blooms. It grows in semi-shade in a sheltered woodland situation on moist, neutral to acid soil. Cold winds damage the leaves, and the plants are damaged by strong sunshine and dry soil. No pruning is required.

Tetrapanax papyrifer 'Rex'

3 × 1.5m (10 × 5 ft.)
UK H4 USDA 6–10

Commonly known as rice paper tree, *Tetrapanax papyrifer* is a large, suckering shrub that can eventually grow into a small tree. The upright stems are topped by huge, deeply lobed leaves, up to 90cm (3 ft.) across in ideal conditions. It is dramatic and almost prehistoric in appearance. 'Rex' is the clone most frequently grown, selected for the size of its leaves and hardiness. In frost-free conditions the foliage is evergreen, but even with mild frosts the shrub is deciduous. In colder regions it can be knocked back to ground level in winter, growing again from the roots the following spring. Creamy flowers are produced in large sprays in fall; these may be followed by black fruits. Plant in full sun or partial shade on any well-drained fertile soil. It needs a sheltered site and is perfect for a walled town garden.

Viburnum rhytidophyllum

3 × 3m (10 × 10 ft.)
UK H6 USDA 5–8

Sometimes known as leather leaf or wrinkled viburnum, this large shrub is rarely grown, partly because of its eventual size, partly because it is unappealing as a young plant in a pot. Light tan–coloured stems carry the large, elongated oval, dark green, textured leaves which are silvery on the undersides. The habit is loose, upright, and often open. Clusters of small creamy flowers are produced in late spring, developing into red, oval fruits which eventually turn black. It grows quickly in sun or shade on any well-drained soil but is happiest on alkaline soil, especially chalk. Prune only to control size and shape in spring.

Yucca gloriosa 'Variegata'

1.5 × 1.5m (5 × 5 ft.)
UK H5 USDA 6–11

The variegated form of Spanish dagger or Adam's needle is a striking subject for a situation where it can be kept at arm's length. It forms a dense rosette head of straight, spine-tipped leaves which are stiff and aggressive but magnificent. Mature specimens may eventually produce a short, stout stem. The stately flower stem rises from the centre of the plant in summer or early fall. The elegant lily-like flowers are creamy white and hang from side branches of the stem. Best in full sun on any well-drained soil, *Yucca gloriosa* is extremely drought tolerant and suits a rocky or gravelled planting scheme. No pruning is needed apart from the removal of dead or damaged leaves and old flower stems. Handle with extreme care and protect your eyes.

OTHER GOOD SHRUBS WITH ARCHITECTURAL OR DRAMATIC FOLIAGE

Astelia 'Silver Shadow'

Aucuba japonica 'Rozannie'

Catalpa bignonioides 'Aurea' *

Hydrangea aspera Kawakamii Group

Magnolia grandiflora

Paulownia tomentosa *

Phormium cookianum subsp. *hookeri* 'Tricolor'

Rhus typhina Tiger Eyes

Trochodendron aralioides

Viburnum davidii

* Trees that need hard pruning annually to 60cm (2 ft.) to encourage the production of vigorous shoots and large leaves.

PLANTING PARTNERS FOR ARCHITECTURAL AND DRAMATIC FOLIAGE EFFECTS

Australian tree fern, *Dicksonia antarctica*, has become a leading architectural and exotic addition for temperate gardens. With its fibrous brown trunk and long, delicate, palm-like leaves, it makes a dramatic statement as soon as it is in leaf. Collected under licence from natural habitats, it is exported as dormant logs of considerable size. The growing tip of each plant is tucked safely among the bases of old leaves, and most of the root system is in the trunk. It withstands a few degrees of frost but hates drought. It needs enough moisture on the stem and around the growing tip to thrive. In a semi-shaded corner it can make a magnificent feature when rising above big, glossy leaves such as those of fatsia and aucuba.

The true castor oil plant, *Ricinus communis*, is a familiar roadside weed in parts of the Mediterranean. A perennial in warmer climes, it is usually grown as an annual bedding subject in temperate regions. It grows quickly from seed, producing large, palmate leaves on upright stems. Later in summer clusters of spiky fruits are held at the tops of the stems and in the leaf axils. The red-leaved forms are the most attractive and can be extremely effective. It should never be grown where there is too much risk of physical contact or a chance of the fruits being eaten; the seeds are highly poisonous.

Varieties of Indian shot, *Canna indica*, have long been cultivated for their dramatic foliage and brightly coloured flowers. The Victorians probably grew more varieties for exotic bedding schemes than are in cultivation today. It is a useful addition to sunny, warm borders or pots and containers where its upright shoots and dramatic colouring make it a good planting partner for phormiums and cordylines.

Amicia zygomeris, a native of Mexico, is a curious half-hardy, woody perennial with upright stems and large clover-like leaves. The yellow pea flowers are typical of the bean family, but its main features are the purple stipules on the stems that cling to the leaf bases. Growing to around 90cm (3 ft.), it forms an attractive clump and works well with euphorbia and melianthus.

Colocasia esculenta, commonly known as taro, is a tropical food crop; the corms are edible. It produces slender, upright stems that carry very large shield-like leaves of silky, delicate beauty. The species is dark green, but there are most attractive purple-leaved forms. It is often used as a summer subject in pots in warmer regions, but it is also effective in a sheltered border. It is best in semi-shade, so perfect with eriobotrya or tetrapanax.

above Australian tree fern, *Dicksonia antarctica*, adds a tropical touch to a sheltered, shaded corner in this garden near the south coast of the UK.

left The dark leaves and bright flowers of cannas are perfect with big leaves and bold grasses.

Amicia zygomeris, a member of the bean family, has striking foliage and interesting colouring.

When it comes to exotic summer blooms, lilies and dahlias excel. They offer a vast choice of colours and flower forms and are easy to grow. Lilies are the hardiest and in most areas are best left in the ground as herbaceous perennials where they will re-emerge and flower year after year. The waxy bulbs hate to dry out, so should be planted soon after purchase. Plant three times the depth of the bulb with the bulbs on their sides; this prevents water from collecting in the base of the bulbs which can cause rotting. Many, such as the magnificent

Lilium 'Scheherazade', grow to considerable height, 1.8m (6 ft.) or more. The blooms are often fragrant; their elegant forms are perfect with bold foliage.

Arum lily, *Zantedeschia aethiopica*, thrives in milder locations in sheltered narrow borders if the soil is reasonably moist. At its best in semi-shade, it carries its exotic arrow-head leaves and creamy blooms on fleshy, upright stems, gradually forming substantial clumps. In cold winters it may be knocked back by frost, but in sheltered town gardens and near the coast it often remains evergreen. It looks particularly good alongside, or even in, shallow water.

Peruvian lily, alstroemeria, is most familiar as a cut flower. The long-lasting, delicately marked blooms are also a lovely addition to the summer garden, both with more traditional perennials and in exotic schemes. There are a vast number of hybrids in a wide colour range from pastel to hot and fiery. There are tall forms, perfect for borders, and dwarf varieties that are good in pots and containers. In most areas they are hardy and can be left in the ground over winter, especially if mulched with bark or bracken in the fall.

above The magnificent foliage of colocasia, taro, makes a bold summer statement in a warm, sheltered garden.

left The elegant lines of stately *Lilium* 'Scheherazade' are strong enough to balance big, bold leaves.

The rich, dark foliage of *Physocarpus opulifolius* 'Diablo' contrasts beautifully with the light, bright backdrop of *Elaeagnus* 'Quicksilver'. Both fast-growing shrubs soon make an impact.

FAST MOVERS FOR IMPACT, SCREENING, AND SHELTER

Most gardeners are impatient and want to see impact from what they plant sooner rather than later. This has led to an increased demand for larger specimen trees and shrubs that deliver a more instant garden for those who want to see a finished result, rather than to watch it grow. Of course the alternative is to select fast-growing subjects that achieve potential sooner, and there are many occasions when these shrubs really come into their own.

In new gardens where the landscape is no more than an area of grass and a few paving slabs, fast-growing subjects soon add height and maturity. They can also define the boundaries and provide screening and privacy, which are valuable in existing gardens as well, especially when surroundings change, as when a neighbouring property is extended or an unwelcome development comes within view.

Often, in mature gardens, plants need to be removed, simply due to age or damage. Here a fast-growing shrub may be the solution to filling a gap in the planting. On an exposed site this may be all the more necessary to provide shelter where removal of a tree or large shrub can leave others exposed.

Very few shrubs grow to exactly the desired size and then stop; even if they do not gain height, they continue to spread. For this reason hedges are often the favoured option because they can be trimmed regularly to maintain manageable proportions. However, their visual effect is different: they form a defined wall, whereas large, individual shrubs can become part of foreground planting, especially if they are well chosen and put together with some imagination.

For example, a purple-leaved subject such as *Cotinus* 'Grace' or *Corylus maxima* 'Purpurea' makes an excellent backdrop for a variegated pittosporum or cornus. The silver leaves of *Elaeagnus* 'Quicksilver' are a striking contrast behind a dark-leaved physocarpus. Where space allows the use of these large, fast-growing shrubs, greater depth in the planting can be achieved.

Berberis ×*ottawensis* f. *purpurea* 'Superba'

2.4 × 2.4m (8 × 8 ft.)
UK H7 USDA 4–9

A vigorous barberry forming a large, broad mound of arching, spiny branches clothed in neat, softly shining, deep purple leaves. The foliage turns crimson-red in autumn before it falls. Tiny pale yellow flowers are carried on the underside of the stems in spring. These develop into small, oval, shining berries that persist on the branches after the leaves have fallen, then are soon taken by wild birds. It grows on any soil that is not waterlogged in sun or partial shade and tolerates fairly exposed situations. It is ideal as a thorny barrier or a colourful screening shrub in large spaces. Prune in winter, if necessary, to remove some of the older stems and give new ones space to develop. It is thorny and unpleasant to handle so regular pruning is best avoided.

Buddleja davidii 'Dartmoor'

3 × 3m (10 × 10 ft.)
UK H6 USDA 5–9

A vigorous butterfly bush with arching branches and large, green, lance-shaped leaves, silver on the undersides. The huge, branched flower panicles appear in late summer at the tips of the shoots. They weigh down the branches in a cascade of light purple, sweetly fragrant blooms that are highly attractive to bees and pollinating insects. Easy to grow and hardy, it thrives on any well-drained soil in full sun and is perfect for the back of the border with other shrubs and perennials. It grows quickly and will make an impact after one growing season. Prune hard in winter, cutting back the stems to around 90cm (3 ft.). This encourages vigorous growth and abundant flowers the following summer.

Ceanothus 'Skylark'

2.4 × 1.8m (8 × 6 ft.)
UK H4 USDA 8–10

Most California lilacs are fast growing and flower from their first season, making them ideal for new gardens where an immediate impact is needed. 'Skylark' is a vigorous evergreen shrub with stiff branches and veined, shiny, emerald green leaves. The sapphire blue flowers appear in midsummer, later than many other spring-flowering ceanothus. They are gathered near the tips of the shoots in abundant fluffy clusters and are very attractive to bees and butterflies. Plant in any well-drained soil in full sun; excellent for coastal gardens but not for cold areas or wet soil. Most ceanothus resent pruning; however, 'Skylark' can be pruned to control size and shape immediately after flowering.

Cornus sericea 'Hedgerows Gold'

1.8 × 1.8m (6 × 6 ft.)
UK H7 USDA 2-8

An exceptionally vigorous variety of red osier dog-wood with dark red stems and green leaves, irregularly and boldly edged with gold, becoming cream later in the season. Some shoots occasionally produce all gold leaves. The leaves usually colour well before they fall. Upright in habit at first, it becomes broader and more spreading if left unpruned, quickly growing to form a substantial shrub on any soil in sun or semi-shade. It thrives on clay and tolerates wet and compacted soils. If pruned hard in late winter, it will still grow quickly to a height of 1.5m (5 ft.) or more in a season. This pruning produces brightly coloured winter stems.

Corylus maxima 'Purpurea'

4 × 3m (13 × 10 ft.)
UK H6 USDA 4-9

Purple filbert is a large, vigorous shrub with ascending branches and large, broad leaves. The foliage is deep purple in early summer becoming green-purple later in the year, often tinted with flame and gold before falling. A few catkins appear in early spring, occasionally followed by nuts, but these are sparse in comparison to the green-leaved species. An excellent choice for country gardens or to create a dark background to a planting scheme. Foliage colour is best in full sun although it will tolerate some shade. It thrives on any soil that is not waterlogged including clay and chalk. Cut back hard every few years to encourage new, upright shoots; otherwise prune only to control size and shape in winter.

Cotinus 'Grace'

4 × 3m (13 × 10 ft.)
UK H5 USDA 4–8

A big, strong-growing hybrid smokebush with vigorous stems and large, rounded, purple-red leaves that colour brilliant scarlet in autumn before they fall. In mid- to late summer the large reddish, smoky flower plumes appear in profusion creating a spectacular effect with the dark foliage. A hardy shrub that grows on any fertile, well-drained soil, it is at its best in full sun where the leaf colour will be richest. Good to grow as a stand-alone specimen or to add colour alongside large evergreens. Hard pruning in winter results in larger leaves and strong, upright shoots that can reach 1.8m (6 ft.) in a season. Lighter pruning promotes branched stems and more flowers.

Cotoneaster franchetii

1.8 × 1.5m (6 × 5 ft.)
UK H5 USDA 6–10

Graceful, upright, arching branches carry small, dark, evergreen leaves, silver on the undersides. In spring the profuse, pink-white flowers are attractive to bees. These are followed by prolific small clusters of orange-scarlet fruits that light up the shrub through autumn and into winter. The flowers and fruit are more prolific in an open, sunny position. Plant at the back of a border or as part of an informal hedge or screen. A good choice alongside a bird feeder and perfect for country and naturalistic gardens. It thrives in sun or semi-shade on any reasonably fertile, well-drained soil. It can be pruned in late winter or early spring to control size and shape and to stimulate new growth.

Griselinia littoralis

3 × 2.4m (10 × 8 ft.)
UK H5 USDA 6–9

Commonly known as broadleaf, *Griselinia littoralis* is a New Zealand native of coastal areas. Upright flexible olive green branches carry oval, shining leaves of bright apple green. Both colouring and habit provide contrast to other evergreens. Tiny, yellow-green flowers in spring are inconspicuous and often go unnoticed. There are separate male and female plants; females sometimes carry purple fruits if a male pollinator is present. It prefers full sun and dislikes cold, wet conditions. It is also best on neutral to acid soils and rarely thrives on chalk. In the right growing conditions it grows quickly and soon achieves a good height; it makes an excellent hedge and windbreak in coastal gardens. Prune in spring as required to control shape and size.

Ligustrum ovalifolium 'Aureum'

3 × 1.8m (10 × 6 ft.)
UK H5 USDA 6–9

Golden privet was a familiar sight in gardens when it was extensively used for hedging. Left to grow naturally it forms an upright shrub with slender branches and evergreen, oval, pointed leaves of rich gold, green in the centres, sometimes entirely golden. In summer small sprays of fragrant creamy white flowers appear at the tips of the shoots. These are highly attractive to pollinating insects. Small, black, shining fruits sometimes follow the flowers. It is not as free flowering as plain green privet but is an easy shrub to grow in sun or shade and to liven up plain evergreens used for screening. Prune in early spring to control shape and size as necessary. It can be clipped with shears or hedge trimmer to promote dense bushy growth for hedging or topiary.

Photinia ×*fraseri* 'Red Robin'

2.4 × 1.8m (8 × 6 ft.)
UK H5 USDA 7–9

One of the most widely planted evergreen shrubs in the world. Ascending, flexible branches carry elliptical dark green leaves that mature from bright scarlet new shoots emerging at the tips of the branches. Loose clusters of red flower buds open to pinkish white flowers on unpruned plants. Photinia grows on any well-drained soil in sun or partial shade. It dislikes cold, wet conditions where foliage becomes sparse and often suffers from leaf spot diseases. It responds well to pruning, making it useful as a colourful hedge and a small standard tree for garden or container. Pruning in late spring and again after midsummer produces at least two flushes of colourful new growth. If possible cut back the stems to just above a cluster of leaf nodes: this results in more new shoots from that point.

Pittosporum tenuifolium

4 × 2.4m (13 × 8 ft.)
UK H4 USDA 8–11

A light and bright evergreen shrub forming a broad column of dark, almost black twigs and small, waved, shiny bright green leaves. Small chocolate flowers appearing in the leaf axils in spring may go unnoticed, apart from the sweet fragrance that can fill the garden. It grows best in an open, sunny situation but will tolerate some shade. Not for cold areas but thriving near the coast, it grows quickly on any well-drained soil. It makes an excellent specimen or screening shrub and responds well to pruning and trimming, so makes an attractive hedge; it can also be trained as a small standard tree. Excellent for cutting for floral decoration.

Prunus laurocerasus

5 × 5m (16 × 16 ft.)
UK H5 USDA 6–9

Cherry laurel is a vigorous, large shrub with big, glossy, evergreen leaves. It is widely used for hedging and screening and has become invasive in many areas, but planted wisely and controlled it is a valuable garden plant used for centuries in formal and informal gardens. Spikes of white flowers appear in spring on unpruned plants; these mature to small, marble-like red fruits which soon turn black. It grows on any soil that is not waterlogged, in sun or shade, and is tolerant of exposure and drought. Prune in spring ideally, although growth is so strong it can be cut back at virtually any time. Using pruners rather than shears avoids unsightly cut leaves.

Rhamnus alaternus 'Argenteovariegata'

3 × 1.8m (10 × 6 ft.)
UK H5 USDA 7–9

Variegated Italian buckthorn is a fast-growing evergreen shrub forming a bushy cone-shaped plant, becoming broader and more irregular as it matures. The stiff, ascending branches carry abundant, small, shiny, dark green and cream variegated leaves. The tiny inconspicuous flowers are followed by red berries which soon turn black; they are insignificant. It grows in sun or partial shade on any well-drained soil. It is best grown against the shelter of a wall or fence as it can be unstable in a more exposed situation and dislikes cold, wet growing conditions. Prune in early spring to control size and shape. Cut out any shoots that have reverted to plain green leaves; these are more vigorous and soon take over.

Taxus baccata

5 × 4m (16 × 13 ft.)
UK H7 USDA 5–8

English yew can be a substantial tree; however, it often serves as a screening shrub, hedge, or subject for topiary. Probably because of its historic use in gardens and its long life, it is seen as slow growing. Left to grow naturally, though, it grows quickly and soon makes a dense, sizable shrub with straight twigs and narrow, deep green leaves. The tiny flowers are insignificant, but they develop into attractive red fruits on mature female plants. It grows in sun or shade on any well-drained soil. Prune or trim at any time to control shape and size. For hedging or formal effect, clip with shears or a trimmer, usually in late summer. All parts of the plant are toxic, so avoid planting near livestock.

Thuja plicata 'Atrovirens'

10 × 5m (33 × 16 ft.)
UK H6 USDA 5–8

Left to grown naturally, western red cedar is ultimately a substantial, conical, coniferous tree that can reach even larger proportions than stated here. However, in gardens it is widely used as a tall, evergreen hedge and is by far the best conifer for this purpose. It responds far better to clipping than fast-growing, controversial ×*Cupressocyparis leylandii* and has denser, fragrant, emerald green foliage. It also thrives in sun or partial shade on a wide range of soil types including chalk and fairly heavy, wet conditions. It is best planted at least 90cm (3 ft.) apart as a hedge and clipped regularly when it reaches a height of 1.5m (5 ft.), even if a taller screen is ultimately required.

above At The Laskett, near Hereford, England, the garden created by Sir Roy Strong and his late wife, Julia Trevelyan Oman, hedges of *Taxus baccata* and *Buxus sempervirens* create a series of formal garden rooms and dramatic vistas.

left *Prunus spinosa*, blackthorn, has spiny stems, white blossoms in spring, and purple-black "sloes" in fall. The fruits can be used to flavour gin.

Copper and green beech, *Fagus sylvatica*, used to create stunning waved hedges in a large garden. Although height can be achieved quickly, this maturity takes several years and immaculate maintenance.

MORE SUGGESTIONS FOR HEDGING

A great many shrubs can be used to create a hedge, but the choice should always be based on the type and size of hedge required as well as on the growing conditions. If a tall, screening hedge is needed, then a large fast-growing subject such as *Thuja plicata* or *Taxus baccata* is ideal. For a shorter dividing hedge, a bushy evergreen such as common box, *Buxus sempervirens*, would be perfect, hence its wide use in gardens.

In rural or more naturalistic settings deciduous hedges, perhaps using native subjects, are more appropriate. Where climatic conditions allow, some evergreen elements such as holly, ivy, or even yew can be incorporated to increase variety. This type of hedge is also a valuable wildlife habitat and in time can host a variety of wild birds and insects.

Deciduous "country" hedges are normally planted using hedging whips. These are young plants sold bare root, lifted from the field in a dormant state. They can only be transplanted from late autumn through to early spring. Plant in two parallel rows that are 45cm (18 in.) apart, staggering the plants so that they are 45cm (18 in.) apart in a zigzag pattern. Suitable subjects include blackthorn, *Prunus spinosa*; hawthorn, *Crataegus monogyna*; and bloodtwig or common dogwood, *Cornus sanguinea*.

Some deciduous shrubs are also widely used for more formal hedges, particularly hornbeam, *Carpinus betulus*, and beech, *Fagus sylvatica*. These respond well to regular clipping and form dense, well-branched hedges up to 1.8m (6 ft.) in height. Unlike evergreens they present a changing picture with the seasons, from the fresh green of spring to the warm brown leaves that hang on the branches into winter.

Hornbeam and beech are similar in appearance. Hornbeam likes heavy soil and tolerates damp conditions, whereas beech likes dry, alkaline soil. In both cases they are best planted when no more than 1.2m (4 ft.) high and clipped from an early age. This can be done in late summer or spring.

OTHER GOOD FAST-MOVING SHRUBS

Cornus alba 'Sibirica'

Forsythia ×*intermedia*

Hippophae rhamnoides

Leycesteria formosa

Lonicera ×*purpusii* 'Winter Beauty'

Ribes sanguineum

Salix alba var. *vitellina* 'Britzensis'

Sambucus nigra f. *laciniata*

Spiraea ×*vanhouttei*

Viburnum opulus

PLANTING PARTNERS FOR FAST MOVERS, SCREENING, AND SHELTER

Shrubs are the obvious choice where big, bold permanent planting is required, whether more organized in the form of a hedge or as an informal backdrop to lower planting in the foreground. However, most big, fast-growing shrubs are broad as well as tall, so they take up more space in a garden. Where space is more limited, well-behaved bamboos may be an alternative option. These can provide dramatic height in narrow spaces, making effective screens while adding another dimension to the garden. Some bamboos are runners and spread rapidly—these are best avoided. Others, such as varieties of phyllostachys and fargesia, are clump forming and well behaved. To control spread, place root barriers into the ground at the time of planting. These are effective at confining the plants and restricting their spread.

Although they are deciduous, the clump-forming grasses such as miscanthus are also worth considering. The more vigorous varieties soon make a strong statement in a border with their upright stems and narrow leaves. Many also have the benefit of attractive flower plumes in late summer and autumn; these, and the leaves, look attractive right into winter. Rows of taller, stronger varieties can be used to make effective screens and cope with windy, open situations.

For a big, bold, dramatic impact few plants deliver more effectively and quickly than the larger-growing varieties of New Zealand flax. *Phormium tenax* quickly reaches massive proportions and the vigorous purple- and yellow-leaved cultivars reach a similar size in mild areas. Used as a contrast in form against large, fast-growing screening shrubs in a wide border, it creates an impressive effect. As the plants mature they also produce dramatic architectural inflorescences in summer.

Large, dark-leaved shrubs can present rather a gloomy background. Often subjects such as common laurel and yew, planted for screening, become rather overpowering in time. If variegated subjects such as *Pittosporum* 'Garnettii' or *Rhamnus alaternus* 'Argenteovariegata' are planted in front, or alongside, the effect is soon lifted. Planting a tall, airy perennial in front adds a stunning seasonal transformation. Providing the soil is not too dry, the shining white flowers of *Anemone* ×*hybrida* 'Honorine Jobert' are a delight in late summer and stand out beautifully against dark foliage.

Where large fast-growing shrubs can be left to grow naturally without pruning, it may be possible to introduce vigorous climbers to add another season of interest. There is always the danger that a strong-growing climber will be too vigorous and will eventually swamp the shrubs or trees that it grows through. *Vitis coignetiae* is a good example. This robust vine reaches 12m (40 ft.) or more and has strong tendrils that are difficult to untwine once it gets a hold. However, the large leaves are striking and the fall colour stunning in shades of scarlet, flame, and gold.

Miscanthus sinensis forms clumps of upright stems and slender green leaves. In late summer the stems are topped by attractive flower plumes that persist, along with the leaves, through winter.

above Phormiums, known as New Zealand flax, make a bold statement in a wide border, their sword-shaped leaves contrasting dramatically with large deciduous and evergreen shrubs.

left *Vitis coignetiae* is a strong-growing climber that can overpower trees and shrubs it uses for support; however, it creates a dramatic foliage effect.

The spring-flowering *Clematis montana* can also be overpowering in time, although less vigorous varieties will bring their garlands of open blooms to light up the foliage of plants that support them. *Clematis* 'Broughton Star' is among the finest, with dark leaves and glorious semi-double long-lasting blooms in late spring and early summer.

Climbers planted to grow through mature shrubs will require extra care and regular watering until they are fully established.

above The delightful *Clematis* 'Broughton Star' would be lovely growing over a plum-purple berberis or through a large purple hazel.

top Autumn anemone, *Anemone ×hybrida* 'Honorine Jobert', carries its cup-shaped blooms on tall stems, perfect against a backdrop of dark-leaved shrubs.

Cercis canadensis 'Forest Pansy' fulfils the role of a small tree on the edge of this informal bed. Its rich purple foliage and glorious autumn colour enhance the planting scheme, but it also provides height and shade.

SHRUBS GROWN AS TREES

It is really impossible to define the difference between a shrub and a tree. Both are perennial plants with woody stems that remain through winter, even if the leaves fall. Both shrubs and trees can have a single or multiple stems. There are large- and small-growing types of both, although large trees grow far bigger and live for much longer than the largest shrubs. Generally trees are perceived as larger plants that are often too big to be accommodated in smaller gardens. They can also have a profound effect on the growing environment in the garden, casting shade and robbing the soil of water and nutrients as their roots spread.

A tree in a garden adds a three-dimensional element to the landscape. Its height and presence give the garden maturity and add interest above eye level. Some shrubs also have the ability to do this, and these offer a less threatening alternative, especially where space is limited. They are often a good alternative as part of a planting scheme, rather than as a stand-alone specimen.

Some shrubs lend themselves to training into tree-like form. Bay, photinia, and holly are often grown as standards with a single stem and a manicured round crown. These are ideal for pots and containers, especially in town gardens and formal settings. Other evergreens including *Buxus sempervirens*, *Euonymus fortunei* and *Ligustrum delavayanum* are also used in this way, often as more compact subjects for small, sheltered gardens. Although they require more maintenance, rosemary and lavender have become standards as summer subjects for pots and in warmer regions. All of these offer a different plant form in a garden, but they do not really fulfil the role of a naturally growing tree, whereas some shrubs can, especially those that achieve height before their branches spread.

Even the smallest gardens have space for a tree of some sort. Consider the use of bonsai and *Acer palmatum* varieties in Japanese gardens. These can give a sense of scale and perspective just through their form and position in the garden. A similar effect can be achieved on terraces, in courtyards, and on balconies through the use of well-chosen shrubs in containers.

Size is particularly difficult to define with this selection; it depends greatly on timescale and growing conditions. Sizes shown are an estimate of size after ten years in reasonable growing conditions.

Acer palmatum 'Bloodgood'

3 × 2.4m (10 × 8 ft.)
UK H6 USDA 5–8

Probably the best red-leaved Japanese maple with dark ascending branches, becoming more spreading as the plant matures. The abundant deep, wine-red maple leaves remain clean and healthy throughout the season, turning rich flame-red before they fall. A hardy small tree, it is more wind resistant than more delicate varieties and is at its best in full sun for the richest foliage colour; red maples take on a muddy hue in shade. It grows on any reasonably moist fertile soil but struggles on shallow dry soils including chalk. It is an excellent choice for a large pot in a courtyard or on a terrace. Avoid waterlogged conditions as these can cause death of roots and disease. No pruning is required, although when in full leaf the plant can be pruned to control size; avoid winter pruning which risks disease entering the wounds.

Acer shirasawanum 'Jordan'

1.8 × 1.5m (6 × 5 ft.)
UK H6 USDA 5–9

A fine, recently introduced cultivar of the full moon maple, more vigorous than *Acer shirasawanum* 'Aureum', which can be painfully slow growing. The rounded, sharply lobed leaves unfold apricot-gold, becoming bright golden yellow, elegantly carried on straight, slender twigs. They remain healthy throughout the season, as long as the soil is moist, turning flame-orange before they fall. Reputedly it tolerates full sun, but it is at its best in semi-shade in a sheltered position. It prefers reasonably moist, neutral to acid soil; dry conditions result in browning of the leaf tips. It is ideal for a large pot with a loam-based growing medium. No pruning is necessary, although it can be pruned selectively to control shape when the plant is in leaf.

Aralia echinocaulis

3.7 × 1.2m (12 × 4 ft.)
UK H6 USDA 5–8

Similar in growth to the Japanese angelica tree, *Aralia elata*, this suckering shrub produces straight, upright spiny stems reaching considerable height in a season. These are topped by delicately branched compound leaves consisting of many leaflets and red leaf stalks. The leaves look like leaves and branches, the upright stems the tree trunks; the overall impression is exotic. It casts little shade and the foliage colours well in fall after finely branched sprays of small white flowers have appeared at the tips of the shoots. Originally raised from seed brought back from China by Jimi Blake of Huntingbrook Garden, Ireland, it grows on any reasonably moist soil and thrives in sheltered conditions. Prune in winter, if necessary, to reduce the height of the stems, or remove unwanted ones.

Cercis canadensis 'Forest Pansy'

4 × 4m (13 × 13 ft.)
UK H5 USDA 5–9

This variety of North American redbud is one of the finest purple-leaved woody plants, growing to form a broad, spreading shrub or small tree with slender dark twigs. In early spring tiny purple pea-like flowers appear in clusters on the branches before the foliage unfurls. The delicate heart-shaped leaves are soft and velvety, contrasting with the ruby red, shining young leaves at the tips of the shoots. The foliage colours beautifully in fall in shades of flame, pink, and gold, spreading a colourful carpet on the ground beneath. Usually grown as a grafted plant, it needs a reasonably sheltered site; the graft union can be weak and easily damaged. It grows best on any deep, fertile soil that is not too dry. Prune as necessary in winter to control shape and size.

Cercis chinensis 'Avondale'

3 × 1.8m (10 × 6 ft.)
UK H5 USDA 5–9

Stiffly ascending branches carry softly shining heart-shaped mid-green leaves that colour rich butter yellow in fall. In early spring before the leaves unfurl, deep purple buds are crowded all up the branches. These open to a magnificent display of bright purple-pink flowers; a plant in full bloom is an arresting sight. Raised in New Zealand, this variety seems hardier than the species but still prefers a sheltered position as the blossoms can be damaged by frost. It thrives on fertile, reasonably moist soil and dislikes drought. It can be grown as a bush with branches to the ground but is increasingly seen as a short standard tree. Prune after flowering if necessary, cutting out dead and damaged wood.

Cornus controversa 'Variegata'

3 × 2.4m (10 × 8 ft.)
UK H5 USDA 4–8

Often referred to as wedding cake tree because of its layered branches, this is an excellent foliage shrub with the additional benefit of late spring flowers. It grows awkwardly at first, eventually producing one or more upright stems with layers of horizontal or downward-sweeping branches. The leaves are soft green broadly edged and variegated with creamy white. Flattened heads of tiny white flowers are carried on the tops of the branches creating an even lighter and more frothy effect. Even in winter the silhouette of branches is attractive after the leaves have fallen. It likes a deep, fertile reasonably moist soil in sun or partial shade and it needs time to mature to be seen at its best. No pruning is necessary apart from the removal of dead branches.

Cornus 'Eddie's White Wonder'

3 × 1.5m (10 × 5 ft.)
UK H5 USDA 6–9

A stunning flowering dogwood raised by H. M. Eddie in Vancouver, Canada, it is among the earliest dogwoods to flower. This hybrid of *Cornus florida* and *Cornus nuttallii* produces large, rounded blooms, consisting of four pure white, waved bracts; they float on the horizontal branches like butterflies in late spring. Its habit is very upright and tree-like, usually with a single main stem and layers of short branches radiating from it. The soft green leaves colour brilliantly in fall on moist, neutral to acid soil, which it prefers. It will grow in sun or semi-shade and is very hardy. No pruning is required apart from the removal of any dead or damaged wood.

Cornus florida 'Cherokee Princess'

3 × 1.5m (10 × 5 ft.)
UK H5 USDA 5–9

A beautiful cultivar of the North American flowering dogwood with masses of large white bracts in late spring. It forms a large, loose shrub with stiff, but elegant greyish branches, eventually tree-like in habit. The flower buds appear as small knobs on the branches in winter, tightly enclosed within the folded bracts. As the bracts unfurl in spring they remain joined at the tips before they open fully. The floral display is long lasting and is followed by fabulous fall foliage colour. A hardy subject, it is at its best on moist, fertile, neutral to acid soil in a position sheltered from cold winds. No pruning is necessary and it is best avoided.

Cornus 'Porlock'

3 × 2.4m (10 × 8 ft.)
UK H5 USDA 5–9

Perhaps the most reliable flowering dogwood, 'Porlock' grows quickly and flowers from an early age. Upright at first, it soon becomes broad and spreading with arching branches and semi-evergreen leaves. The blooms are freely produced and stand on upright stalks all along the branches in early summer. The bracts are green at first, then cream, gradually turning white before blushing pink before they fall. These are followed by pendent strawberry-like fruits that hang all along the branches in autumn. Truly a plant for two seasons and better value than most trees planted for their blossoms, it grows on any reasonably fertile soil except for shallow chalk. No pruning is needed, but it can be pruned lightly after flowering to control size.

Cotoneaster 'Cornubia'

5 × 4m (16 × 13 ft.)
UK H6 USDA 6–9

A big, vigorous shrub with wide spreading flexible branches. The narrow, willow-like leaves are olive to dark green, leathery and veined. The foliage is semi-evergreen; the older leaves turning gold and falling when the shrub is in fruit. Loose clusters of small white flowers appear in spring, followed by large, shining scarlet berries that weigh down the branches in fall, probably the best fruit of any cotoneaster. An excellent shrub for wildlife, attracting bees in spring and birds in fall and early winter. It thrives on any reasonable soil and makes an excellent screening shrub where space allows. Prune if necessary after flowering to control shape and size; however, hard pruning results in even more vigorous growth.

Cryptomeria japonica 'Sekkan-sugi'

3 × 1.5m (10 × 5 ft.)
UK H6 USDA 6–9

An interesting conifer for colouring and texture, it mixes well with broad-leaved shrubs. The appealing feathery foliage is light peridot green, cream or primrose towards the tips of the shoots. It grows naturally to form an elegant flame-shaped shrub, but the habit is quite unlike that of any other conifer. It makes a fine specimen and is excellent as a focal point in a planting scheme. Growing on any well-drained soil, it seems to succeed on poor dry soils as well as in more fertile conditions in sun or partial shade. No pruning is necessary although it responds well to shaping and makes an interesting topiary subject, even trimmed as a large ball.

Eucryphia ×nymansensis 'Nymansay'

3 × 1.5m (10 × 5 ft.)
UK H4 USDA 8–10

For those gardening on acidic soil this evergreen shrub is a must. With upright branches, it grows to form a loose column of dark green, evergreen foliage. In summer the round buds develop, opening to exquisite cupped blooms with silky white petals and a mass of fine stamens. A shrub in full bloom is an arresting sight and all the more surprising as there are few other flowering shrubs performing at that time of the year. It grows in sun but is often at its best in semi-shade on moist, fertile soil; perfect for the woodland garden. No pruning is required, but dead, damaged, or stray shoots can be cut out in spring.

Ilex ×altaclerensis 'Golden King'

3 × 1.5m (10 × 5 ft.)
UK H6 USDA 6–8

Despite its name this is a female holly producing a heavy crop of showy scarlet berries in the presence of a male pollinator. Like most hollies it is rather a rangy shrub when young, becoming bushier and more conical in shape as it matures. The broad leaves are almost spineless, green with a clear gold margin. It is considered the best of the golden-variegated hollies and makes a bold, bright statement in a planting scheme in sun or semi-shade. Suitable for any reasonably fertile soil and drought resistant once established. Best pruned in early spring just before new growth commences to encourage branching and maintain shape. A good structure shrub to plant as a long-term subject in the garden.

Magnolia ×*loebneri* 'Leonard Messel'

3 × 1.5m (10 × 5 ft.)
UK H6 USDA 4–9

An elegant tall shrub with ascending branches and soft green leaves. The buff-grey, furry winter buds open in early spring into starry blooms with strap-like petals of soft mauve-pink before the leaves unfurl. Despite their delicacy the flowers are more weather resistant than many of the large-flowered magnolias. It flowers freely even on young plants and is easy to grow on any fertile soil including clay and chalk. It prefers a sheltered position in full-sun or semi-shade and sits well with other shrubs, especially dark evergreens. Prune to control shape and size if necessary, after flowering.

Prunus lusitanica 'Myrtifolia'

2.4 × 1.5m (8 × 5 ft.)
UK H5 USDA 7–10

A dense, bushy form of Portuguese laurel that is becoming increasingly popular as an evergreen tree. The leathery, dark green, shining leaves are smaller and narrower than those of the species. It grows naturally to form a dense cone. In late spring or early summer upright spikes of round buds open to small, white, lightly scented flowers on the branches. It grows on any well-drained soil in sun or shade and is very tolerant of chalk. A hardy plant, it is a better choice than *Laurus nobilis* for cold gardens. No pruning is necessary, but it responds well to trimming and shaping, best carried out before growth commences in early spring.

OTHER GOOD SHRUBS TO USE AS TREES

Cordyline australis	*Crinodendron hookerianum*	*Syringa vulgaris*
Cornus mas	*Mahonia ×media* 'Charity'	*Tamarix ramosissima*
Corylus avellana 'Purpurea'	*Photinia ×fraseri* 'Red Robin'	
Crataegus monogyna	*Pittosporum tenuifolium*	

PLANTING PARTNERS FOR SHRUBS GROWN AS TREES

As shrubs grown as trees are smaller and less demanding when it comes to root space and water consumption than mature trees, it is easier to associate other plants alongside them or under their branches. Many shade-loving shrubs such as sarcococca, skimmia, *Mahonia aquifolium*, and *Viburnum davidii* are ideal, as are hellebores, pulmonarias, vinca, and ground-covering ivies which appear in so many planting combinations.

Where there is a little headroom and space allows, *Kerria japonica* is an attractive choice for early spring flowers. With arching green stems and small green leaves, it is unobtrusive but comes into its own in spring when the stems are garlanded with soft orange buttercup-like blooms. The single-flowered species or the larger-flowered 'Golden Guinea' are more graceful and pleasing than the popular double-flowered cultivar. It is particularly useful in shade with evergreens and lovely underplanted with blue-flowered pulmonarias or brunnera.

Deadnettles grow well in dry shade and once established make excellent groundcover with the benefits of attractive foliage and spring flowers. There are several varieties of *Lamium maculatum* to choose from with variously marked foliage and purple or white blooms. Yellow archangel, *Lamium galeobdolon* 'Florentinum', has soft golden flowers and green leaves marked with silver. It is very shade tolerant and ideal under large shrubs such as *Cercis canadensis* 'Forest Pansy' or *Cotoneaster* 'Cornubia'.

Epimediums, commonly called barrenworts, are ideal in the dry soil under large shrubs and trees. *Epimedium* 'Amber Queen' is an evergreen variety, the new leaves flushed red in spring as they emerge. The finely branched stems of dancing winged flowers rise above the leaves over a long period from midspring. Another excellent groundcover is *Tellima grandiflora* or fringe-cups, a member of the saxifrage family. It forms clumps of rounded, soft green leaves, and in spring slender upright stems carry small, fringed greenish yellow flowers, often stained purple or red. A native of North American woodlands, it is well adapted to growing under trees and large shrubs. Perfect with foxgloves around flowering dogwoods.

Annual honesty, *Lunaria annua*, is in fact a biennial, flowering the spring after the plants have grown, then fading to leave its silvery seedheads to grace the winter garden. Perennial honesty, *Lunaria rediviva*, may be considered less showy, but it produces its delicate white spring flowers year after year. These are followed by flat, oval seed pods that hang green in summer before turning to parchment in fall. A good choice under shrubs grown as trees with a high enough canopy.

Those gardening on acid, woodland soil should not miss the opportunity to grow *Trillium grandiflorum*, wake-robin. It likes light shade and reasonably moist ground rich in leaf mould where it thrives with spring-flowering bulbs and ferns. Those elegant three-petalled blooms

The delicate single flowers of *Kerria japonica* are carried on graceful arching stems in spring. Best in shade, it makes an excellent planting partner for bold evergreen shrubs and thrives under the canopy of deciduous trees.

The attractively marked foliage of the deadnettle *Lamium maculatum* makes good groundcover in dry shade. It is ideal under large, deciduous shrubs.

set against collars of fresh green leaves are a delight under flowering dogwoods, magnolias, or the deep green leaves of eucryphia.

Many low-growing spring-flowering bulbs are ideal to grow under large shrubs. They add early spring colour and interest while deciduous shrubs are still sleeping and enjoy the shade of the foliage later in the season. Of course cultivation should be avoided where they grow. Small bulbs, corms, and tubers grow near the surface and most spread by seeding; careless weeding may limit their success. *Anemone blanda* is particularly successful on a variety of soil types, including chalk. If planted in autumn, dry tubers should be soaked for a few hours prior to planting.

top Many varieties of epimedium make excellent groundcover under shrubs and trees. *Epimedium* 'Amber Queen' has striking spring flowers, similar to erythronium blooms in shape and character. It is particularly attractive under Japanese maples.

above left Among the most desirable of spring-flowering perennials, *Trillium grandiflorum* opens its striking blooms in midseason.

left The starry blooms of *Anemone blanda* appear in greater numbers every year once established under deciduous shrubs, a spring delight before the foliage unfurls overhead.

Skimmias put on an attractive display for several months, first their buds, then fragrant flowers. Female and hermaphrodite varieties also produce colourful berries.

LONG-BLOOMING SHRUBS

Most flowering shrubs bloom for three to four weeks once a year, often a disappointment to gardeners who expect more from their plants. In large gardens the length of flowering of individual subjects is less of an issue; for much of the year another plant will take over. But in smaller gardens and key positions, a longer season of interest is desirable. Of course shrubs that are grown for their foliage have the edge, especially evergreens, but most of us have a weakness for flowers.

Interestingly some of our most familiar flowering shrubs such as philadelphus, weigela, deutzia, and lilac have a single, short flowering period. Rhododendrons, perhaps the most colourful and exotic, bloom just once, then revert to plain evergreens for the rest of the year. Magnolias too have a single spectacular but fragile display that is easily cut shorter by frost.

Today most roses grown in gardens repeat flower, even if they have one main flowering season in summer and then another later flush. Originally nearly all roses were what we now call summer flowering; in other words they bloom only once in midsummer. The repeat flowering of modern roses made them the most popular flowering shrubs, especially in the heyday of hybrid tea and floribunda roses in the 1960s and '70s.

Sometimes spring-flowering shrubs surprise with a few late blooms depending on the weather conditions and rarely affecting the ability to flower the following season. *Viburnum plicatum* f. *tomentosum* 'Mariesii', various magnolias, and some rhododendrons seem prone to this unscheduled flower production.

However, for a more reliable, longer flowering period or repeat blooming it is worth being selective; some shrubs will consistently produce an exceptionally long display of flowers. With a few exceptions these mostly start to bloom in midsummer and will continue right into fall. All varieties of *Potentilla fruticosa* fall into this category and can be relied upon for several months of flowers when grown in sunny situations. Hydrangeas too are exceptional in the length of their flowering periods; in many cases the faded blooms continue to be attractive throughout the winter months.

Several winter-flowering shrubs are also in bud or bloom for many weeks. Winter-flowering heathers remain attractive for three months or more. *Viburnum* ×*bodnantense* blooms intermittently from late autumn until midspring, only really affected by severe weather. *Viburnum tinus* and *Skimmia* are perhaps the most enduring, putting on a display of buds and flowers for months.

Calycanthus ×*raulstonii* 'Hartlage Wine'

1.8 × 1.5m (6 × 5 ft.)
UK H5 USDA 5–8

A hardy deciduous sweetshrub with upright, then spreading branches and broad, mid-green leaves that colour golden yellow in fall. The large lotus-like flowers are delicately fragrant, wine red, with small creamy petals in the centres. Elegantly poised on the branches, they open in succession from fat, red-brown buds from late spring through to midsummer, sometimes later. It grows in sun or partial shade and is best on moist, fertile soil with plenty of organic matter. A hybrid between *Calycanthus chinensis* and *C. floridus* raised by Richard Hartlage at North Carolina State University, it was introduced into cultivation by the J. C. Raulston Arboretum in North Carolina. Prune after flowering to control size and shape if necessary. Light pruning from an early age encourages branching and promotes flower production.

Ceanothus ×*delileanus* 'Gloire de Versailles'

1.8 × 1.2m (6 × 4 ft.)
UK H4 USDA 7–10

Many gardeners overlook the deciduous California lilacs in favour of evergreen varieties. However, when it comes to length of flowering period, deciduous varieties excel. 'Gloire de Versailles' has an exceptionally long flowering period in summer and again in fall. The large, cloud-like clusters of powder blue flowers are carried loosely on the arching branches. Somewhat lax and open in habit, the stems are upright, then spreading, and may need some support. It needs a sunny situation and well-drained soil and is perfect for a mixed border or alongside a wall or fence. It should be pruned lightly in early spring or after flowering to encourage branching and bushy growth.

Choisya ×*dewitteana* 'Aztec Pearl'

1.8 × 1.5m (6 × 5 ft.)
UK H4 USDA 8–9

An elegant hybrid Mexican orange with deep green, evergreen leaves, each composed of three to five finger-like leaflets. The foliage is strongly aromatic when crushed. A rounded and bushy shrub, it retains a light airy habit and fulfils the role of both a structure subject and an excellent flowering shrub. Pink flower buds open to fragrant white single blooms in large, loose clusters in both spring and autumn. Exceptionally free flowering, 'Aztec Pearl' is smothered with blooms right down to ground level when grown in full sun. It thrives in sun or semi-shade on any well-drained soil. It resents waterlogged ground. Prune if necessary to control size and shape.

Cistus ×*obtusifolius* 'Thrive'

60 × 60cm (2 × 2 ft.)
UK H4 USDA 7–10

One of the hardier sun roses with dense, bushy growth and small, deep green, evergreen leaves. It forms a rounded mound, studded with pale green flower buds from late spring. The cupped, pure white flowers with tissue-paper petals and golden stamens open in profusion from early summer. Unlike many other cistus, 'Thrive' continues to bloom right through summer. The falling petals cover the ground around the plant in white confetti. It needs full sun and well-drained, preferably alkaline soil to thrive. Drought tolerant, it is perfect for dry, gravel gardens. Although not a long-lived shrub, it is very rewarding and reliable. Unlike other cistus, 'Thrive' can be clipped lightly in early spring to keep the plant in shape and promote bushy growth.

Cornus kousa 'Miss Satomi'

1.5 × 1.5m (5 × 5 ft.)
UK H6 USDA 5-8

A beautiful flowering dogwood with broadly spreading branches and soft green leaves that turn rich red before they fall. The showy bracts appear in early summer, green, tinged with pink at first, becoming deep salmon-pink as they mature. The display is long lasting, for eight weeks or more, if the soil is moist and the weather not too hot. The flower colour is paler in shade. Smaller in stature than most flowering dogwoods, this lovely shrub fits well into most gardens and mixes well with other shrubs and perennials. It grows in sun or shade and is best on reasonably moist, neutral to acid soils. It dislikes shallow chalk. Pruning is unnecessary and should be avoided. Dead and damaged wood can be removed in spring when plants are in leaf.

Erica ×darleyensis 'Darley Dale'

30 × 45cm (12 × 18 in.)
UK H6 USDA 6-8

The winter-flowering heathers bloom over a long period from early winter through to mid- or late spring. They are attractive in bud and colourful in flower, their early blooms particularly appreciated by bees. 'Darley Dale' is an enduringly popular variety with mid-green bristling foliage with cream and pink tips to the shoots in spring. Abundant pale pink flowers smother the shoots over a long period from early winter to midspring, the colour darkening as the flowers age. Selected in Derbyshire, UK, it has been in cultivation since 1900. It thrives in sun or semi-shade on well-drained soil and is lime tolerant although at its best on neutral to acid soil. Trim lightly after flowering to remove faded flowers. Left to grow, it produces longer stems that make excellent cut flowers.

Grevillea 'Canberra Gem'

1.8 × 1.8m (6 × 6 ft.)
UK H4 USDA 8–11

This hybrid grevillea is surprisingly hardy for a shrub of Australian origin. With spreading branches it forms a loose shrub with narrow, soft, needle-like leaves that resemble those of a conifer. The foliage is bright green and aromatic. It grows quickly in the right conditions and is an ornamental evergreen from an early age. The curious, crimson waxy flowers appear between the slender leaves anytime from winter through to late summer, their intriguing form earning the plant its common name, spider flower. It needs a position in full sun on well-drained neutral to acid soil. No pruning is necessary; any light pruning to control shape or size is best done in spring at the expense of flowers.

Hydrangea 'Blue Deckle'

90 × 90cm (3 × 3 ft.)
UK H5 USDA 5–8

A light and pretty lacecap hydrangea with upright tan-coloured stems and mid-green leaves, sometimes flushed with purple-red in sun. In mid-summer the refined lacecap flower heads appear, lilac-pink on alkaline soils, sky blue on acid soils. Each flower head consists of a flattened cluster of tiny fertile florets surrounded by larger, showier, ray florets. As the season progresses the flower colour changes to lilac-green. A shrub for sun or light shade, it grows on any moist, fertile soil. Remove faded flower heads in early spring if possible. Cut out some of the older stems each year to encourage new growth from ground level. These older stems are easily identified by their more branching habit and dull brown colouring.

Hydrangea paniculata 'Phantom'

1.5 × 1.8m (5 × 6 ft.)
UK H5 USDA 4–8

A magnificent variety of paniculate hydrangea, upright and spreading in habit with strong, stiff stems and soft green leaves. The massive flower heads appear in late summer, broadly conical with abundant florets. They are white at first, becoming coral pink as they age, eventually green flushed with dark pink, turning to parchment in winter and remaining attractive if the weather is not too damp. Perfect for the back of a border or under the light shade of deciduous trees, it grows in sun or semi-shade on any fertile soil that is not too dry. Prune in late winter, cutting back to around 60cm (2 ft.) each year; this promotes strong, upright stems.

Hypericum ×*hidcoteense* 'Hidcote'

1.2 × 1.2m (4 × 4 ft.)
UK H5 USDA 5–9

A tough, semi-evergreen shrub with tan-coloured stems and oval dark green leaves forming a rounded bush. The golden yellow saucer-shaped blooms reliably smother the plant from midsummer to late fall. Their shining petals, golden stamens, and nectar are attractive to bees and pollinators. It grows easily in sun or semi-shade on any soil, thrives on clay and chalk, and is more disease resistant than most hypericums. It will tolerate heavier shade but does not flower as well. Once a popular shrub, it is often disregarded probably because of its unfashionable bright yellow flowers and the fact that other hypericums have had disease problems. Prune in late winter, cutting back by one third to encourage branching and vigorous growth.

LONG-BLOOMING SHRUBS

Potentilla fruticosa 'Abbotswood'

60 × 60cm (2 × 2 ft.)
UK H7 USDA 3–7

Among the most useful flowering shrubs. A small, very hardy, bushy shrub with fine branches and small, dark green divided leaves. The buttercup-like blooms are freely produced from early summer through to late fall. The petals are pure white surrounding centres with golden stamens. It is at its best in full sun but tolerates some shade on any well-drained soil, especially chalk. It combines well with other shrubs and perennials. Potentillas are little more than a tangle of dark twigs in winter, but their performance through the summer months more than compensates. Prune in late winter, clipping over with shears to remove spindly growth and faded flowers.

Rosa Bonica

90 × 90cm (3 × 3 ft.)
UK H6 USDA 4–9

Many hybrid roses repeat bloom, but few perform as reliably as Bonica. It forms a tidy shrub with green stems and few thorns. The emerald green, shining foliage is plentiful and remarkably disease free. The rose-pink blooms are double, carried in loose clusters; the petals are perfect, clean, and weather resistant. Sadly it has only a very light fragrance. The first flowers appear in early summer and continue right through to late fall, even winter in milder districts. Growing well in sun or semi-shade on any fertile soil, like other roses it is at its best on clay. Feed generously with rose fertilizer in early spring and again in midsummer. Prune lightly in winter to encourage branching and more flowers.

Rosa ×*odorata* 'Mutabilis'

1.5m × 90cm (5 × 3 ft.)
UK H5 USDA 5–10

Sometime known as butterfly rose because of the delicate beauty of its flowers, this is a slender, open branched shrub, quite different from any other rose. With new red shoots and red-flushed leaves composed of narrow leaflets on thornless stems, it produces large, branched flower clusters at the tops of the shoots. The single flowers open from elegant orange buds, soft apricot gold, blushing pink, becoming crimson as they age. All colours appear in a flower cluster at any one time, the blooms reminiscent of butterflies or sweet peas. It likes a sheltered position in full sun on rich fertile soil and can be grown as a wall shrub. Prune lightly in late winter to remove any old flower stems and weak growth.

Viburnum plicatum f. *tomentosum* 'Nanum Semperflorens'

1.5 × 1.2m (5 × 4 ft.)
UK H5 USDA 5–9

Narrower in habit than the wide-spreading 'Marie-sii', this variety grows slowly to form a conical shrub with layered branches and bright green, pleated leaves that colour purple-red and bronze before they fall. The more compact habit makes it ideal for smaller gardens and mixed borders. The small lace-cap flower heads are green-cream at first, maturing to pure white, appearing along the tops of branches from early summer until fall. Also offered as 'Wata-nabe' and as the very similar 'Summer Snowflake', it grows on any reasonably fertile soil in sun or partial shade and is particularly effective alongside white and green variegated evergreens. No pruning is necessary.

Viburnum tinus Spirit

1.8 × 1.5m (6 × 5 ft.)
UK H4 USDA 7–11

A superb variety of laurustinus forming a compact, bushy, evergreen shrub with dark green foliage. The pink flower buds on dark red-brown stems appear in flattened clusters anytime from late fall onwards. These open into lacy heads of white flowers with dark stamens, giving a pink glow to the long-lasting blooms which can still be present on the shrub in late spring. Its smaller habit, tolerance of a wide variety of growing conditions, and attractive flowers make it ideal for smaller gardens and use as a low, informal hedge. It grows in sun or shade on any well-drained soil. No pruning is necessary, but it can be pruned to shape after flowering or trimmed for a more formal effect.

OTHER GOOD LONG-BLOOMING SHRUBS

Abelia ×*grandiflora*

Calluna vulgaris

Choisya ternata

Daphne bholua 'Jacqueline Postill'

Daphne ×*transatlantica* Eternal Fragrance

Erica carnea

Erysimum 'Bowles's Mauve'

Fuchsia 'Riccartonii'

Rosa rugosa

Salvia 'Hot Lips'

PLANTING PARTNERS FOR LONG-BLOOMING SHRUBS

For those who want to achieve a long-lasting floral effect, there are plenty of planting partners that also have a long flowering season. For shrubs that bloom in summer, perennials and annuals are the obvious choices. For the winter-flowering heathers and others that bloom in the colder months, evergreen planting partners are the obvious choice.

Salvias are a vast plant group, including small shrubs, annuals, and herbaceous perennials. Many are blessed with long flowering periods, especially later in the season. Some are not reliably hardy and may need winter protection in a frame or cold greenhouse before being planted out in the border after frost has passed. However, the display of flowers is rewarding enough to justify the effort.

Salvia guaranitica 'Blue Enigma' is a good example, Tall, slender stems carry intense lapis-blue flowers from midsummer through to late fall, stunning as the season progresses against hot autumn tints. In a sunny border it is ideal between cistus, potentilla, silver foliage shrubs, and other sun lovers.

Another salvia, *Salvia horminum* or clary, is a favourite of the cottage garden and cutting garden. An annual, it is easily raised from seed, either sown directly or started indoors and planted out. Plants have either inky blue, white, or pink bracts arranged on upright spikes. The mixture is perfect for the summer garden with a rose like Bonica or at the base of the soft blue *Ceanothus* ×*delileanus* 'Gloire de Versailles'. Drift plants between lavenders and low hebes to add light height.

We tend to think of diascias as dwarf spreading plants suitable for hanging baskets and patio containers. *Diascia personata* is an altogether taller plant for the border, with upright stems reaching 75cm (30 in.), topped with clouds of dainty salmon-pink flowers. The variety 'Hopleys' is excellent and particularly floriferous. This lovely perennial is perfect with *Rosa* ×*odorata* 'Mutabilis' which has a similar character.

Blue-flowered hardy geraniums are deservedly popular and perfect for the front of a border. Blue flowers mix so readily with other colours and

there are simply never enough in any garden. The problem with many of our favourite geraniums such as *Geranium* ×*johnsonii* 'Johnson's Blue' is that their flowering season is just a few weeks. There may be one or two flowers later in the season, but they are few and far between. *Geranium* Rozanne is often slightly later to get going, starting to bloom in midsummer, but once it starts it keeps going through autumn. It spreads and billows; one plant is sufficient in any single planting position.

Although recommended for any well-drained soil, achilleas only really grow well on alkaline soils and thrive on chalk. They hate waterlogged sites and sulk on acid soils. However, on ground they like, in full sun they are wonderful plants with upright stems, finely cut leaves, and flattened flower heads loved by bees and butterflies. They come in a wide range of colours to suit just about any planting scheme, and they flower for many weeks. They also make good cut flowers.

Catmints are perhaps the longest blooming perennials of all and perfect mixers. Great with roses, shrubs,

Hardy annual clary, *Salvia horminum*, is a delightful subject to
grow between shrubs and roses.

above Soft salmon-pink fading to cream, the long-lasting flowers of yarrow *Achillea* 'Lachsschönheit' (Galaxy Series) mix well with many shrubs..

top Few other perennials bloom for as long as *Diascia personata*. The flowers keep coming from early summer until well into autumn.

above Annual cosmos, *Cosmos bipinnatus*, is easy to grow from seed, flowers for weeks, and is excellent for cutting.

and perennials, they thrive on most soils as long as they have enough sun. *Nepeta* 'Six Hills Giant' is among the best to grow with shrubs. Forming vigorous clumps of strong stems with small, aromatic leaves, it produces clouds of soft blue flowers throughout the season.

Of all the annuals suitable for the mixed border, cosmos seem to keep blooming for longest, flowering late into the season. The plants are easily raised from seed, best started indoors and planted out after danger of frost has passed. Their feathery foliage and open blooms add bold flower form to the planting; the taller varieties are ideal to extend the season alongside early-flowering shrubs.

Of course the most effective and lasting planting combinations are created with the right foliage. For example, *Calycanthus* ×*raulstonii* 'Hartlage Wine' would be perfect with the coppery leaves of *Physocarpus opulifolius* 'Diable D'Or'. *Hydrangea paniculata* always works well with the soft green and white variegations of *Cornus alba* 'Elegantissima'. Shrubs with purple foliage, such as cotinus and the red-leaved berberis cultivars, add depth to the planting and bring out the best in any coloured flowers.

A cloud of blue in the border, *Nepeta* 'Six Hills Giant' keeps producing its bee-attracting flowers through summer and autumn.

The flowers of sweet box, *Sarcococca confusa*, may look insignificant but their fragrance is powerful, filling the whole garden early in the new year.

SHRUBS WITH FRAGRANT FLOWERS

Fragrant flowers and aromatic foliage are magical ingredients in any planting scheme. Plants with scented blooms are among our favourites: lily of the valley, sweet peas, and lilies all have distinctive perfumes to stir the emotions. They are fragrances we look forward to in our gardens, ones we recognize instantly when we encounter them by chance.

Flowering shrubs offer so many possibilities of scent in the garden through all the seasons. What is more, they offer the promise of that fragrance at the same time year after year. Take the humble sweet box, sarcococca, for example. Sometime just after midwinter, every year, it will fill the garden with its sweet perfume, far more powerful and with greater impact than the appearance of the modest flowers. Some regard winter as the most important season for scent. Proportionately there are more shrubs with fragrant flowers in winter than there are in other seasons. This highlights the reason: plants blooming in the coldest months have to work hard to attract the few insects that are out and about. Perfume on cold winter air does the trick.

The fabulous orange-blossom fragrance of philadelphus, however, is a scent of the summer garden. Somewhat reminiscent of sweet honeysuckle, it seems to be made for the warm air of a summer evening.

Some shrubs, notably roses and lavender, possess our favourite fragrances. Since ancient times man has extracted the essential oils from their flowers to use in perfumes. The fragrance is such an important characteristic that varieties lacking in this quality are often regarded as inferior and undesirable while varieties that excel in the perfume department become enduring favourites.

Fragrances vary greatly. They can be sweet, spicy, fresh, fruity, to name just a few different characteristics. Personal preferences also vary. Some like light, delicate scents; others prefer powerful and strong. A scent in the open air can be quite different to how it smells in the confines of the house.

Chimonanthus praecox

1.8 × 1.5m (6 × 5 ft.)
UK H5 USDA 7–9

Commonly known as wintersweet, this rather plain deciduous shrub redeems itself with the powerful fragrance of its winter flowers. Forming a medium-sized bushy plant with narrow, pointed, plain green leaves, it is not a subject for a prominent position but ideal for the back of a border. In winter rounded buds open to translucent, stemless, waxy flowers of creamy yellow, sometimes almost beige, stained purple towards the centres. The scent is strong, sweet, and spicy and hangs on the cool winter air. Wintersweet grows on most well-drained soils but prefers alkaline conditions or chalk. Plant in a sunny position where the sun can ripen the shoots for flowering; in shade it rarely blooms. It is ideal as a wall shrub and was traditionally grown in walled gardens where shoots could be cut for the house. Prune after flowering to control shape and size.

Clerodendrum trichotomum var. *fargesii*

3 × 3m (10 × 10 ft.)
UK H5 USDA 6–9

A large, spreading shrub, often of tree-like habit, with broad, dark green, deciduous leaves. In late summer clusters of buds appear at the tips of the shoots, hidden in capsule-like pink calyces. These open to white, jasmine-like blooms, wonderfully fragrant and beautifully displayed against the dark green foliage. The nectar-rich flowers earn the plant the common names: peanut butter bush and Farges harlequin glorybower. As the blooms fade the calyces split, becoming dark pink, surrounding the bead-like fruits in spiky collars as they turn from green, through red, to iridescent dark blue. It grows on any well-drained but reasonably moist soil in sun or semi-shade. Prune in early spring to control size and shape.

Daphne bholua 'Jacqueline Postill'

1.8m × 90cm (6 × 3 ft.)
UK H4 USDA 6-8

If you only grow one shrub for fragrance, this is the one to choose. Commonly known as Nepalese paper plant, it is an open and upright shrub with tan-coloured, flexible stems and narrow semi-evergreen leaves. Clusters of purple-pink flower buds develop at the tips of the shoots in winter, opening to clusters of starry, lilac-white flowers, purple on the reverse of the petals. The perfume is sweet, strong, and delicious, and a plant in flower will fill the whole garden with its fragrance. Best planted as a young specimen on well-drained soil in a sheltered position where it will retain its foliage through winter. Growing in sun or semi-shade, it is a good choice close to a wall or fence. Prune after flowering if necessary to control size and shape. Old plants are subject to virus and produce little or no foliage; when this happens they are best replaced.

Edgeworthia chrysantha

1.2 × 1.2m (4 × 4 ft.)
UK H4 USDA 7-9

Paperbush is so called because the bark is used to make high-quality paper for bank notes. It forms a rounded shrub with straight, flexible stems topped with clusters of grey, furry buds in winter. These open to small creamy white, tubular flowers, yolk-yellow within; they are highly fragrant and a delight in the winter garden. After flowering the small, oval, green leaves unfurl on the branches and the plant becomes quite ordinary for the rest of the year. It needs a sheltered position in sun or semi-shade, ideally close to the house where the fragrance can be enjoyed. Plant on moist but well-drained soil. No pruning is necessary, but damaged or stray shoots can be removed straight after flowering.

Hamamelis ×intermedia 'Vesna'

1.5 × 1.8m (5 × 6 ft.)
UK H5 USDA 5–8

A vigorous, vase-shaped shrub with ascending branches and leaves that resemble those of common hazel. The ribbon-petalled flowers open on the bare branches in mid- to late winter, rich orange-yellow, paler towards the tips of the petals. The blooms are remarkably weather resistant, defying frost and snow. The fragrance is strong, sweet, and spicy, bewitching on cold winter air. The leaves colour brilliantly in shades of orange and red before they fall, giving the plant another main season of interest. Thriving in sun or semi-shade on moist, fertile, neutral or acid soil, it struggles and often fails on chalk. No pruning is necessary and if possible should be avoided, apart from the removal of suckers from the rootstock.

Mahonia ×media 'Winter Sun'

1.8 × 1.5m (6 × 5 ft.)
UK H5 USDA 7–9

An excellent cultivar of Oregon grape forming a large but compact evergreen shrub with upright stems and abundant architectural foliage. The holly-like leaflets are shining and deep green, arranged on stiff, horizontal leaf stalks. Clusters of spikes of small yellow flowers appear at the tips of the shoots in fall and last for several weeks, attracting attention from late bees and butterflies. The blooms are sweetly fragrant, more so than many other early-flowering mahonias. Attractive blue-black berries often follow. Growing on any well-drained soil, it is ideal for a shady corner, although it will tolerate sun. Prune in spring if necessary, cutting back hard to rejuvenate a leggy plant.

Myrtus communis

1.5 × 1.2m (5 × 4 ft.)
UK H4 USDA 8–11

Common myrtle is a delightful evergreen shrub with fine tan-coloured stems and bright green, shining, pointed leaves that are wonderfully aromatic when crushed. In late summer the fragrant pure white flowers appear in the leaf axils. Opening from pin-like buds, they are filled with delicate white stamens, giving a dainty pincushion effect. Not the hardiest of shrubs, it loves a warm, sheltered wall where it will attain greater height and spread. It grows on any well-drained soil and is particularly happy in coastal gardens. Long regarded as a symbol of long life, health, and fertility, it is used in bridal bouquets and for decoration. Prune in early spring to control size and shape.

Osmanthus delavayi

1.5 × 1.8m (5 × 6 ft.)
UK H5 USDA 7–10

With arching, light brown stems and small, leathery, very dark, evergreen leaves, this is a broad spreading shrub of grace, despite its rather stiff growth habit. The flower buds appear in the leaf axils in early spring, soon opening to small white tubular flowers with a sweet and powerful fragrance. Although the floral display only lasts for a couple of weeks the enduring foliage makes this a useful structure shrub for sun or partial shade. It grows on any well-drained soil and is particularly effective when planted with green and white variegated shrubs. No pruning is required, but selective pruning to control height and spread can be carried out straight after flowering.

Philadelphus maculatus 'Sweet Clare'

1.5 × 1.5m (5 × 5 ft.)
UK H6 USDA 5–9

Of all the varieties of mock orange this one has the sweetest and most powerful fragrance. Unlike many others it forms a bushy shrub with finely branched twiggy growth that appears lifeless in winter. In spring the tiny new leaves appear, grey-green at first becoming green as they mature. The growth is quite arching in habit, becoming more so as the round grey buds appear along the branches from late spring. The single blooms open on the underside of the branches in early summer, pure white, four-petalled, and stained with purple towards the centres. A shrub for full sun on well-drained soil, it thrives on chalk. Pruning is less important than it is with other philadelphus. It should be carried out immediately after flowering, but on older plants some of the oldest stems can be cut out in winter.

Pittosporum tobira

1.8 × 1.5m (6 × 5 ft.)
UK H3 USDA 8–11

A fairly slow-growing evergreen shrub with flexible branches and whorls of mid-green leaves unusually rounded at the tips. It is upright in habit when young, becoming more spreading as it matures. Clusters of creamy white flowers appear at the tips of the shoots in early summer, the blooms becoming darker and more yellow as they age. They are strongly fragrant, reminiscent of orange blossom. It thrives in sun or partial shade and is often hardier than expected. It grows on any well-drained soil and is drought tolerant and ideal for coastal gardens. It can be grown as a hedge in warmer regions and is excellent for pots. Prune after flowering to promote new growth and a bushier habit.

Rhododendron 'Irene Koster'

1.2 × 1.2m (4 × 4 ft.)
UK H5 USDA 5–7

Among the best deciduous azaleas with an elegantly branched habit and soft green leaves towards the tips of the shoots. The delicate salmon-pink flowers are carried in large heads, opening in late spring from deeper salmon buds. Each bloom has a golden orange flare in the throat and on the upper petal. The fragrance is strong and sweet. The foliage develops warm orange and red tints in fall. At its best in semi-shade, like other rhododendrons it needs a reasonably moist neutral to acid soil. In a pot, use a lime-free growing medium and water regularly with rainwater if possible. No pruning is necessary, but older plants may be pruned after flowering to stimulate new growth.

Rhododendron luteum

1.5 × 1.5m (5 × 5 ft.)
UK H6 USDA 5–8

The powerful fragrance of this deciduous azalea is a real delight of the late spring garden. It can eventually form a large shrub of open habit with sticky young shoots and soft green leaves. The creamy yellow flower buds burst in late spring into heads of slender, trumpet-shaped blooms of rich golden yellow, reminiscent of large heads of honeysuckle in both appearance and fragrance. In fall the leaves colour richly in shades of crimson, orange, and sometimes purple: this shrub excels in autumn colour as well as scent. It grows in sun or semi-shade and requires a neutral to acid, reasonably moist soil. Prune after flowering if necessary to control shape and size and to rejuvenate older plants.

Rosa Gertrude Jekyll

1.2m × 90cm (4 × 3 ft.)
UK H6 USDA 5–10

Considered the most fragrant of the English roses, this is a vigorous shrub with thorny stems and healthy foliage. The blooms are sumptuous flattened rosettes of deep rose-pink with a powerful old-rose fragrance, so strong that this variety has been grown for the production of essential oil used for perfume. Flowering starts in early summer and continues into fall, the blooms making excellent cut flowers. Best in full sun, although it will tolerate shade for some of the day. As with most other roses it likes a fertile, reasonably moist soil and thrives on clay. Summer prune as the blooms fade to encourage further flowers. Prune again in late winter, shortening the stems by about a third to encourage branching. Feed with slow-release fertilizer after summer and winter pruning. *Rosa* Gertrude Jekyll can be grown as a short climber.

Sarcococca hookeriana var. *hookeriana* 'Ghorepani'

60 × 60cm (2 × 2 ft.)
UK H5 USDA 6–9

A recently introduced variety of sweet box with upright stems and narrow, dark, evergreen, shining leaves, forming dense, spreading clumps. The flowers appear later than on other varieties, usually opening in early spring; white and tuft-like in the leaf axils, they are profuse and conspicuous against the dark leaves. The flowers have a strong, sweet fragrance that will fill any garden. At its best in shade but more tolerant of sun than other sarcococcas, it grows on any reasonable soil that is not too dry. Tolerant of chalk, it thrives on clay and is a good choice under deciduous trees. No pruning is required, but the foliage is good for cutting for floral decoration.

Viburnum carlesii 'Diana'

1.2 × 1.2m (4 × 4 ft.)
UK H6 USDA 4–8

Commonly known as arrowwood or Korean spice, this is a rounded shrub of open habit, with straight twigs and soft, slightly downy, grey-green leaves sometimes tinged with purple when young. In leaf it is unremarkable; its moment of glory is in late spring when clusters of red-pink buds open to pure white flowers, salmon-pink on the outside of the petals and tube. The scent is strong, sweet, and powerful. Plant in full sun or partial shade on any well-drained fertile soil. It can be pruned lightly immediately after flowering to control shape and spread, but this is rarely necessary. It is usually grown as a grafted plant, so it is important to look out for suckers arising from the rootstock. Left to develop, these will quickly take over and weaken the shrub.

┌───┐

OTHER GOOD SHRUBS
WITH FRAGRANT FLOWERS

Daphne odora
  'Aureomarginata'

Elaeagnus 'Quicksilver'

Elaeagnus ×*submacrophylla*

Magnolia grandiflora

Mahonia japonica

Osmanthus ×*burkwoodii*

Philadelphus 'Belle Étoile'

Rosa gallica var. *officinalis*

Sarcococca confusa

Skimmia ×*confusa* 'Kew Green'

PLANTING PARTNERS
FOR FRAGRANT SHRUBS

The majority of flowers have some sort of fragrance, but it may be light and easily missed by all but those with a keen sense of smell and the curiosity to seek it out. Some flowers only smell when the reproductive parts of the flower are ripe for pollination; the perfume attracts pollinating insects to work their magic. These are not the ones to choose if you want fragrance to be a feature. Instead go for planting partners with powerful perfume and ideally ones with a different flowering season from that of the fragrant shrubs in your garden.

Flower bulbs are easy planting partners to add, and these offer a number of fragrant possibilities. Narcissi are particularly useful because they are deer resistant, reasonably hardy, and tolerant of some shade. Many also thrive on moister soil than other varieties. The sweetly scented paperwhite narcissus, *Narcissus papyraceus*, frequently grown for indoor decoration, is not hardy, so is only suitable for warmer areas. True pheasant's eye

or poet's narcissus, *Narcissus poeticus* var. *recurvus*, flowers in late spring. Its pure white rounded flowers with deep red and gold eyes have a wonderful fragrance. It is ideal for warmer borders near sunny walls and fences with shrubs like myrtle and daphne.

The double blooms of *Narcissus* 'Sir Winston Churchill' are carried in twos and threes on stout stems. Clotted cream in colour with hints of yolky yellow, they are particularly effective with cream and green variegations and useful under deciduous shrubs before they are in full leaf. Because the foliage takes time to die down, a position further back in the border where shrubs and perennials will hide the fading leaves is perfect.

Hyacinths are often used in pots and containers. However, they also offer early colour around shrubs, a good home for them after their first year in the house or on the patio. The flower spikes become lighter and sparser in subsequent years which makes their

appearance more suited to garden beds and borders, especially around philadelphus and other shrubs that are later in leaf.

Few flowers have such an iconic perfume as *Convallaria majalis*, lily of the valley. Its sweet scent is so well known it is often used to describe the fragrance of other flowers. Modest in stature and appearance but sometimes rampant and invasive in growth habit, it is perfect for shady situations with shrubs like sarcococca and skimmia. It is also useful in narrow shaded borders where little else will grow, as long as the soil is moist enough.

Fragrant flower bulbs continue the season into summer with the lilies. Not all are scented, so check before you choose. The trumpet-flowered varieties are usually perfumed, few more so than the beautiful species *Lilium regale*. This is also an easy, hardy lily to grow which will fit into any border between shrubs and perennials. It likes fertile soil that is not too dry and is

The clotted cream blooms of *Narcissus* 'Sir Winston Churchill'
have a delicious orange-blossom fragrance in midspring. Perfect
among later-flowering shrubs.

above The lovely *Convallaria majalis*, lily of the valley, blooms in shade in late spring. Modest in stature, it can be rampant in growth.

right Elegant *Lilium regale*, a wonderful addition to the summer border. Waxy blooms have a powerful, delicious fragrance.

Few can resist the scent of sweet peas. The old-fashioned varieties with smaller flowers often have the most perfume.

Pinks, varieties of *Dianthus plumarius*, are wonderfully fragrant and perfect for the front of sunny beds and borders.

best planted early in the season before the waxy bulbs dry out. It blooms in midsummer, perfect following early-flowering shrubs such as *Osmanthus delavayi* or among shrub roses where it usually follows the first flush of flowers.

The heavy, sweet scent of jasmine is one to be savoured. Hardy *Jasminum officinale* f. *affine* is pleasant, but nothing compared to the less hardy *Jasminum polyanthum,* star of the Mediterranean night. It grows quickly and vigorously in sheltered town gardens, and its evergreen foliage is attractive throughout the year. Clusters of pointed pink buds open into starry white flowers in late spring in sun or semi-shade. It is the ideal

plant for a wall or fence in a courtyard garden, perhaps with green and white variegated euonymus and *Pittosporum tobira.*

Few can resist the fresh fragrance of sweet peas, *Lathyrus odoratus.* These old-fashioned annual climbers are easily raised from seed and need not be confined to regimented rows for the production of show-quality blooms. Growing up obelisks or simple wigwams of canes or twigs, they add height and colour among shrubs, roses, and perennials. The secret is regular dead-heading, to avoid the production of seed pods which eventually prevent further flowering.

Simple pinks, varieties of *Dianthus plumarius*, often have a powerful, spicy, clove-like fragrance. They bloom for several weeks in summer and are a great addition at the front of a border, alongside paving or in pots. Their grey-green foliage sets off the flowers perfectly and provides a welcome contrast to other plants. They prefer alkaline soil and are ideal on shallow chalk.

289

Erica ×darleyensis provides nectar and pollen from late winter through to midspring. It is a favourite food source for bees.

SHRUBS TO ATTRACT WILDLIFE

Shrubs are beneficial to wildlife in many ways. Larger shrubs and hedges provide shelter and nesting places for wild birds. Small bushes and groundcovers are a haven for ground-dwelling insects and other small creatures. Leaves of some shrubs may be where insects deposit their eggs, or they are the food for certain insects and their larvae. Leaf litter from deciduous shrubs often provides winter shelter and nesting material. But the most important way that shrubs are beneficial to wildlife is as a source of food: pollen and nectar for bees, butterflies, and other pollinating insects and berries and seeds for wild birds.

Buddleja, or butterfly bush, is perhaps the best known garden plant that is sure to attract wildlife. Easy to grow, it has established itself widely outside gardens, managing to colonize the most inhospitable areas. Although it is considered invasive in many places, its value as a source of nectar in mid- to late summer is undeniable. Dead-heading as the blooms fade prolongs the flowering season, extending the food supply for several weeks.

Many berry-bearing shrubs are beneficial to wildlife more than once in a year. Take cotoneaster for example: small, single, white flowers in spring attract bees and other pollinators; orange-red berries are enjoyed by birds when they ripen in early winter. The same is true of pyracantha and single-flowering varieties of rose.

Insects and birds may not use your garden as a place to live or breed, but they will visit to feed, especially if there is good continuity of food supply throughout the year. Choosing the right succession of flowering and fruiting shrubs, in association with flower bulbs and perennials, makes a garden wildlife friendly as well as attractive for the garden owner. A garden does not need to be an unkempt wilderness to be attractive to wildlife. However, it is important to choose the right plants, basically those with single flowers, even tiny ones, where the pollen and nectar is easily accessible.

Winter and early spring–flowering shrubs are particularly important. Bumblebees, for example, do not store food reserves in the same way that honey bees do. Therefore on warm, sunny days in late winter bumblebees will be out searching for food. Mahonia, erica, and viburnum are just some of the winter blooming shrubs that will be waiting for them. *Erica carnea* and *Erica ×darleyensis* varieties are particularly important because of their long flowering season and abundance of nectar and pollen.

Berberis thunbergii

1.2 × 1.2m (4 × 4 ft.)
UK H7 USDA 4–9

Japanese barberry is a tough shrub with stiff, arching, spiny stems and small, rounded, soft green leaves that turn rich shades of red and orange in fall. Small solitary flowers appear along the branches in spring, offering a rich source of nectar and pollen for bees and other insects. They are followed in autumn by small, shining, egg-shaped berries that persist on the branches after the leaves have fallen, eventually enjoyed by wild birds during winter. An easy shrub for sun or semi-shade on any well-drained soil, it comes in numerous forms with red and gold foliage, varying in stature from dwarf and compact to large and loose in habit; some are freer flowering and fruiting than others. The species requires no pruning, except the occasional removal of some old stems in winter. It is invasive in parts of North America.

Caryopteris ×clandonensis 'White Surprise'

75 × 75cm (30 × 30 in.)
UK H4 USDA 5–9

All varieties of bluebeard are highly attractive to bees, butterflies, and other pollinating insects when in bloom in late summer. 'White Surprise', a variegated sport of 'Heavenly Blue', is a recent introduction forming a rounded shrub with stiff, upright stems and neat, grey-green leaves edged with creamy white. The whorls of bright blue tubular flowers appear in late summer and early fall. An excellent choice for a warm, sunny spot on well-drained or dry soil. Although tolerant of most conditions, it prefers alkaline soil and is excellent on chalk. There are many varieties of *Caryopteris ×clandonensis* with both plain and variegated foliage. The white and green foliage of this variety mixes particularly well with lavenders and silver-leaved shrubs. Prune hard every year in late winter, cutting back to where small grey buds are crowded on the stems.

Clethra alnifolia

1.5 × 1.2m (5 × 4 ft.)
UK H5 USDA 4-9

Sweet pepper bush or summersweet is a suckering shrub with upright branched stems and attractive alder-like green leaves that often turn yellow before they fall. In mid- to late summer the spikes of tiny, fragrant, creamy white flowers appear flecked with golden stamens. These are highly attractive to butterflies which seek them out as the blooms open. The flower spikes are reminiscent of those of a hebe. A hardy shrub that prefers neutral to acid soil, it grows in sun or partial shade. It likes moist or wet growing conditions and does not tolerate dry soil. More compact forms such as *Clethra alnifolia* 'Hummingbird' are ideal for smaller gardens. No pruning is necessary.

Cornus sanguinea

1.8 × 1.5m (6 × 5 ft.)
UK H6 USDA 4-8

Common dogwood is a hardy British native shrub of bushy, upright habit. The green leaves turn red-purple before they fall in autumn to reveal reddish winter stems. Clusters of small white flowers develop in spring, producing round, shining black berries in fall. Although the more colourful cultivars are often grown in gardens, the species is an excellent wildlife shrub, ideal for naturalistic planting and as an addition to mixed hedgerows. It grows on any well-drained soil, thrives on chalk, and is tolerant of cold, exposed situations. Like other dogwoods grown for their stems, it can be pruned hard in early spring to encourage vigorous, upright growth.

Cotoneaster horizontalis

90cm × 1.5m (3 × 5 ft.)
UK H7 USDA 4–7

Herringbone cotoneaster is a spreading shrub with stiff, regularly branched sprays of dark twigs clothed in small, shining, dark green leaves. Tiny, pinkish white flowers stud the branches in spring; these are very attractive to bees. They are followed by rounded scarlet berries that persist after the foliage has turned orange and red in fall. The berries are welcome food for wild birds in winter. Often used as a low wall shrub, it is also excellent as ground-cover, especially on slopes and banks. It grows on any well-drained soil in sun or shade and is extremely hardy. *Cotoneaster horizontalis* is widely naturalized and considered invasive in some areas, but there is no denying its value as a food source for wildlife. No pruning is required except the removal of branches to control spread.

Crataegus monogyna

4 × 4m (13 × 13 ft.)
UK H7 USDA 4–8

Common hawthorn is a versatile plant that can be used as a tree, trimmed as a hedge, or allowed to grow as a large, bushy shrub. It is an excellent wild-life subject as a roosting and nesting site for birds, a habitat for insects, and a food source for both. Clusters of fragrant white flowers in spring are an excellent source of pollen and nectar. When they ripen, abundant dark red fruits or haws are soon devoured by wild birds. The attractive dark green foliage stays in good condition through the summer and often colours rich gold in fall. Hawthorn grows on any soil that is not waterlogged and thrives on clay and chalk in sun or semi-shade. Prune in winter to control size and shape.

Erica arborea var. *alpina*

1.5 × 1.2m (5 × 4 ft.)
UK H4 USDA 7–9

Alpine tree heather is smaller in stature than *Erica arborea*, though the fire-resistant root nodules of both are used to make briar pipes. It is an upright shrub with dense, bright green foliage that is soft to the touch. In spring the shoots are crowded with tiny creamy white flowers with brown stamens; when fully open they produce clouds of pollen when brushed. The blooms are highly attractive to bees. A lovely shrub for neutral to acid soil that is moist but well-drained, at its best in full sun. Although some do not recommend pruning, it is best cut back after flowering as it will respond with bold, upright spikes of foliage that display the flowers to greatest advantage.

Euonymus europaeus 'Red Cascade'

3 × 1.8m (10 × 6 ft.)
UK H6 USDA 5–8

An excellent cultivar of spindle with vigorous, green, ascending and arching stems. The narrow oval green leaves turn rich red before they fall, at the same time as the fruits ripen. The small yellow-green flowers appear in early summer; they may seem insignificant, but they are much appreciated by pollinating insects. The crimson-pink, plump, triangular fruits hang from the branches in fall; they split when they ripen to reveal bright orange seeds. A hardy shrub that grows on any well-drained soil in sun or semi-shade, it is at its best on chalk and is very tolerant of cold, exposed sites. Prune in winter or early spring to control size and shape.

Hedera helix

8 × 3m (26 × 10 ft.)
UK H5 USDA 4–9

Common ivy is often regarded as an enemy in the garden and is sometimes classified as invasive. As a climber it scales tall trees with its self-clinging stems and glossy, evergreen leaves with characteristically pointed lobes. Mature plants produce non-clinging branched shoots with triangular leaves and spherical inflorescences of small green flowers that develop into round black fruits. The flowers are a magnet for insects in search of pollen and nectar, and the berries are food for wild birds. The bushy growth of mature plants is an important habitat that makes common ivy one of the most useful wildlife plants. It grows on any soil in sun or shade. Except where it is invasive, it can be controlled by regular pruning at any time and is useful to clothe unsightly walls and old fences.

Ilex aquifolium

5 × 3m (16 × 10 ft.)
UK H6 USDA 5–9

Common holly may ultimately be a substantial medium-sized tree, but it is slow to grow when young and often open and bony in character, becoming bushy and handsome as it matures. The dark green, shining, undulating, spiny leaves are evergreen and the perfect setting for the shining red berries that develop from tiny, dull-white spring flowers. Both flowers and fruit are food for wildlife and a mature plant a safe haven and nesting site. There are separate male and female plants, and both are needed for pollination and the production of fruit. There are hermaphrodite, self-fertile varieties and a host of variegated and ornamental cultivars. Holly grows in sun and shade on any well-drained soil. It can be pruned to shape or trimmed as a hedge or even as topiary.

Lavandula angustifolia

90 × 90cm (3 × 3 ft.)
UK H5 USDA 5–8

English lavender is a bushy shrub with stiff, ascending stems and narrow grey-green, strongly aromatic leaves. The slender spikes of pale to deep purple-blue flowers open in mid- to late summer and last for several weeks. Even when fading they are highly attractive to bees and butterflies, and a plant in full flower is buzzing with life from dawn to dusk. If left on the plants the oil-rich seeds are picked from the seedheads by small wild birds in winter. Lavender needs full sun and well-drained soil to thrive. It is at its best on sand and chalk and is extremely drought tolerant. There are many named cultivars in shades of purple, blue, pink, and white. For best results prune immediately after flowering, cutting back the flower stems into the top of the foliage. Leave a plant or two unpruned for the birds.

Ligustrum vulgare

3 × 1.8m (10 × 6 ft.)
UK H6 USDA 4–8

Wild or common privet is a semi-evergreen or deciduous shrub with straight twigs and small, dark green, shiny leaves that often turn burgundy-brown in late summer. Loose panicles of small, creamy tubular flowers are characteristically strongly scented and very attractive to insects. They develop into sprays of small, round green fruits that eventually turn black. These are soon eaten by wild birds. It grows on any well-drained soil, especially chalk, in sun or shade. It is ideal under the light shade of deciduous trees and as a transitional shrub in country gardens. Prune as necessary to control shape and size in winter.

Ribes sanguineum

1.8 × 1.5m (6 × 5 ft.)
UK H6 USDA 6–9

Commonly known as flowering currant, this is a strong shrub with upright brown stems and soft green lobed leaves that are powerfully aromatic, reminiscent of blackcurrants. Drooping clusters of pink flowers are produced all the way up the stems in spring, unfurling along with the new leaves. They are a sought-after early source of nectar for bees and other insects. Small blackcurrants, covered in grey-white bloom, are produced in late summer; these are soon taken by wild birds while the scent of the leaves usually prevents attack by deer and rabbits. A shrub for any well-drained soil and perfect for clay and chalk, it grows best in full sun but tolerates partial shade. Prune after flowering, cutting out some of the flowered shoots each year.

Rosa canina

3 × 1.5m (10 × 5 ft.)
UK H7 USDA 3-7

Sometimes more like a short climber than a shrub, dog rose has vigorous arching stems with sharp thorns and neat mid-green leaves. The sweetly fragrant single blooms are pale pink, sometimes white, opening in early summer, providing nectar for bees. These are followed by small, oval, orange-red hips, a familiar sight in autumn hedgerows and welcome winter food for birds and small mammals. Dog rose grows on any soil in sun or semi-shade. It can either be grown as a loose shrub or incorporated in a mixed hedgerow, perfect for informal country gardens. Prune in winter as required.

Viburnum opulus

4 × 3m (13 × 10 ft.)
UK H6 USDA 3-8

Guelder rose is a vigorous deciduous shrub with upright stems and fresh green, maple-like leaves. In spring the white lacecap flower heads are visited by pollinators. In fall drooping clusters of juicy redcurrant-like fruits are nutritious food for wild birds. The foliage colours flame and red in autumn before it falls, striking with the shining red fruits. A hardy shrub that thrives on any soil including clay and chalk in full sun or partial shade, it grows in shade but does not flower or fruit well. It is useful to incorporate in mixed rural hedgerows but also makes a good specimen shrub to grow in rough grass. The compact form is ideal for smaller gardens. Prune periodically in winter, cutting out some of the older stems.

OTHER GOOD SHRUBS TO ATTRACT WILDLIFE

Amelanchier lamarckii

Buddleja davidii

Buxus sempervirens

Calluna vulgaris

Cistus ×hybridus

Erica carnea

Escallonia macrantha

Hebe albicans

Mahonia aquifolium

Perovskia atriplicifolia

PLANTING PARTNERS WITH SHRUBS TO ATTRACT WILDLIFE

There is no shortage of planting partners that are attractive to wildlife. Many perennials, annuals, biennials, and flower bulbs are excellent sources of nectar and pollen and many of these go on to produce seeds that are eaten by wild birds. Here again these are the single- and semi-double–flowered varieties where stamens are exposed and the nectar is easily accessible. For the plants it is a way of achieving pollination; for wild creatures it is a lifeline.

As many berry-bearing shrubs display good autumn foliage colour, as well as richly coloured berries, hot-coloured blooms make good planting partners. In addition to fiery crocosmias, heleniums in particular make a fine fall show in shades of gold, orange, rust, and flame. They send out a strong signal to bees and butterflies and make easy landing platforms for creatures to feed on nectar and pollen.

Sedum 'Herbstfreude' is the real bee and butterfly destination in the late summer border. Often referred to as *Sedum* 'Autumn Joy', it is now correctly *Hylotelephium* (Herbstfreude Group), commonly called stonecrop or ice plant. The flattened heads of deep purple-pink starry flowers are buzzing with insect activity for several weeks alongside Michaelmas daisies and other autumn-flowering daisies such as the ever-popular purple coneflower, *Echinacea purpurea*.

The popularity of echinaceas has led to extensive breeding and the introduction of cultivars in a wide range of colours. However, the simple purple-pink– and white-flowered ones are the easiest to grow and most successful in the mixed border. They like good drainage but adequate moisture below the surface.

Single and semi-double dahlias come in a variety of sizes and a wide colour range. The tall Bishop Series are now often seen, both as border plants and as flowers to grow for cutting; they mix well with other perennials and shrubs and require little support. Tall and elegant in stature, they are ideal to grow among shrub roses and taller shrubs with the light and airy *Verbena bonariensis*, another excellent wildlife plant. Its tiny purple flowers with orange eyes are gathered in clusters. Although it may not be obvious, these tiny blooms are easily accessed by hungry insects.

Monarda, commonly known as bergamot or bee balm, has slender tube-shaped flowers arranged in whorls. Colours are bright and showy, a useful addition to the summer border. Although it likes good drainage and is excellent on chalk, it is prone to mildew if the soil is too dry beneath the surface.

Bees find allium flowers quite irresistible. Grow a few different varieties in the border and you can provide an excellent supply of nectar from late spring through to late summer. Although it does not have the longest flowering period, no wildlife-friendly garden should be without honey garlic, *Nectaroscordum siculum.* The chandelier-like blooms are a favourite destination of bees in search of nectar. Grow it among perennials and shrubs, or naturalize it in thin, long grass.

above The golden blooms of *Helenium* 'Wyndley' are clearly attractive to bees and other insects as they stand out in the late summer border.

left Clump-forming perennial sedums make a bold statement in the late summer border, the blooms remaining attractive long after their nectar supply has been exhausted.

The lovely *Dahlia* 'Bishop of Leicester' is useful to extend the summer season both in terms of colour and as a source of nectar and pollen for insects.

The aromatic foliage and whorls of tubular blooms of bergamot *Monarda* 'Prärienacht' (or Prairie Night) are a showy addition to the summer border with silver or purple leaves.

opposite The spectacular *Echium nervosum* is only suitable for the most favoured gardens with mild climates. Where it thrives the insects also do.

Those gardening in milder areas can enjoy the amazing echiums. Some reach incredible heights, but the most spectacular flower heads are produced by the shrubbier *Echium nervosum* with its euphorbia-like growth and plump columnar heads of tiny sapphire flowers. A plant in bloom is a spectacular sight and certainly attracts any bee or butterfly in the neighbourhood. It is ideal to grow with lavenders and silver foliage shrubs, cistus, and Mediterranean natives.

Early in the year many spring flower bulbs are a valuable food source; they are also easy to incorporate alongside shrubs and are an easy way of creating exciting planting combinations. Some of the best are the smaller bulb flowers such as fritillaria and galanthus. Crocus, especially the species such as *Crocus tommasinianus*, are particularly good and very popular with early bumblebees.

Ruta graveolens or common rue and other woody herbs with aromatic foliage are usually avoided by deer and rabbits.

DEER- AND RABBIT-RESISTANT SHRUBS

Gardening where deer and rabbits roam can be a real challenge. Both can cause serious damage to established and newly planted stock. They are often a problem in large, rural gardens, where fencing would be expensive or impractical and is often considered undesirable. Many repellents are available; sonic devices and various solutions can be applied. There are also those remedies that are passed on by others who have clearly never suffered from a deer or rabbit invasion: human hair, lion dung, garlic, and other mythical concoctions. In reality, none work. You either have to fence a garden properly, or plant what they are less likely to eat.

Unfortunately it is impossible to predict the actual dietary preferences of a particular deer or rabbit population. Even if they do not eat a plant, this will not prevent them from ripping it apart as part of the decision-making process. This often happens with evergreen rhododendrons: they are rarely eaten but may suffer damage.

Certain shrubs are likely to survive. Needless to say they are rarely at the top of a gardener's wish list: favourites, especially roses, are also very popular with deer. Highly aromatic leaves are a good choice and are usually avoided. Some people do not like the smell of choisya; deer and rabbits don't either. Lavender, rosemary, and sage may not be totally resistant, but they are usually left alone once established. Ribes is fairly resistant because of its strong blackcurrant aroma.

There are differing opinions on the resistance of hydrangeas to deer and rabbit attack. Here in the UK deer seem to avoid them which is good news as they have enjoyed such a rise in popularity. In North America the situation can be different, however.

In addition to mophead and lacecap hydrangeas, *Hydrangea arborescens*, *H. quercifolia*, and *H. paniculata* varieties are all worth trying. With a little planning you could have one in flower from early summer through to late fall. Most find buddlejas resistant, and they also attract more desirable landscape wildlife. They are easy to manage, requiring only hard winter pruning, and suit naturalistic gardens.

One thing is certain: deer and rabbits are always attracted by new plantings, so it is essential to protect new shrubs with mesh or some other barrier after planting. This can be removed once resistant plants are established.

Berberis thunbergii 'Starburst'

90cm × 1.2m (3 × 4 ft.)
UK H7 USDA 4-7

A striking variety of Japanese barberry with spreading, arching stems clothed in rounded pale green leaves, mottled white and pink in summer, turning brilliant orange and red in fall. In spring small yellow flowers are attractive to bees, followed by oval, shiny, red fruits that persist on the branches after the leaves have fallen. The thorny, tough stems are resistant to deer and rabbit attack, and the plant is drought tolerant. It grows in sun or semi-shade on any soil; the foliage colour is at its best in an open, sunny situation. Prune in winter if necessary to control shape and size, cutting out a few older stems at the base to preserve the open character of the plant. The species is invasive in parts of North America.

Buddleja 'Pink Delight'

1.8 × 1.5m (6 × 5 ft.)
UK H5 USDA 5-9

A superb variety of the popular butterfly bush with characteristic upright, arching silvery stems and grey-green leaves. The large conical sprays of mauve-pink flowers are freely produced in mid- to late summer; they are sweetly fragrant and very attractive to bees and butterflies. Buddlejas grow on any well-drained soil, including very poor, dry ground. They are at their best in full sun and are very drought tolerant. As they are deciduous and have tough, unappealing older stems, they are unattractive to deer and rabbits in winter and seem to avoid attack at other times. Prune hard in late winter, cutting back to less than 90cm (3 ft.) to encourage vigorous growth. Dead-heading prolongs the flowering period considerably. It is invasive in parts of North America.

Buxus sempervirens

1.8 × 1.5m (6 × 5 ft.)
UK H6 USDA 5–8

A familiar evergreen shrub, common box is most often seen trimmed and trained as topiary or hedging; therefore size is in the hands of the gardener. Left to develop naturally, it is a slow-growing, bushy shrub with stiff stems and small, rounded, leathery olive or dark green leaves. Tiny, insignificant yellow flowers appear in the leaf axils in spring. It grows in sun or shade and is tolerant of drought. It thrives on any soil that is not waterlogged and is particularly successful on clay and chalk. Prune in midsummer; early pruning can result in soft growth that is susceptible to frost damage. Box blight disease is a problem in many areas. Regular feeding with a balanced, slow-release fertilizer helps resistance.

Choisya ternata

1.5 × 1.8m (5 × 6 ft.)
UK H4 USDA 7–10

A widely grown evergreen shrub that forms a broad dome of dark green, shining leaves, each with three leaflets. It is commonly known as Mexican orange blossom because of the clusters of fragrant pure white blooms that appear in spring and again in early fall, the flowers resembling those of citrus. As for other members of the rue family, the foliage is highly aromatic, the taste and smell making the plant unattractive to deer and rabbits. Growing and flowering in sun or partial shade, it will tolerate heavier shade at the expense of flowers. It thrives on any reasonably fertile well-drained soil. Prune after the first flush of flowers, cutting back the longer shoots to encourage new growth from within the plant. The frosted tips of shoots many need removing after winter.

Cistus ×*purpureus* 'Alan Fradd'

75 × 90cm (30 in. × 3 ft.)
UK H4 USDA 8–10

A lovely variety of rock rose forming a loose, bushy shrub with ascending branches and narrow ever-green leaves, grey-green on the undersides. The large, rounded blooms appear in midsummer with pure white tissue-paper petals, blotched crimson towards the centre of the flower which is filled with golden stamens. Cistus are usually ignored by deer and rabbits once established. They need full sun and good drainage to thrive, growing on any soil but at their best on alkaline and chalk soils. Drought tolerant and undemanding, they are not long-lived shrubs and do not respond well to pruning, espe-cially when older.

Clerodendrum trichotomum var. *fargesii* 'Carnival'

1.8 × 1.5m (6 × 5 ft.)
UK H5 USDA 6–9

This variegated shrub deserves wider planting for both its foliage and welcome autumn flowers. It usually grows to form a characterful shrub with grey branches and pale green leaves with soft yellow mar-gins when young, maturing to sage green and cream. The foliage smells of rubber when lightly crushed, which makes it unpalatable to wildlife. It also appears to be pest- and disease-resistant. The white flowers open from prominent pink calyces that per-sist after the flowers fall. The characteristic metallic blue fruits of the species do not usually develop. It grows in sun or semi-shade on any reasonable soil. Prune in late winter to control shape and size if necessary.

Daphne odora 'Aureomarginata'

90cm × 1.2m (3 × 4 ft.)
UK H4 USDA 7–9

Daphnes are among the most sought-after flowering shrubs, prized for their fragrant blooms. *Daphne odora* 'Aureomarginata' is among the best known and easiest to grow. It forms a low, mounded shrub that becomes more open in character as it ages. The elongated, oval, evergreen leaves are gathered at the ends of the branches, mid- to dark green in colour, with very fine gold margins. In winter purple-pink buds form in clusters at the tips of the shoots, opening to small mauve-pink blooms with a strong, sweet fragrance. It grows in sun or semi-shade on any well-drained, reasonably moist soil, but it is at its best on chalk or in alkaline conditions. It does not grow well in a pot or container. No pruning is needed. The plants are short lived and usually need replacing after ten to fifteen years.

Forsythia ×*intermedia* 'Spring Glory'

1.8 × 1.5m (6 × 5 ft.)
UK H5 USDA 3–9

The yellow flowers of forsythia may not be to everyone's taste, but they do provide a welcome blast of colour in early spring. The upright, arching, tan-coloured stems are garlanded with golden yellow starry blooms before the leaves appear. They can be cut when in tight bud and will open in water in the house. The plain green, narrow, oval leaves unfurl after the flowers fade and transform the plant into a healthy structure shrub for the rest of the season. Forsythia grows on any soil, including heavy clay and shallow chalk. It thrives in sun or semi-shade and is very hardy. Prune immediately after flowering, cutting back some of the flowered shoots to where new growth is emerging. It can also be trimmed to shape with shears to encourage bushy, branched growth.

Hydrangea serrata 'Bluebird'

90 × 75cm (3 ft. × 30 in.)
UK H5 USDA 5–9

The perfect choice for any garden without the space for a larger lace-cap hydrangea variety. 'Bluebird' is a slender shrub, with upright tan-coloured stems and pointed dark green leaves flushed with purple-red. In midsummer the delicate lacecap flower heads appear; these are purple-pink on alkaline soils but bright gentian blue on acid soils. Each flower head consists of a flattened cluster of tiny fertile florets surrounded by larger, showier, ray florets. Later in the season the flower colour changes to purple-green. The wine-red colour of the foliage becomes more intense towards fall. It is at its best in semi-shade on any reasonably moist, fertile soil but prefers neutral to acid conditions. Prune in late winter, removing faded flower heads and cutting back some of the oldest stems to ground level.

Laurus nobilis

3 × 1.8m (10 × 6 ft.)
UK H4 USDA 8–11

The leaves of bay laurel are well known as a culinary herb, and the plants are a familiar sight gracing doorways as trimmed cones and standards. Left to grow naturally, bay forms a large, upright evergreen shrub with thin but leathery, dark, evergreen leaves that are strongly aromatic when crushed. Small greenish yellow flowers appear in clusters in late spring. These develop into green, oval fruits that turn black with age. Growing in sun or semi-shade on any well-drained soil, bay is a tough, drought-resistant plant, although not one of the hardiest. It grows well as a trained long-term subject for a pot or container and suits town gardens when grown this way. As a large, natural evergreen it is an ideal background shrub in rural gardens and is avoided by deer and rabbits. Prune in spring as required.

Lonicera nitida 'Baggesen's Gold'

1.5 × 1.8m (5 × 6 ft.)
UK H5 USDA 6–9

Boxleaf honeysuckle is widely used because it is such a tolerant, easy-to-grow, evergreen shrub. With bushy habit and straight twigs clothed in tiny yellow-green leaves, it forms a loose mound, the small leaves and light character contrasting handsomely with large-leaved heavier evergreens. Many designers may regard it as too utilitarian, but its versatility and durability cannot be denied. It grows in sun or shade, the colour more golden yellow in sun, lime green in shade. It grows on any reasonably well-drained soil and is drought tolerant once established, ideal under deciduous trees. It can be left to grow naturally or trimmed to shape and makes a good hedge given a little time.

Rhododendron 'Catawbiense Grandiflorum'

1.8 × 1.5m (6 × 5 ft.)
UK H6 USDA 4–8

Mountain rosebay is a very hardy rhododendron forming a large, domed shrub with leathery, dark green, evergreen leaves. The flowers are freely produced in late spring or early summer, usually at the end of the rhododendron flowering season. They are held at the tips of the shoots in rounded clusters, the individual, funnel-shaped blooms are bright mauve-pink with delicate orange-red markings on the upper petal. At its best in semi-shade, it is more tolerant of sun than some rhododendrons. It needs neutral to acid soil with adequate moisture; yellowing of the foliage usually indicates a high pH. No pruning is necessary, but older plants can be cut back after flowering to rejuvenate them.

Rosa rugosa

1.5 × 1.5m (5 × 5 ft.)
UK H7 USDA 2–8

Deer love roses, the first choice for grazing animals, usually when there are new leaves and developing flower buds. However, the prickly upright, suckering stems and tough-veined, wrinkled leaves of *Rosa rugosa* are avoided. The bright green foliage is healthy and disease resistant. The single or semi-double blooms are large, purple-pink or white, and very fragrant; with open centres and golden stamens, they are loved by bees in search of nectar and pollen. Flowers appear from early summer to fall and are followed by large, tomato-like fruits that remain on the stems after the leaves have fallen. When ripe the hips are enjoyed by wild birds. This rose thrives in sun or semi-shade on any well-drained soil including poor sandy ground. No pruning is required, but old stems can be removed in winter and tall shoots shortened.

Viburnum plicatum f. *plicatum* 'Rotundifolium'

1.5 × 1.8m (5 × 6 ft.)
UK H5 USDA 5–8

Japanese snowball is a wonderful flowering shrub with layered, spreading branches. The broad, oval leaves are conspicuously veined and pleated, green through summer, turning rich purple-red before they fall. In late spring the rounded clusters of sterile florets are carried in pairs along the branches, at first pale green, then rich cream, creamy white, and finally salmon-pink before they fade. The floral display lasts for several weeks. This hardy shrub thrives in sun or shade on any well-drained fertile soil. All *Viburnum plicatum* varieties are generally left alone by deer and rabbits once established. No pruning is required and should be avoided to preserve the shape; therefore plant with enough space for it to spread its branches.

OTHER GOOD DEER- AND RABBIT-RESISTANT SHRUBS

Calluna vulgaris

Cistus ×pulverulentus 'Sunset'

Helichrysum italicum

Lavandula angustifolia 'Hidcote'

Leucothoe fontanesiana 'Rainbow'

Lonicera ×purpusii 'Winter Beauty'

Phlomis fruticosa

Prunus laurocerasus

Sambucus nigra f. *porphyrophylla* 'Eva'

Sarcococca confusa

SHRUBS TO AVOID WHERE DEER AND RABBITS ARE A PROBLEM

Cornus sanguinea

Euonymus fortunei

Euonymus japonicus

Hebe albicans

Ilex aquifolium

Rhododendron luteum

Rosa Flower Carpet

Rubus thibetanus 'Silver Fern'

Vaccinium corymbosum

Viburnum tinus

DEER- AND RABBIT-RESISTANT PLANTING COMPANIONS

Just as some shrubs escape damage, some perennials also seem to be avoided. However, many produce juicy shoots that are a delicacy for deer and rabbits even if the mature plants are wildlife-proof later in the season.

Deer and rabbits dislike hellebores, so any *Helleborus ×hybridus* varieties are a good choice for big clumps of architectural foliage and late winter and early spring flowers. They grow on any well-drained but moist soil and, once established, seed themselves and spread. The foliage is probably at its best in shadier situations, but they flower better with enough sun. Therefore they make good planting companions for a wide range of shrubs. They are particularly useful for under-planting deciduous shrubs such as buddleja and clerodendrum where they can provide early interest.

The hybrids of *Helleborus argutifolius*, *Helleborus ×nigercors*, and *Helleborus ×ericsmithii*, which are all evergreen and more shrub-like, are also excellent planting partners. These suit open positions in sun or semi-shade with good air circulation. Damp, sheltered shady sites can result in leaf spot diseases which also ruin the flowers.

Deer and rabbits hate euphorbias because they have irritant milky sap that makes them impossible to eat. *Euphorbia griffithii* 'Fireglow' dies down to ground level in winter and spreads by underground runners. It erupts like rust-coloured asparagus in spring and produces

The glowing shoots and bracts of *Euphorbia griffithii* 'Fireglow' are spectacular for several weeks in spring and early summer, later the foliage often develops good fall colour.

It may be rampant and rather invasive, but *Euphorbia cyparissias* 'Fens Ruby' makes effective groundcover and is left untouched by wildlife.

The delicate pale green spikes of perennial foxglove, *Digitalis lutea*, are a delightful addition to any planting scheme.

spectacular glowing bracts at the tops of orange-tinted stems. Few perennials deliver such a long-lasting and colourful display.

Although it is considered invasive, *Euphorbia cyparissias* 'Fens Ruby' can be used as effective groundcover around deer-resistant shrubs. Brilliant lime green bracts top feathery purple-green foliage and stems from spring into summer. In fall the plants become a rusty, smoky haze. Grow it where you do not need to cultivate between tough shrubs such as choisya and rhododendron.

Digitalis or foxgloves are given a wide berth by deer and rabbits and can be encouraged to self-seed and naturalize. Their vertical flower spikes add a different dimension to a planting scheme. Most are biennial but some, such as *Digitalis lutea*, are longer lived and useful to drift between other plants. They seed themselves easily on most soils and are easily transplanted.

When it comes to flower bulbs, narcissi are safe and certainly the best choice to naturalize in grass and to plant in groups in beds and borders. They are avoided by deer and rabbits and are long lived. Their greatest disadvantage is their foliage, which takes

a long time to die down and can be unsightly. Plant the wild daffodil, *Narcissus pseudonarcissus*, where you do not need to mow or where deciduous shrubs will conceal the fading foliage as the season progresses.

Alliums are also usually safe, although some grazing animals seem to develop a taste for ornamental onions and nip off the leaf shoots when they emerge. Fortunately the leaves come through well before the flowers and even though they may be nibbled early in the season, the blooms usually emerge unscathed. Alliums are long-lived flower bulbs; some varieties will also seed and spread. The larger-growing

Allium 'Globemaster' makes an impressive statement in a border in midsummer. The flowers are loved by bees but fortunately avoided by deer and rabbits.

English bluebell, *Hyacinthoides non-scripta*, is a lovely subject to naturalize in grass under trees. Most deer and rabbits leave it untouched.

ones make impressive additions to mixed borders as they rise above other subjects in midsummer.

Snowdrops, *Galanthus nivalis* and other species, avoid damage because they are quite toxic. English bluebell, *Hyacinthoides non-scripta*, is avoided by some types of deer but seems to be sought after by others. This lovely wildflower is worth cultivating in naturalistic, informal gardens where it will thrive if left undisturbed under the light shade of trees.

For pots and containers hyacinths, related to bluebells, are normally safe. However, tulips should be avoided or very well protected. Deer love them and will devour the emerging shoots or wait until the buds are about to burst. Crocus often fall victim to birds and squirrels even before the rabbits get to them.

Although some may regard it as a last resort, cortaderia or pampas grass can be effective. If you have tried to clean up your pampas to remove the old foliage you will know just why deer and rabbits give it a wide berth. Large varieties are messy and difficult to accommodate, but *Cortaderia selloana* 'Pumila' is compact and attractive for several months.

Further Reading

Anderton, Stephen. *Rejuvenating a Garden*. London: Kyle Cathie, 1998.

Brickell, Christopher, and David Joyce. *The Royal Horticultural Society Pruning and Training: The Definitive Practical Guide to Pruning Trees, Shrubs, and Climbers*. New York: Dorling Kindersley, 2011.

Brown, George E., and Tony Kirkham. *Essential Pruning Techniques: Trees, Shrubs, Conifers*. Portland, Oregon: Timber Press, 2017.

Clausen, Ruth Rogers. *50 Beautiful Deer-Resistant Plants: The Prettiest Annuals, Perennials, Bulbs, and Shrubs that Deer Don't Eat*. Portland, Oregon: Timber Press, 2011.

Cooke, Ian. *Shrubs: A Gardener's Handbook*. Ramsbury, Wiltshire: Crowood Press, 2012.

Cushnie, John. Shrubs for the Garden. London: Kyle Cathie, 2004.

Dirr, Michael A. *Dirr's Encyclopedia of Trees & Shrubs*. Portland, Oregon: Timber Press, 2011.

Dirr, Michael A. *Hydrangeas for American Gardens*. Portland, Oregon: Timber Press, 2004.

Dirr, Michael A. *Viburnums: Flowering Shrubs for Every Season*. Portland, Oregon: Timber Press, 2007.

Gardiner, Jim. *The Timber Press Encyclopedia of Flowering Shrubs: More Than 1700 Outstanding Garden Plants*. Portland, Oregon: Timber Press, 2011.

Gossler, Roger, Eric Gossler, and Marjory Gossler. *The Gossler Guide to the Best Hardy Shrubs: More than 350 Expert Choices for Your Garden*. Portland, Oregon: Timber Press, 2009.

Hogan, Sean. *Trees for All Seasons: Broadleaved Evergreens for Temperate Climates*. Portland, Oregon: Timber Press, 2008.

Houtman, Ronald. *Variegated Trees and Shrubs: The Illustrated Encyclopedia*. Portland, Oregon: Timber Press, 2004.

Kukielski, Peter E. *Roses Without Chemicals: 150 Disease-Free Varieties That Will Change the Way You Grow Roses*. Portland, Oregon, Timber Press, 2015.

McIndoe, Andy. *The Creative Shrub Garden: Eye-Catching Combinations for Year-Round Interest*. Portland, Oregon: Timber Press, 2014.

Miller, Diana M. *400 Trees and Shrubs for Small Spaces: How to Choose and Grow the Best Compact Plants for Gardens*. Portland, Oregon: Timber Press, 2008.

Photography Credits

Bob Purnell, page 209 bottom
David Austin Roses, page 284 bottom
Dianna Jazwinski, page 266
New Place Nurseries / Steven Lee, page 169 bottom
Osberton Nursery / Will Murch, page 137 bottom

All other photos are by the author.

Index

Abbotsbury Gardens, 23
Abelia ×grandiflora, 118, 272
Abelia ×grandiflora Confetti, 162
Abelia parvifolia 'Bumblebee', 170
Abeliophyllum distichum, 212
Abutilon 'Kentish Belle', 212
Abutilon 'Souvenir de Bonn', 204
Acer palmatum, 112, 249
Acer palmatum 'Beni-maiko', 162
Acer palmatum 'Bloodgood', 250
Acer palmatum 'Jerre Schwartz', 148
Acer palmatum 'Katsura', 156
Acer shirasawanum 'Aureum',
    157, 250
Acer shirasawanum 'Jordan', 250
achillea, 272
Achillea 'Lachsschönheit' (Galaxy
    Series), 274
Achillea millefolium, 73
acid soil, 103–115
    improving, 103
    listed shrubs for, 47, 104–112
    planting partners for, 112–115
Actinidia kolomikta, 214, 215
Adam's needle, 227
aeoniums, 119, 153
African blue lily, 186
agapanthus, 184, 186
Agapanthus Headbourne, 184
Agapanthus 'Northern Star', 184
ajuga, 56
Akebia quinata, 214, 215
Alchemilla mollis, 140, 141
alkaline and chalk soils, 89–101
    improving, 89
    listed shrubs for, 90–98
    planting partners for, 98–101
allium, 37, 98, 128, 172,
    300, 316–317

Allium atropurpureum, 172
Allium cernuum, 128, 129
Allium cristophii, 172, 173
Allium 'Globemaster', 317
Allium sphaerocephalon, 98, 100
alpine tree heather, 295
alstroemeria, 230
Amelanchier canadensis, 84, 132
Amelanchier lamarckii, 300
American wake-robin, 112–115
Amicia zygomeris, 228, 230
Anemone blanda, 261
Anemone ×hybrida 'Honorine
    Jobert', 184, 244, 247
annual honesty, 258
aphids, 119
apothecary's rose, 80
Aquilegia vulgaris, 140
Aralia echinocaulis, 251
Aralia elata, 251
Aralia elata 'Variegata', 220
architectural and dramatic foliage
    effects, 219–231
    listed shrubs for, 220–228
    planting partners for, 228–231
Argyrocytisus battandieri, 204
Armeria maritima, 70
aromatic foliage and flowers. See
    fragrant flowers, shrubs with
Aronia arbutifolia 'Erecta', 84
arrowwood, 285
Artemisia 'Powis Castle', 119
arum lily, 84, 230
Astelia 'Silver Shadow', 48, 156, 228
astilbes, 84
astrantias, 99
attributes, selecting for, 35
Aubrieta deltoidea, 200
aucuba, 228

Aucuba japonica, 90
Aucuba japonica 'Rozannie',
    49, 56, 228
Aucuba japonica 'Variegata', 90
Australian tree fern, 228, 229
autumn anemone, 247
azaleas, 109, 111, 137, 140, 283, 284
Azara microphylla, 212

Ballota pseudodictamnus, 119
balm-leaved red deadnettle, 198
bamboo, 14–15, 244
barberry, 176, 234
bare-root shrubs, planting
    instructions, 42
barrenwort, 56, 59, 258
bay, 249, 311
bearberry cotoneaster, 191
bee balm, 300
beech, for hedging, 243
berberis, 61, 142, 145, 247, 275
Berberis darwinii, 49, 105
Berberis darwinii 'Compacta', 49
Berberis ×ottawensis f. purpurea
    'Superba', 234
Berberis thunbergii, 292
Berberis thunbergii f. atropurpurea
    'Admiration', 31, 148, 184
Berberis thunbergii f. atropurpurea
    'Harlequin', 90, 101, 112
Berberis thunbergii f. atropurpurea
    'Helmond Pillar', 184
Berberis thunbergii 'Orange Ice',
    176, 186
Berberis thunbergii 'Orange
    Rocket', 176
Berberis thunbergii 'Starburst', 306
bergamot, 300, 302
berry-bearing shrubs, 291, 300

birches, 28, 109, 112, 140

black-leaved elder, 89

blackthorn, 242, 243

bloodtwig, for hedging, 243

bluebeard, 292

blue comfrey, 112

blue lavender, 126

blue passion flower, 184

bonsai, 249

botanists, shrub definition, 12, 13

boundaries, defining, 32, 170, 233

box blight, 180, 307

boxleaf honeysuckle, 193, 311

boxwood, 17, 165

Brachyglottis (Dunedin Group) 'Sunshine', 62, 98, 126

bridal wreath, 81

Briza maxima, 99

broadleaf, 238

brunnera, 258

Brunnera macrophylla, 58

Brunnera macrophylla 'Jack Frost', 58

Brunnera macrophylla 'Looking Glass', 57, 58

buddleja, 126, 291, 305, 314

Buddleja davidii, 300

Buddleja davidii Buzz Indigo, 98, 120

Buddleja davidii Buzz Series, 120, 170

Buddleja davidii 'Dartmoor', 234

Buddleja 'Pink Delight', 306

bugles, 56

bull bay, 210

bumblebees, 291, 302

bunchberry, 140

burning bush, 134

butcher's broom, 54

butterfly bush, 120, 234, 291, 306

butterfly rose, 270

Buxus sempervirens, 17, 242, 243, 249, 300, 307

Buxus sempervirens 'Elegantissima', 149, 157, 158

cabbage palm, 221

cacti and succulents, 128

calamagrostis, 143

calico bush, 107

California lilac, 190, 205, 235, 264

California poppy, 126, 129

Callistemon citrinus 'Splendens', 120

Calluna vulgaris, 140, 198, 272, 300, 314

Calluna vulgaris 'Silver Knight', 104

Calycanthus floridus, 84

Calycanthus ×*raulstonii* 'Hartlage Wine', 264, 275

camellia, 158

Camellia japonica, 212

Camellia japonica 'Adolphe Audusson', 104

Camellia ×*williamsii* 'Jury's Yellow', 156, 177

camouflage fatsia, 223

Campanula lactiflora, 101

Canary spurge, 222

canna, 219, 229

Canna indica, 228

Carpinus betulus, 243

Caryopteris ×*clandonensis*, 292

Caryopteris ×*clandonensis* 'Heavenly Blue', 177

Caryopteris ×*clandonensis* 'White Surprise', 292

Catalpa bignonioides 'Aurea', 228

Catalpa ×*erubescens* 'Purpurea', 220

Catananche caerulea, 72, 73

catmints, 272–275

ceanothus, 30, 200, 203, 212

Ceanothus ×*delileanus* 'Gloire de Versailles', 212, 264, 272

Ceanothus 'Italian Skies', 30, 205

Ceanothus 'Skylark', 235

Ceanothus thyrsiflorus var. *repens*, 126, 190

Ceratostigma willmottianum, 178, 186

Cercis canadensis 'Forest Pansy', 249, 251, 258

Cercis chinensis 'Avondale', 252

Chaenomeles speciosa, 184

Chaenomeles speciosa 'Moerloosei', 205

chalk soil, 89. *See also* alkaline and chalk soils

checkerberry, 106

cherry laurel, 30, 53, 89, 95, 240

Chilean guava, 155

Chilean lantern tree, 207

Chimonanthus praecox, 212, 278

Chinese bramble, 195

Chinese plumbago, 178

chionodoxa, 56, 172

chocolate vine, 214, 215

choisya, 305

Choisya ×*dewitteana* 'Aztec Pearl', 163, 265

Choisya ×*dewitteana* White Dazzler, 163, 170

Choisya ternata, 17, 163, 272, 307

Christmas box, 54, 96, 169

Christmas rose, 101

cistus, 30, 65, 98, 192, 200

Cistus ×*dansereaui* 'Decumbens', 198
Cistus ×*hybridus*, 70, 91, 112, 300
Cistus ×*obtusifolius* 'Thrive', 265
Cistus ×*pulverulentus* 'Sunset', 121, 314
Cistus ×*purpureus* 'Alan Fradd', 308
clary, 272, 273
clay soil, 27, 40, 41, 75, 103. *See also* wet and compacted soil
clematis, 98, 170, 212, 213
Clematis alpina, 143
Clematis 'Broughton Star', 247
Clematis cirrhosa, 212
Clematis 'Minuet', 101
Clematis montana, 247
Clematis 'Perle d'Azur', 212
Clematis 'Princess Diana', 212–214
Clematis The Countess of Wessex, 170–172
Clematis viticella, 101, 143
clerodendrum, 314
Clerodendrum bungei 'Pink Diamond', 221
Clerodendrum trichotomum var. *fargesii*, 278
Clerodendrum trichotomum var. *fargesii* 'Carnival', 37, 308
Clethra alnifolia, 140, 293
Clethra alnifolia 'Hummingbird', 293
climbers
    alternatives to, 203–215
    with fast-growing shrubs, 244, 246–247
    for narrow beds and borders, 175, 184
    in small gardens, 170
    for steep slopes and banks, 198
climbing hydrangea, 184
coastal situations, 61–73
    listed shrubs for, 62–70

planting partners for, 70–73
colocasia, 231
Colocasia esculenta, 228
color schemes in the garden, 35–37
columbine, 140
common box, 149, 243, 307
common dogwood, 243, 293
common foxglove, 200
common hawthorn, 70, 71, 294
common holly, 297
common honeysuckle, 72, 73
common ivy, 51, 198, 296
common laurel, 244
common myrtle, 281
common periwinkle, 196
common privet, 298
common rosemary, 124
common rue, 305
common snowball, 83
common snowdrop, 143
compacted soil. *See* wet and compacted soil
conifers, planting instructions, 41–42
containers and pots, gardening in. *See* pots and containers, gardening in
Convallaria majalis, 286, 288
Convolvulus cneorum, 121, 128, 156, 170
copper and green beech, 243
copper-leaved heucheras, 156
Coprosma repens 'Tequila Sunrise', 150, 156
cordyline, 23, 228
Cordyline australis, 258
Cordyline australis 'Torbay Dazzler', 221
cornus, 143, 233
Cornus alba, 87
Cornus alba 'Baton Rouge', 132
Cornus alba 'Elegantissima', 76, 275

Cornus alba 'Sibirica', 132, 244
Cornus alba 'Sibirica Variegata', 70, 163, 173
Cornus canadensis, 140, 198
Cornus controversa 'Variegata', 23, 24, 38, 59, 252
Cornus 'Eddie's White Wonder', 253
Cornus florida 'Cherokee Princess', 253
Cornus kousa 'Miss Satomi', 266
Cornus mas, 258
Cornus 'Porlock', 112, 217, 254
Cornus sanguinea, 37, 243, 293, 314
Cornus sanguinea 'Midwinter Fire', 131
Cornus sericea 'Bud's Yellow', 84, 133
Cornus sericea 'Flaviramea', 133
Cornus sericea 'Hedgerows Gold', 236
Corokia cotoneaster, 62
Coronilla valentina subsp. *glauca*, 206
cortaderia, 317
Cortaderia selloana 'Pumila', 70, 317
Corylus avellana 'Purpurea', 258
Corylus maxima 'Purpurea', 233, 236
cosmos, 159, 274
Cosmos bipinnatus, 274
cotinus, 23, 275
Cotinus 'Grace', 233, 237
cotoneaster, and wildlife, 291
Cotoneaster atropurpureus 'Variegatus', 190, 198
Cotoneaster 'Cornubia', 255, 258
Cotoneaster dammeri, 191
Cotoneaster franchetii, 98, 112, 237
Cotoneaster horizontalis, 198, 294
Cotoneaster naoujanensis 'Berried Treasure', 35
Cotoneaster salicifolius 'Gnom', 191

cotton lavender, 125
Crataegus monogyna, 70, 71, 243, 258, 294
creeping blue blossom, 190
creeping rosemary, 194
creeping thyme, 200, 201
creeping wintergreen, 106
crimson bottlebrush, 120
Crinodendron hookerianum, 112, 207, 258
crocosmias, 300
crocus, 172, 317
Crocus tommasinianus, 302
Cryptomeria japonica 'Sekkan-sugi', 255
cupid's dart, 73
×*Cupressocyparis leylandii*, 241
currant, 15
cut-leaf sumac, 138
cut-leaved elder, 81
Cyclamen hederifolium, 56, 57

Daboecia cantabrica, 63
dahlia, 230, 300
Dahlia 'Bishop of Leicester', 302
daisies, 73, 300
daphne, 35, 286
Daphne bholua 'Jacqueline Postill', 272, 279
Daphne odora, 8
Daphne odora 'Aureomarginata', 98, 170, 286, 309
Daphne ×*transatlantica* Eternal Fragrance, 164, 272
Darwin's barberry, 49
daylilies, 87
deadnettle, 56, 200, 258, 260
deciduous azaleas, 109, 283, 284
deciduous clematis, 143
deciduous shrubs, 17, 21
deciduous trees, selective crown thinning of, 28

deer- and rabbit-resistant plants, 58, 305–317
  listed shrubs, 306–314
  planting companions, 314–317
  protecting new plants, 43
  shrub selection, 37
  shrubs to avoid, 314
Desfontainia spinosa, 105
deutzia, 87, 263
Deutzia ×*elegantissima* 'Rosealind', 92
Deutzia ×*hybrida* 'Strawberry Fields', 76
Deutzia setchuenensis var. *corymbiflora*, 178
Dianthus plumarius varieties, 289
diascia, 272
Diascia personata, 272, 274
Diascia personata 'Hopleys', 272
Dicentra 'Stuart Boothman', 112
Dicksonia antarctica, 228, 229
Digitalis lutea, 316
Digitalis purpurea, 200
disease and pests, 156, 210. *See also specific pest and disease names*
dog rose, 299
dogwoods, 76, 136, 143
  and deer, 37
  planting partners for, 84, 85
Drimys winteri, 207
drought conditions and drought-resistant plants, 21, 27, 117, 126. *See also* exposed sites; hot and dry conditions
drumstick allium, 98, 100
dry conditions, 103. *See also* hot and dry conditions
Dryopteris filix-mas 'Cristata', 112
dry shade, selecting shrubs for, 47, 54
dwarf mountain pine, 136

dwarf winged euonymus, 134

Echinacea purpurea, 142, 143, 300
Echinops ritro, 142, 143
Echium nervosum, 302
Edgeworthia chrysantha, 279
Elaeagnus ×*ebbingei*, 61, 63, 70
Elaeagnus pungens 'Frederici', 50, 56
Elaeagnus 'Quicksilver', 92, 101, 140, 233, 286
Elaeagnus ×*submacrophylla*, 61, 63, 70, 286
elder, 84, 96, 140
English bluebell, 317
English lavender, 89, 297
English roses, 33, 183, 212, 284
English yew, 241
Enkianthus campanulatus, 105
Epimedium 'Amber Queen', 258, 261
Epimedium ×*versicolor* 'Sulphureum', 56
erica, and wildlife, 291
Erica arborea var. *alpina*, 295
Erica carnea, 156, 198, 272, 291, 300
Erica carnea f. *alba* 'Winter Snow', 133
ericaceous plants, 27, 103
  fertilizer for, 27, 43, 103
  planting instructions, 41
  planting partners for, 112
  and soil pH, 89
Erica ×*darleyensis*, 291
Erica ×*darleyensis* 'Darley Dale', 266
Erigeron glaucus 'Sea Breeze', 73
Erigeron karvinskianus, 73
eriobotrya, 228
Eriobotrya japonica, 222
eryngium, 100, 126
Eryngium giganteum, 126, 127
erysimum, 200
Erysimum 'Apricot Twist', 201

Erysimum 'Bowles's Mauve', 126, 170, 272
Escallonia laevis Pink Elle, 64
Escallonia macrantha, 300
Eschscholzia californica, 126, 129
eucryphia, 261
Eucryphia ×nymansensis 'Nymansay', 256
eulalia, 70
euonymus, 186, 289
Euonymus alatus 'Bladerunner', 134
Euonymus alatus 'Compactus', 134
Euonymus europaeus 'Red Cascade', 98, 296
Euonymus fortunei, 51, 131, 184, 211, 249, 314
Euonymus fortunei 'Emerald Gaiety', 70, 170, 179, 198
Euonymus fortunei 'Emerald 'n' Gold', 131
Euonymus fortunei 'Silver Queen', 50, 56, 57, 212
Euonymus japonicus, 314
Euonymus japonicus 'Bravo', 184
Euonymus japonicus 'Chollipo', 179
Euonymus japonicus 'Green Rocket', 180
Euonymus japonicus 'Green Spire', 180
Euonymus japonicus 'Microphyllus Albovariegatus', 156, 180
Euonymus japonicus 'Ovatus Aureus', 179
Eupatorium purpureum, 84–87
euphorbia, 186, 228, 314
Euphorbia characias, 37
Euphorbia cyparissias 'Fens Ruby', 316
Euphorbia griffithii 'Fireglow', 314–316
Euphorbia ×martini 'Ascot Rainbow', 186, 187

Euphorbia mellifera, 222
European gorse, 63, 69
European red elder, 138
evergreen broom, 209
evergreen euonymus, 37
evergreen shrubs, 17, 43, 89, 186
exposed sites, 61–73
    listed shrubs for, 62–70
    planting partners for, 70–73

Fagus sylvatica, 243
fall foliage, 24
false castor oil plant, 223
false dittany, 119
false holly, 167
false spiraea, 139
Farges harlequin glorybower, 278
fargesia, 244
fast-growing shrubs, 234–247
    planting partners for, 244–247
    selecting, 234–244
×*Fatshedera lizei*, 56, 208
fatsia, 219, 228
Fatsia japonica, 51
Fatsia japonica 'Murakumo-nishiki', 223
Fatsia japonica 'Variegata', 51
ferns, 112, 158
fertilizer, 27, 43
    for common box, 307
    for container gardening, 147
    for ericaceous plants, 27, 43, 103
    for perennials, 115
    for roses, 27, 80, 183, 270, 284
firethorn, 210
flaky juniper, 192
flame creeper, 115
floribunda roses, 73
flower bulbs, 56, 128, 143, 158, 172, 286
Flower Carpet roses, 194
flowering currant, 298

flowering dogwood, 253, 254, 258, 261, 266
flowering maple, 204
flowering season, extended. *See* long-blooming shrubs
foam flower, 140
forsythia, 15
Forsythia ×intermedia, 244
Forsythia ×intermedia 'Spring Glory', 309
Forsythia suspensa, 212
Fothergilla major Monticola Group, 106
foxglove, 258, 316
fragrant flowers, shrubs with, 277–289
    choosing, 35, 278–286
    planting partners for, 286–289
fringe-cups, 258
fritillaria, 172, 302
Fritillaria meleagris, 86, 87
frost, and shrub care, 43, 131
Fuchsia 'Riccartonii', 93, 272
Fuji cherry, 168
full moon maple, 250

galanthus, 56, 172, 302
Galanthus nivalis, 56, 87, 143, 317
garden designers, shrub definitions, 12, 13
gardeners, shrub definitions, 13–14
garrya, 203
Garrya elliptica 'James Roof', 208
Gaultheria procumbens, 106, 198
gaura, 172
Gaura lindheimeri 'The Bride', 172
Gaura lindheimeri 'Whirling Butterflies', 172
Genista 'Porlock', 209
geranium, 58, 100, 143
Geranium 'Azure Rush', 173

Geranium ×*johnsonii* 'Johnson's Blue', 272
Geranium macrorrhizum, 58
Geranium 'Orion', 98, 99
Geranium Rozanne, 98, 172, 272
geum, 98
Geum 'Totally Tangerine', 98
globe thistle, 142, 143
glory flower, 221
golden Irish yew, 183
golden privet, 238
gorse, 73
grasses, 70, 84–87, 126, 128
Grecian horehound, 119
Grevillea 'Canberra Gem', 267
Griselinia littoralis, 238
Griselinia littoralis 'Dixon's Cream', 64
Griselinia littoralis 'Variegata', 64
groundcovers, 58, 112, 140, 189, 198, 258
guelder rose, 299

Hamamelis ×*intermedia* 'Barmstedt Gold', 107
Hamamelis ×*intermedia* 'Jelena', 34
Hamamelis ×*intermedia* 'Vesna', 280
hardiness ratings, 8–9
hardy fuchsias, 89, 101
hardy geraniums, 73, 98, 143, 172, 272
hawthorn, 243
heather, 104, 111, 115
hebes, 73, 165, 172, 186, 272
Hebe albicans, 300, 314
Hebe pinguifolia 'Sutherlandii', 73, 165
Hebe rakaiensis, 18
Hebe 'Red Edge', 65, 165
Hebe 'Silver Dollar', 165
Hebe 'Spender's Seedling', 93

Hebe 'Youngii', 170
Hedera algeriensis 'Gloire de Marengo', 170
Hedera colchica, 58
Hedera colchica 'Sulphur Heart', 198, 199
Hedera helix, 198, 296
Hedera helix 'Erecta', 51
Hedera helix 'Green Ripple', 198
hedges, 32, 42, 233, 243
heleniums, 300
Helenium 'Wyndley', 301
helianthemums, 192, 200
Helianthemum 'Rhodanthe Carneum', 192
Helianthemum 'The Bride', 126
Helichrysum italicum, 314
Helichrysum italicum 'Korma', 126
hellebores, 58, 101, 314
Helleborus argutifolius, 314
Helleborus ×*ericsmithii*, 101, 314
Helleborus ×*hybridus*, 101, 186, 187, 314
Helleborus niger, 101
Helleborus ×*nigercors*, 314
hemerocallis, 186
Hemerocallis 'Summer Wine', 87
herbicides, 189
herbs, woody, 117, 124, 192, 200, 305
herringbone cotoneaster, 190, 294
heucheras, 145, 156
Heuchera 'Plum Pudding', 156
heucherellas, 156
Heucherella 'Brass Lantern', 156, 158
×*Heucherella* 'Tapestry', 156, 159
Hibiscus syriacus 'Hamabo', 98
Himalayan honeysuckle, 77
Hippophae rhamnoides, 65, 140, 244
holly, 243, 249, 256
holly-leaved sweet spire, 209
honey bees, 291

'Honey Bee' viola, 159
honey flower, 224
honey garlic, 300
hornbeam, 243
horticulturists, shrub definitions, 13
hostas, 84, 112, 143, 156
Hosta 'Blue Wedgwood', 156
Hosta 'Halcyon', 156
Hosta 'Patriot', 156, 157
Hosta 'So Sweet', 84
Hosta (Tardiana Group) 'June', 156
hot and dry conditions, 117–129
   dry acidic soils, 103
   listed shrubs for, 118–126
   planting partners for, 126–129
   soil improvements for, 117
houseplants, 208
Hyacinthoides non-scripta, 317
hyacinths, 286, 317
hydrangea, 16, 263, 305
Hydrangea anomala subsp. *petiolaris*, 175, 184
Hydrangea arborescens, 305
Hydrangea arborescens 'Annabelle', 134
Hydrangea aspera Kawakamii Group, 228
Hydrangea 'Blue Deckle', 267
Hydrangea macrophylla, 84
Hydrangea macrophylla Magical Amethyst, 16
Hydrangea macrophylla 'Zorro', 77
Hydrangea paniculata, 140, 184, 275, 305
Hydrangea paniculata Bobo, 147, 150
Hydrangea paniculata Confetti, 181
Hydrangea paniculata 'Limelight', 135
Hydrangea paniculata 'Phantom', 268
Hydrangea quercifolia, 223, 305

Hydrangea serrata 'Bluebird', 310
Hylotelephium (Herbstfreude
    Group), 128, 300
Hypericum ×*hidcoteense* 'Hidcote',
    84, 98, 269

ice plant, 300
Ilex ×*altaclerensis* 'Golden
    King', 56, 256
Ilex aquifolium, 297, 314
Ilex aquifolium 'Ferox Argentea', 56
Ilex crenata 'Convexa', 112
Ilex crenata (Fastigiata Group)
    'Fastigiata', 181
Ilex crenata (Fastigiata Group) 'Sky
    Pencil', 181
Indian shot, 228
invasive species
    bamboos, 15
    Euphorbia cyparissias 'Fens
        Ruby', 316
    grasses, 70
    ivies, 58, 296
    lily of the valley, 286
Irish heath, 63
Irish juniper, 182
Iris sibirica, 84, 86
irrigation systems, 31, 117. *See also*
    watering and water supply
Italian buckthorn, 240
itea, 203
Itea ilicifolia, 209
ivies, 58, 198, 243

Japanese anemones, 184
Japanese angelica tree, 220, 251
Japanese aralia, 51
Japanese barberry, 292, 306
Japanese holly, 181
Japanese laurel, 49
Japanese maple, 105, 109, 148, 151,
    162, 261

Japanese mock orange, 154
Japanese quince, 205
Japanese snowball, 313
Japanese spiraea, 82, 97
Japanese spurge, 53
japonica, 205
jasmine, fragrance of, 289
Jasminium nudiflorum, 198
Jasminum officinale f. *affine*, 289
Jasminum polyanthum, 289
Jerusalem sage, 123
Juniperus communis
    'Compressa', 184
Juniperus communis 'Hibernica', 182
Juniperus ×*pfitzeriana* 'Sulphur
    Spray', 66
Juniperus squamata 'Blue Carpet',
    189, 192

Kalmia latifolia, 107
Kerria japonica, 258, 259
Kerria japonica 'Golden
    Guinea', 258
Knautia macedonica, 100, 101
Korean spice, 285

lace shrub, 195
lady's mantle, 140, 141
Lamium galeobdolon
    'Florentinum', 258
Lamium maculatum, 258, 260
Lamium maculatum 'Beacon
    Silver', 56
Lamium maculatum 'White
    Nancy', 56
Lamium orvala, 198, 200
The Laskett (garden), 242
Lathyrus odoratus, 289
Laurus nobilis, 257, 311
laurustinus, 271
Lavandula angustifolia, 70, 297

Lavandula angustifolia 'Hidcote',
    122, 170, 314
Lavandula stoechas 'Spring-break
    Princess', 15
Lavatera ×*clementii*, 94
Lavatera ×*clementii* 'Candy
    Floss', 94
lavender
    for combination planting, 73,
        100, 124, 125, 214, 272
    and deer and rabbits, 305
    fragrance of, 277
    popularity of, 15–16, 249
    timescale of, 30
leaf spot disease, 64, 65, 239
leather leaf viburnum, 226
Leptospermum scoparium, 214
Leptospermum scoparium 'Red
    Damask', 214
lesser periwinkle, 197
Leucothoe axillaris 'Curly Red', 151
Leucothoe fontanesiana 'Rainbow',
    56, 108, 314
Leucothoe Scarletta, 151
leycesteria, 84
Leycesteria formosa, 77, 244
lifespan of shrubs, 30
Ligularia dentata 'Desdemona', 84
Ligustrum delavayanum, 249
Ligustrum ovalifolium
    'Argenteum', 56
Ligustrum ovalifolium
    'Aureum', 238
Ligustrum vulgare, 298
lilac, 15, 41, 97, 263
lilies, 230, 286–289
Lilium regale, 286–289
Lilium 'Scheherazade', 230, 231
Lily of the Nile, 184, 186
lily of the valley, 286, 288
lily of the valley bush, 111, 153
lilyturf, 56

Linaria purpurea 'Canon Went', 172
Liriope muscari, 56, 59
Lithodora diffusa 'Heavenly
    Blue', 115
long-blooming shrubs, 263–275
    listed shrubs, 264–272
    planting partners for, 272–275
Lonicera nitida 'Baggesen's
    Gold', 311
Lonicera nitida 'Maigrün', 193
Lonicera periclymenum, 72, 73
Lonicera ×purpusii 'Winter Beauty',
    78, 98, 244, 314
Lophomyrtus ×ralphii 'Magic
    Dragon', 152
loquat, 222
Loropetalum chinense var. *rubrum*
    'Fire Dance', 108
Luma apiculata 'Glanleam Gold',
    166, 184
Lunaria annua, 258
Lunaria rediviva, 258
lungworts, 58
Lysimachia ciliata 'Firecracker', 84

magnolia, 261, 263
Magnolia grandiflora, 203, 210,
    228, 286
Magnolia ×loebneri 'Leonard
    Messel', 257
Magnolia ×soulangeana, 78, 112
Magnolia stellata 'Water Lily', 166
mahonia, 219, 291
Mahonia aquifolium, 300
Mahonia aquifolium 'Apollo',
    52, 70, 198
Mahonia japonica, 35, 56, 224, 286
Mahonia ×media 'Charity', 258
Mahonia ×media 'Winter Sun', 280
maidenhair vine, 198
maintenance needs for gardens,
    17–21, 33

melianthus, 228
Melianthus major, 224
Mexican hydrangea, 221
Mexican orange, 17, 163, 265
Mexican orange blossom, 307
Michaelmas daisies, 300
Microbiota decussata, 193
mirror plant, 150
miscanthus, 70, 87, 244
Miscanthus nepalensis, 70, 72
Miscanthus sinensis, 245
Miscanthus sinensis
    'Variegatus', 86, 87
Miss Willmott's ghost, 126, 127
mock orange, 94, 282
monarda, 300
Monarda 'Prärienacht', 302
Moroccan broom, 204, 214
mountain laurel, 107
mountain pine, 67
mountain rosebay, 312
Muehlenbeckia complexa, 198
mulches and mulching, 117, 122,
    125, 156, 194, 230
mycorrhizal fungi, 41, 42, 43
myrtle, 286
Myrtus communis, 170, 281

Nandina domestica, 182
Nandina domestica 'Fire
    Power', 167
Nandina domestica Obsessed, 19,
    152, 156
Nandina domestica
    'Richmond', 182
narcissi, 56, 87, 286, 316
Narcissus papyraceus, 286
Narcissus poeticus var. *recurvus*, 286
Narcissus pseudonarcissus, 316
Narcissus 'Sir Winston Churchill',
    286, 287
narrow beds and borders, 175–187

listed shrubs for, 176–184
    planting partners for, 184–187
Nectaroscordum siculum, 300
Nepalese paper plant, 279
nepeta, 37
Nepeta 'Six Hills Giant', 275
nerines, 184, 185
Nerine bowdenii, 184
New Zealand broadleaf, 64
New Zealand flax, 66, 153, 225,
    244, 246
ninebark, 79, 136
Nippon spiraea, 139
North American flowering
    dogwood, 253
North American redbud, 251
nursery professionals, shrub
    definitions, 12

oak-leaved hydrangea, 223
Olearia ×haastii, 61, 70
Olearia ×scilloniensis, 122
Olearia traversii, 61
oleaster, 92
Oregon grape, 52, 280
oriental poppies, 126
Osmanthus ×burkwoodii, 286
Osmanthus delavayi, 281, 289
Osmanthus heterophyllus
    'Goshiki', 167
Osmanthus heterophyllus
    'Variegatus', 52

Pachysandra terminalis, 53, 198
pampas grass, 70, 317
panicum, 143
Papaver orientalis, 126
paperbush, 279
paperwhite narcissus, 286
Parrotia persica, 20
Passiflora caerulea, 184
Paulownia tomentosa, 228

peanut butter bush, 278

peaty soil, 103. *See also* acid soil

penstemon, 186, 187

Penstemon 'Raven', 187

perennial honesty, 258

perennials, 84, 115, 140, 219

perovskia, 126

Perovskia atriplicifolia, 300

Perovskia 'Blue Spire', 184

Perovskia Lacey Blue, 123

Persicaria amplexicaulis, 87

Persicaria amplexicaulis 'Firetail', 86, 87

Peruvian lily, 230

pests and disease, 156, 210. *See also specific pest and disease names*

Pfitzer juniper, 66

pheasant berry, 77

pheasant's eye narcissus, 286

philadelphus, 35, 263, 277, 286

Philadelphus 'Belle Étoile', 94, 101, 286

Philadelphus coronarius, 18

Philadelphus maculatus 'Sweet Clare', 282

Phlomis fruticosa, 37, 123, 314

Phlomis italica, 19, 126

pH of soil, 25–27, 89

phormium, 14, 23, 37, 145, 156, 219, 228, 246

Phormium cookianum subsp. *hookeri* 'Tricolor', 66, 228

Phormium 'Crimson Devil', 153, 159

Phormium tenax, 244

Phormium 'Yellow Wave', 225

photinia, 249

Photinia ×*fraseri* 'Little Red Robin', 170

Photinia ×*fraseri* 'Red Robin', 98, 239, 258

Photinia serratifolia Pink Crispy, 16

phyllostachys, 244

physocarpus, 140, 233

Physocarpus opulifolius 'Dart's Gold', 84, 136, 143

Physocarpus opulifolius 'Diable D'Or', 112, 275

Physocarpus opulifolius 'Diablo', 79, 86, 87, 142, 233

pieris, 158

Pieris 'Forest Flame', 111

Pieris japonica 'Little Heath', 153

pincushion flowers, 98–101

pineapple broom, 204

pinks, 289

Pinus mugo, 67, 70

Pinus mugo 'Carsten', 136

Pinus mugo 'Carsten's Wintergold', 136

pittosporum, 145, 233

Pittosporum 'Garnettii', 8, 244

Pittosporum tenuifolium, 32, 112, 239, 258

Pittosporum tenuifolium 'Golf Ball', 154

Pittosporum tenuifolium 'Irene Paterson', 168, 170, 184

Pittosporum tenuifolium 'Tom Thumb', 156

Pittosporum tenuifolium 'Variegatum', 31

Pittosporum tobira, 61, 282, 289

Pittosporum tobira 'Variegatum', 154

planting instructions, 40–42

poet's narcissus, 286

poisonous/toxic plants, 228, 241, 371

Polygonatum ×*hybridum*, 142, 143

Polystichum setiferum 'Herrenhausen', 112, 115

poor man's box, 193

Portugal laurel, 89, 95, 257

potentilla, 8, 33, 98, 143

Potentilla fruticosa, 263

Potentilla fruticosa 'Abbotswood', 20, 269

Potentilla fruticosa 'Pink Beauty', 137

Potentilla fruticosa 'Primrose Beauty', 70, 95

pots and containers, gardening in, 147–159

listed shrubs for, 148–156

planting instructions, 41

planting partners for, 156–159

primrose, 158, 200

Primula vulgaris, 200

privacy in the garden, 32, 233

pruning, 13, 21, 32, 33, 228

Prunus ×*cistena*, 140

Prunus incisa 'Kojo-no-mai', 168

Prunus laurocerasus, 89, 95, 240, 314

Prunus laurocerasus 'Otto Luyken', 53

Prunus lusitanica, 89

Prunus lusitanica 'Myrtifolia', 257

Prunus lusitanica 'Variegata', 56, 95

Prunus spinosa, 242, 243

pulmonarias, 58, 140, 258

purple catalpa, 220

purple coneflower, 142, 143, 300

purple filbert, 236

purple hazel, 247

purple-leaved heucheras, 156

purple rock cress, 200

purple sage, 73, 125

purple toadflax, 172

pyracantha, 203, 291

Pyracantha Saphyr Rouge, 210

rabbit- and deer-resistant plants. *See* deer- and rabbit-resistant plants

rambler roses, 212
red-barked dogwood, 80, 132
red-leaved Japanese maple, 250
red osier dogwood, 236
red-twigged dogwood, 163
redvein enkianthus, 105
restricted planting spaces. *See* small gardens
Rhamnus alaternus 'Argenteovariegata', 240, 244
rhododendrons, 18, 41, 111, 158, 263
Rhododendron 'Cannon's Double', 109
Rhododendron 'Catawbiense Grandiflorum', 312
Rhododendron 'Cunningham's White', 56, 70, 79
Rhododendron 'Daviesii', 103
Rhododendron 'Horizon Monarch', 109
Rhododendron 'Irene Koster', 283
Rhododendron Loderi Group, 110
Rhododendron luteum, 284, 314
Rhododendron macabeanum, 225
Rhododendron 'Northern Hi-Lights', 137
Rhododendron yakushimanum, 156, 169
RHS Rosemoor (garden), 59
RHS Wisley (garden), 219
Rhus typhina Tiger Eyes, 138, 228
ribes, 305
Ribes laurifolium, 212
Ribes sanguineum, 244, 298
rice paper tree, 226
Ricinus communis, 228
rock rose, 121, 192, 308
rodgersia, 84
Rodgersia aesculifolia, 85
root-balled shrubs, planting instructions, 41–42

Rosa Bonica, 270, 272
Rosa canina, 299
Rosa 'Compassion', 212, 213
Rosa 'Felicia', 42
Rosa Flower Carpet, 73, 314
Rosa Flower Carpet White, 194
Rosa 'Fru Dagmar Hastrup', 67
Rosa gallica var. *officinalis*, 80, 286
Rosa Gertrude Jekyll, 212, 284
Rosa 'Jubilee Celebration', 33
Rosa ×*odorata* 'Mutabilis', 212, 270, 272
Rosa Queen of Sweden, 183
Rosa rugosa, 67, 73, 272, 312
Rosa The Pilgrim, 212
rosemary, 65, 68, 192, 249, 305
roses
    fertilizer for, 27, 80, 183, 270, 284
    fragrance of, 277
    and harsh weather, 131
    planting instructions, 41, 42
    and wildlife, 37, 291, 300
Rosmarinus officinalis, 124, 184
Rosmarinus officinalis 'Arp', 124
Rosmarinus officinalis Prostratus Group, 194
Royal Horticultural Society hardiness ratings, 8–9
Rubus thibetanus 'Silver Fern', 314
Rubus tricolor, 56, 195, 198
rue, 305, 307
Ruscus aculeatus 'John Redmond', 54
Russian arbor-vitae, 193
Russian sage, 123, 126
Ruta graveolens, 305

sacred bamboo, 19, 152, 167, 182
sage, 192, 305
Salix alba var. *vitellina* 'Britzensis', 80, 140, 244
Salix irrorata, 75

Salix purpurea 'Gracilis', 84
salty air, 61, 70, 73. *See also* coastal situations
salvia, 272
Salvia guaranitica 'Blue Enigma', 272
Salvia horminum, 272, 273
Salvia 'Hot Lips', 124, 126, 272
Salvia ×*jamensis* 'Hot Lips', 124
Salvia officinalis 'Purpurascens', 125, 198
Sambucus nigra 'Black Lace', 96
Sambucus nigra f. *laciniata*, 81, 244
Sambucus nigra f. *porphyrophylla* 'Eva', 96, 98, 314
Sambucus racemosa 'Plumosa Aurea', 138
Sambucus racemosa 'Sutherland Gold', 84, 138
Sandhill Farm (garden), 7
sandy and stony soils, 103. *See also* acid soil
Santolina chamaecyparissus, 70, 125
sarcococca, 8, 186, 286
Sarcococca confusa, 96, 184, 277, 286, 314
Sarcococca hookeriana var. *digyna*, 54
Sarcococca hookeriana var. *hookeriana* 'Ghorepani', 285
Sarcococca hookeriana Winter Gem, 54, 169, 170
Scabiosa 'Vivid Violet', 101
scabious, 98–101
scilla, 58
scorpion vetch, 206
screening and privacy, shrubs for, 32, 233
sea buckthorn, 65, 68
sea holly, 126
seaside gardens. *See* coastal situations

seasonal bedding plants, 14, 21, 147, 158
seasons of interest, shrub selection for, 34, 151, 161
sea thrift, 70
seaweed extract, 43
sedum, 70, 98, 100, 128, 301
Sedum 'Autumn Joy', 300
Sedum 'Herbstfreude', 128, 300
Sedum 'Red Cauli', 128
selective crown thinning, of deciduous trees, 28
serviceberry, 132
shaded areas, 47–59. *See also* sun and shade
    listed shrubs for, 48–56
    planting partners for, 56–59
shrubby mallow, 94
shrub roses, 289
shrubs, 7–9
    care during establishment, 43
    contribution to garden, 21
    deciduous, 17, 21
    definitions of, 12–15
    evergreen, 17, 43, 89, 186
    as low-maintenance plants, 17–21, 33
    planting instructions, 40–42
    selection of, 23–38
Siberian bugloss, 58
Siberian cypress, 193
silk tassel, 208
silverberry, 63
silverbush, 121
silver foliage subjects, 98, 100, 121, 124, 125, 126, 172
size of shrubs, 30
skimmia, 55, 151, 155, 263, 286
Skimmia ×*confusa* 'Kew Green', 55, 156, 286
Skimmia japonica 'Magic Marlot', 155

slugs and snails, 84, 156
small gardens, 31, 161–173. *See also* narrow beds and borders; pots and containers, gardening in; restricted planting spaces
    listed shrubs for, 162–170
    planting partners for, 170–173
small-leaved ivy, 56
smokebush, 237
snails and slugs, 84, 156
snake's head fritillary, 86, 87
snowberry, 196
snowdrop, 87, 317
soft shield fern, 112
soils and soil types, 25–27, 40, 117. *See also* acid soil; alkaline and chalk soils; wet and compacted soil
solanum, 212
Solanum crispum 'Glasnevin', 211
Solomon's seal, 142, 143
Sophora Sun King, 211
Sorbaria sorbifolia 'Sem', 45, 139
Spanish dagger, 227
spider flower, 267
spindle, 296
spiraea, 33, 98, 143
Spiraea 'Arguta', 81
Spiraea japonica 'Anthony Waterer', 82
Spiraea japonica 'Firelight', 33, 97, 98
Spiraea japonica 'Goldflame', 70
Spiraea japonica 'Little Princess', 68, 73, 170
Spiraea nipponica 'Snowmound', 139
Spiraea ×*vanhouttei*, 244
spotted laurel, 90
spring-flowering bulbs, 261, 302
star of the Mediterranean night, 289
steep slopes and banks, 189–201

listed shrubs for, 190–198
planting partners for, 198–201
Stephanandra incisa 'Crispa', 195
Stipa tenuissima, 128, 129
Stokes' aster, 115
Stokesia laevis, 114, 115
stonecrop, 300
succulents and cacti, 128
sulphur chips, 89
summersweet, 293
sun and shade, 28–29. *See also* exposed sites; shaded areas
sun rose, 91, 265
sweet Betsy, 115
sweet box, 54, 96, 169, 277, 285
sweet pea, 289
sweet pepper bush, 293
sweetshrub, 264
Symphoricarpos albus, 84, 140
Symphoricarpos ×*chenaultii* 'Hancock', 56, 196
Symphytum caucasicum, 112, 113
Syringa 'Pink Perfume', 97
Syringa 'Red Pixie', 20
Syringa vulgaris, 41, 140, 258

Tamarix ramosissima, 258
Tamarix ramosissima 'Rubra', 68
taro, 228, 231
Taxus baccata, 241, 242, 243
Taxus baccata 'Fastigiata Aureomarginata', 183
tea-tree, 214
Tellima grandiflora, 258
tetrapanax, 228
Tetrapanax papyrifer 'Rex', 219, 226
Teucrium fruticans, 126
Thuja plicata, 243
Thuja plicata 'Atrovirens', 241
thyme, 70, 192
Thymus serpyllum, 200, 201
Thymus 'Silver Queen', 126

Tiarella cordifolia, 140
timescale of shrubs, 30
topiary, 13, 149, 255, 307
toxic/poisonous plants, 228, 241, 371
Trachelospermum jasminoides, 170, 171
tree ivy, 208
trees, shrubs grown as, 249–261
    listed shrubs for, 250–258
    planting partners for, 258–261
trillium, 112–115
Trillium cuneatum, 115
Trillium grandiflorum, 112–115, 258, 261
Trillium sessile, 115
Trochodendron aralioides, 228
Tropaeolum speciosum, 115
true castor oil plant, 228
Tulipa tarda, 128, 129
tulip magnolia, 78
tulips, 128, 145, 158, 317

Ugni molinae 'Flambeau', 155, 156
Ulex europaeus, 69, 140
USDA hardiness zones, 9

Vaccinium corymbosum, 314
variegated evergreens, 35
Venus dogwood, 11
Verbena bonariensis, 117, 126, 300
veronicastrum, 101
Veronicastrum virginicum 'Album', 100, 101
viburnum, 87, 291
Viburnum ×*bodnantense*, 263
Viburnum carlesii 'Diana', 285
Viburnum davidii, 55, 56, 57, 156, 228
Viburnum furcatum, 111
Viburnum opulus, 84, 140, 244, 299
Viburnum opulus 'Roseum', 83

Viburnum plicatum f. *plicatum* 'Rotundifolium', 313
Viburnum plicatum f. *tomentosum* 'Mariesii', 30, 263
Viburnum plicatum f. *tomentosum* 'Nanum Semperflorens', 271
Viburnum plicatum f. *tomentosum* 'Watanabe', 271
Viburnum rhytidophyllum, 226
Viburnum tinus, 37, 263, 314
Viburnum tinus Spirit, 271
vinca, 200
Vinca major, 198
Vinca major 'Variegata', 196
Vinca minor, 56, 198
Vinca minor 'Bowles's Variety', 197
vine eyes, 170
vine weevil, 156
violas, 158
Vitex agnus-castus, 126
Vitis coignetiae, 244, 246

wake-robin, 258
wallflower, 200, 201
wall shrubs, alternatives to climbers, 203–215
    listed shrubs for, 204–212
    planting partners for, 212–215
watering and water supply, 31, 41, 42, 43, 117, 147
wedding cake tree, 252
weed suppression, on steep slopes and banks, 189
weigela, 263
Weigela 'Florida Variegata', 83, 98
western red cedar, 241
wet and compacted soil, 75–87
    improving, 75
    listed shrubs for, 76–84
    planting partners for, 84–87
white-barked birch, 67
white willow, 80

wild daffodil, 316
wildlife, shrubs to attract, 35, 243, 291–302
    planting partners for, 300–302
    selecting, 292–300
wild privet, 298
willow, 75, 84, 85
windbreaks, 61
windy sites, 61, 70. *See also* exposed sites
wintercreeper, 179
winter-flowering heather, 263, 266
winter-flowering honeysuckle, 78
winter heath, 133
winter's bark, 207
wintersweet, 278
winter weather, 131–143
    listed shrubs for, 132–140
    planting partners for, 140–143
wire-netting bush, 62
wire vine, 198
witch alder, 106
witch hazel, 34, 107
wood lily, 115
woody herbs, 117, 124, 192, 200, 305
woody salvia, 126
wormwood, 119
wrinkled viburnum, 226

yarrow, 73, 274
yellow archangel, 258
yellowtwig dogwood, 133
yew, 243, 244
yucca, 219
Yucca flaccida 'Golden Sword', 126
Yucca gloriosa 'Variegata', 227

Zantedeschia aethiopica, 84, 230

Craig Fields

Andy McIndoe is a practical horticulturist and author with more than four decades' experience. He designs and advises on gardens of all sizes, specializing in schemes using trees and shrubs. Responsible for twenty-five Gold Medal–winning exhibits at the RHS Chelsea Flower Show, he was awarded the Veitch Memorial Medal in 2017 for outstanding contribution to the science and practice of horticulture. He is a regular contributor to blogs, magazines, and BBC Radio and lectures widely at home and abroad.

He and his wife have a two-acre garden, Sandhill Farm, in Hampshire, UK. Naturalistic in style, it features a native wildflower meadow and informal planting based on foliage to provide year-round colour and interest. Visit him at www.andymcindoe.com and follow @AndyMcIndoe on Twitter. His first Timber Press book was *The Creative Shrub Garden: Eye-Catching Combinations for Year-Round Interest.*

Copyright © 2018 by Andy McIndoe.
    All rights reserved.
Photography credits appear on page 319.

Published in 2018 by Timber Press, Inc.
The Haseltine Building
133 S.W. Second Avenue, Suite 450
Portland, Oregon 97204-3527
timberpress.com

Printed in China

Text design by Debbie Berne
Cover design by Adrianna Sutton

Library of Congress Cataloging-in-Publication Data

Names: McIndoe, Andrew, 1956- author.
Title: Shrubs : discover the perfect plant for every place
    in your garden / Andy McIndoe.
Description: Portland, Oregon : Timber Press, 2019. |
    Includes bibliographical references and index. |
Identifiers: LCCN 2018011962 (print) | LCCN
    2018015770 (ebook) | ISBN 9781604698954 | ISBN
    9781604697674 (hardcover)
Subjects: LCSH: Ornamental shrubs.
Classification: LCC SB435 (ebook) | LCC SB435 .M456
    2019 (print) | DDC 635.9/76—dc23
LC record available at https://lccn.loc.gov/2018011962

A catalog record for this book is also available from the
    British Library.